T0323865

The Black–Scholes Model

The Black–Scholes option pricing model is the first, and by far the best-known, continuous-time mathematical model used in mathematical finance. Here, it provides a sufficiently complex, yet tractable, testbed for exploring the basic methodology of option pricing.

The discussion of extended markets, the careful attention paid to the requirements for admissible trading strategies, the development of pricing formulae for many widely traded instruments and the additional complications offered by multi-stock models will appeal to a wide class of instructors. Students, practitioners and researchers alike will benefit from the book's rigorous, but unfussy, approach to technical issues. It highlights potential pitfalls, gives clear motivation for results and techniques, and includes carefully chosen examples and exercises, all of which makes it suitable for self-study.

MAREK CAPIŃSKI has published over 50 research papers and eleven books. His diverse interests include mathematical finance, corporate finance and stochastic hydrodynamics. For over 35 years he has been teaching these topics, mainly in Poland and in the UK, where he has held visiting fellowships. He is currently Professor of Applied Mathematics at AGH University of Science and Technology in Kraków, Poland, where he established a Master's programme in mathematical finance.

EKKEHARD KOPP is Emeritus Professor of Mathematics at the University of Hull, UK, where he taught courses at all levels in analysis, measure and probability, stochastic processes and mathematical finance between 1970 and 2007. His editorial experience includes service as founding member of the Springer Finance series (1998–2008) and the Cambridge University Press AIMS Library Series. He has taught in the UK, Canada and South Africa, and he has authored more than 50 research publications and five books.

Mastering Mathematical Finance

Mastering Mathematical Finance is a series of short books that cover all core topics and the most common electives offered in Master's programmes in mathematical or quantitative finance. The books are closely coordinated and largely self-contained, and can be used efficiently in combination but also individually.

The MMF books start financially from scratch and mathematically assume only undergraduate calculus, linear algebra and elementary probability theory. The necessary mathematics is developed rigorously, with emphasis on a natural development of mathematical ideas and financial intuition, and the readers quickly see real-life financial applications, both for motivation and as the ultimate end for the theory. All books are written for both teaching and self-study, with worked examples, exercises and solutions.

[DMFM]   *Discrete Models of Financial Markets*,
         Marek Capiński, Ekkehard Kopp

[PF]   *Probability for Finance*,
         Ekkehard Kopp, Jan Malczak, Tomasz Zastawniak

[SCF]   *Stochastic Calculus for Finance*,
         Marek Capiński, Ekkehard Kopp, Janusz Traple

[BSM]   *The Black–Scholes Model*,
         Marek Capiński, Ekkehard Kopp

[PTRM]   *Portfolio Theory and Risk Management*,
         Maciej J. Capiński, Ekkehard Kopp

[NMFC]   *Numerical Methods in Finance with C++*,
         Maciej J. Capiński, Tomasz Zastawniak

[SIR]   *Stochastic Interest Rates*,
         Daragh McInerney, Tomasz Zastawniak

[CR]   *Credit Risk*,
         Marek Capiński, Tomasz Zastawniak

[FE]   *Financial Econometrics*,
         Marek Capiński, Jian Zhang

[SCAF]   *Stochastic Control Applied to Finance*,
         Szymon Peszat, Tomasz Zastawniak

Series editors Marek Capiński, *AGH University of Science and Technology, Kraków*; Ekkehard Kopp, *University of Hull*; Tomasz Zastawniak, *University of York*

The Black–Scholes Model

MAREK CAPIŃSKI
AGH University of Science and Technology, Kraków, Poland

EKKEHARD KOPP
University of Hull, Hull, UK

CAMBRIDGE
UNIVERSITY PRESS

CAMBRIDGE
UNIVERSITY PRESS

University Printing House, Cambridge CB2 8BS, United Kingdom

One Liberty Plaza, 20th Floor, New York, NY 10006, USA

477 Williamstown Road, Port Melbourne, VIC 3207, Australia

314-321, 3rd Floor, Plot 3, Splendor Forum, Jasola District Centre, New Delhi - 110025, India

79 Anson Road, #06-04/06, Singapore 079906

Cambridge University Press is part of the University of Cambridge.

It furthers the University's mission by disseminating knowledge in the pursuit of education, learning and research at the highest international levels of excellence.

www.cambridge.org
Information on this title: www.cambridge.org/9781107001695

© Marek Capiński and Ekkehard Kopp 2012

This publication is in copyright. Subject to statutory exception and to the provisions of relevant collective licensing agreements, no reproduction of any part may take place without the written permission of Cambridge University Press.

First published 2012

A catalogue record for this publication is available from the British Library

Library of Congress Cataloging in Publication data
Capiński, Marek, 1951–
The Black-Scholes model / Marek Capiński, Ekkehard Kopp.
p.   cm. – (Mastering mathematical finance)
Includes index.
ISBN 978-1-107-00169-5 (hardback)
1. Options (Finance) – Prices – Mathematical models.   I. Kopp, P. E., 1944–   II. Title.
HG6024.A3C364   2013
332.64´53 – dc23   2012023180

ISBN 978-1-107-00169-5 Hardback
ISBN 978-0-521-17300-1 Paperback

Additional resources for this publication at www.cambridge.org/9781107001695

Cambridge University Press has no responsibility for the persistence or accuracy of URLs for external or third-party internet websites referred to in this publication, and does not guarantee that any content on such websites is, or will remain, accurate or appropriate.

Contents

Contents

Preface

The development of modern financial markets can be traced back to two events in the USA in 1973, both of which revolutionised market practice, for very different reasons. One of these revolutions was essentially institutional: the opening of the world's first options exchange in Chicago allowed options to be exchanged in much the same way as stocks (that is, through a regulated exchange) rather than having to be traded 'over the counter' as separate contracts between buyer and seller. The second upheaval was purely theoretical: the publication in the *Journal of Political Economy* of the now famous paper by Fischer Black and Myron Scholes (extended by Robert Merton in the same year), which developed arbitrage techniques for pricing and hedging options, and presented the now ubiquitous Black–Scholes formula for the rational pricing of European call options.

By the late 1970s the basis of their arguments, and the link with martingale theory in particular, had become well enough understood to allow the rapid development of this theoretical breakthrough, which has, since the 1980s, pre-occupied a host of financial economists and mathematicians (principally probabilists) and has given rise to the new profession of quantitative analyst (or 'quant'), which has attracted into the finance sector a large section of the best graduates with mathematics, physics, statistics or computer science degrees. This, in turn, has spawned a host of postgraduate courses emphasising market practice and taught in business schools, but increasingly also courses attached to mathematical sciences departments, focusing on the underlying mathematics, much of which is of comparatively recent origin.

At the same time, finance practitioners have led the explosive, largely unregulated, growth of new financial instruments, grouped together under the term 'derivative securities', which are constantly being devised to meet (or create) demand for specific tailor-made financial products in the banking, currency, insurance, energy and mortgage markets. Hedge funds, which specialise in trading these highly leveraged products, involving huge sums, have become major players in most developed economies. While the mathematical theory underlying their activities is based firmly on market models that exclude arbitrage opportunities (colloquially, a 'free lunch'), in practice much of the motivation comes from the search for risk-free profits, or, perhaps more accurately, the exploitation of market imperfections which briefly create highly marginal profits available through rapid, large-scale trading. This leads to secondary markets whose size overshadows global primary trade – by 2007 the annual volume of derivative trades had reached one quadrillion (10^{15}) US dollars, ten times the global industrial output over the past century – and where incautious, sometimes politically driven, decisions can leave banking institutions exposed to colossal losses, as was demonstrated painfully by the global banking crises of 2008–9 that continue to haunt the global economy.

All this suggests that a more thorough understanding of the principles underlying market practice is essential both for the improvement of that practice and for its regulation. Like nuclear power or the combustion engine, modern financial markets cannot be un-invented; instead, clear insight into their purpose, workings and potential benefits, which necessarily involves mastery of their mathematical basis, is a pre-requisite for adjusting market practice and preventing its abuse.

We will focus attention on the development of the Black–Scholes pricing model and its ramifications. Unlike its much simpler discrete-time binomial counterpart, the Cox–Ross–Rubinstein model (see [DMFM]), a proper understanding of this model requires substantial mathematical tools, principally from the stochastic calculus, which are developed carefully in [SCF]. The random dynamics of stock prices in the Black–Scholes model are based upon the Wiener process (often called Brownian motion). Despite its greater mathematical complexity, the continuous-time model produces a unique pricing formula for vanilla European options which is simpler than its discrete-time counterpart (the CRR formula described in [DMFM]), and has been universally adopted as a standard tool by finance practitioners.

Chapters 1–3 present the basic single-stock model for a general European derivative, with a focus on the explicit formulae for pricing calls and puts, and give a careful account of restrictions on admissible trading strategies. Since arbitrage opportunities usually involve trading in derivatives, the assets held in such strategies should include holdings in the derivatives being priced, and we show that, in our model, the prices of derivative and the replicating strategy must coincide if arbitrage is to be avoided. Option prices are derived in detail for vanilla European options and the unique admissible replicating strategy is constructed and related to the Black–Scholes PDE and to sensitivity measures for the option price relative to its parameters. The key roles of the risk-neutral probability and the representation of martingales by stochastic integrals are highlighted.

Chapter 4 extends and applies the Black–Scholes model in a variety of settings: options on foreign currencies, on futures and on other options. A structural model of credit risk is shown to fit the option pricing setting, a pricing model with time-dependent parameters is introduced, American call options are considered briefly, and the chapter closes with a description of the growth-optimal portfolio. Chapter 5 extends the discussion to the more exotic barriers, lookbacks and Asian options. A two-asset Black–Scholes model is first considered in Chapter 6 before presenting a general multi-asset pricing model, requiring more general versions of the Lévy and Girsanov theorems.

We restrict ourselves to the Black–Scholes setting and its immediate generalisations throughout this volume, working with the natural filtration of a given Wiener process and keeping our reliance on general martingale theory to a minimum. Notable features include the justification of derivative prices by means of replicating strategies and the care taken at the outset in defining the class of admissible trading strategies. The emphasis is on honest proofs of the results we discuss, with much attention given to specific examples and calculation of pricing formulae for different types of options. As usual, the many exercises, whose solutions are made available on the linked website www.cambridge.org/9781107001695, form an integral part of the development of the theory and applications.

We wish to thank all who have read the drafts and provided us with feedback.

1

Introduction

In the Black–Scholes option pricing model the stock price dynamics are assumed to follow an Itô process with constant characteristics. This key hypothesis, dating from a 1965 paper by Paul Samuelson, adapts ideas from a remarkable doctoral thesis by the French mathematician Louis Bachelier in 1900. The model makes various simplifying assumptions about the market, not all of which are borne out by market data. Nonetheless, the Black–Scholes prices of European derivatives provide benchmarks against which prices quoted in the market can be judged.

We turn first to a description of the continuous-time price processes for the assets that comprise the basic single-stock Black–Scholes model.

1.1 Asset dynamics

The market model contains two underlying securities.

- The **risk-free** asset (money-market account), described by a deterministic function

$$dA(t) = rA(t)dt,$$

with $A(0) = 1$ (for convenience), where $r > 0$ is the risk-free rate.

This is an ordinary differential equation $A'(t) = rA(t)$ but for consistency with stock prices, which are assumed to be Itô processes, we use differential notation. The equation has a unique solution:

$$A(t) = e^{rt}.$$

1

- The **risky** asset, thought of as a stock, is represented by an Itô process of the form

$$dS(t) = \mu S(t)dt + \sigma S(t)dW(t), \qquad (1.1)$$

with $S(0)$ given, where we call $\mu \in \mathbb{R}$ the **drift**, and $\sigma > 0$ the **volatility**, of the stock price S.

The sign of σ is actually irrelevant. If σ is negative then we change W to $-W$ and we have an equation with positive σ but with respect to $(-W)$, which is again a Wiener process. The probability space underlying W will be denoted by $(\Omega, \mathcal{F}, P)$, and the associated filtration is given by $\mathcal{F}_t^S = \sigma(S(u) : u \le t\})$. Writing out (1.1) we see that

$$S(t) = S(0) + \mu \int_0^t S(u)du + \sigma \int_0^t S(u)dW(u).$$

The stochastic differential equation (1.1) has a unique solution since the coefficients are Lipschitz with linear growth:

$$\mu S(t) = a(t, S(t)), \quad a(t, x) = \mu x,$$
$$\sigma S(t) = b(t, S(t)), \quad b(t, x) = \sigma x,$$

so that

$$|a(t, x) - a(t, y)| \le |\mu||x - y|,$$
$$|b(t, x) - b(t, y)| \le \sigma|x - y|,$$

linear growth being obvious, and we can apply the existence and uniqueness theorem for stochastic differential equations, proved in [SCF] as Theorem 5.8.

We can determine the solution immediately: it takes the form

$$S(t) = S(0) \exp\{\mu t - \frac{\sigma^2}{2}t + \sigma W(t)\}. \qquad (1.2)$$

> **Exercise 1.1** Show that this process solves (1.1).

As the solution is unique, S given by (1.2) is the unique solution of (1.1). Note that the filtration $\mathcal{F}^S$ governing the random fluctuations in the stock price S coincides with the natural filtration of W, where $\mathcal{F}_t^W = \sigma(W(u) : u \le t)$ for each $t \in [0, T]$, since (1.2) shows that W is the only source of randomness in S.

Exercise 1.2 Find the probability that $S(2t) > 2S(t)$ for some $t > 0$.

Model parameters

To understand the role of the parameters μ, σ in this model we compute the expectation of $S(t)$. Recall that for a normally distributed random variable X with $\mathbb{E}(X) = 0$ we have

$$\mathbb{E}(\exp\{X\}) = \exp\{\frac{1}{2}\mathrm{Var}(X)\}. \tag{1.3}$$

We apply this with $X = \sigma W(t)$, so that $\mathrm{Var}(X) = \sigma^2 t$ (we write the expectation of X with respect to P simply as $\mathbb{E}(X)$ rather than $\mathbb{E}_P(X)$ when there is no danger of confusion):

$$\mathbb{E}(S(t)) = S(0)\mathbb{E}(\exp\{\mu t - \frac{1}{2}\sigma^2 t + \sigma W(t)\})$$

$$= S(0)\exp\{\mu t - \frac{1}{2}\sigma^2 t\}\mathbb{E}(\exp\{\sigma W(t)\})$$

$$= S(0)\exp\{\mu t\}.$$

Clearly, if $\mu = 0$ then the expectation of $S(t)$ is constant in time.

The expression for $\mathbb{E}(S(t))$ gives μ as the (annualised) logarithmic return of the expected price

$$\mu = \frac{1}{t}\ln\frac{\mathbb{E}(S(t))}{S(0)}, \tag{1.4}$$

which should not be confused with the expected (annualised) logarithmic return

$$\frac{1}{t}\mathbb{E}(\ln\frac{S(t)}{S(0)}) = \frac{1}{t}\mathbb{E}(\mu t - \frac{\sigma^2}{2}t + \sigma W(t)) = \mu - \frac{\sigma^2}{2}.$$

The variance of the return is

$$\mathrm{Var}(\mu t - \frac{\sigma^2}{2}t + \sigma W(t)) = \mathrm{Var}(\sigma W(t)) \quad \text{(adding a constant has no impact)}$$

$$= \sigma^2 t \quad \text{(since } \mathrm{Var}(W(t)) = t\text{)}.$$

A natural question emerges of how to find these parameters given some past stock prices. The formula (1.4) suggests taking average prices as the proxy for the expected price, but the accuracy of this is poor, according to statistical theory.

Much more effective is the approximation of volatility provided, for instance, by the following scheme. Consider the process

$$\ln S(t) = \ln S(0) + (\mu - \frac{1}{2}\sigma^2)t + \sigma W(t),$$

which is an Itô process with constant characteristics. Its quadratic variation is equal to $\sigma^2 t$ (see [SCF]) and for a partition of $[0, t]$ given by $0 = t_1 < \cdots < t_n = t$, with small mesh $\max |t_{k+1} - t_k|$, we have

$$\sum_k (\ln S(t_{k+1}) - \ln S(t_k))^2 \approx \sigma^2 t.$$

Hence if the times t_k represent past instants at which we know the prices, then we can take

$$\sigma = \sqrt{\frac{1}{t} \sum \ln \frac{S(t_{k+1})}{S(t_k)}}$$

as our estimate of the volatility coefficient, a positive number called the sample volatility.

Exercise 1.3 Find the formula for the variance of the stock price: $\mathrm{Var}(S(t))$.

Exercise 1.4 Consider an alternative model where the stock prices follow an Ornstein–Uhlenbeck process: this is a solution of $dS_1(t) = \mu_1 S_1(t)dt + \sigma_1 dW(t)$ (see [SCF]). Find the probability that at a certain time $t_1 > 0$ we will have negative prices: i.e. compute $P(S_1(t_1) < 0)$. Illustrate the result numerically.

Exercise 1.5 Allowing time-dependent but deterministic σ_1 in the Ornstein–Uhlenbeck model, find its shape so that $\mathrm{Var}(S(t)) = \mathrm{Var}(S_1(t))$.

The above partial differential equation (PDE) is known as the Black–Scholes PDE and solving it will give us the function u, and so the pricing problem will have a sucessful conclusion. With some knowledge from the theory of PDEs one may show that this problem has a unique solution given by a closed-form expression.

In outlining this approach to the pricing problem we have made some powerful assumptions. It will turn out for the Black–Scholes model we are able to prove all these statements – the assumptions will be converted into theorems. We will find the expression for u as well, and then we will revisit the above PDE to see that this is indeed a solution.

2

Strategies and risk-neutral probability

We begin executing some of the elements of the programme outlined in the previous chapter. The first goal is to discuss the martingale properties of strategies. For this we must first construct a risk-neutral probability. Next we define self-financing strategies by analogy with the discrete case and observe that in the present setting pathologies can emerge which are absent in discrete-time models. This leads to conclusions about the class of trading strategies that are admissible in continuous-time models.

2.1 Finding the risk-neutral probability

We consider the discounted stock price process $\tilde{S}(t) = e^{-rt}S(t)$, which, by the definition of $S(t)$, becomes

$$
\begin{aligned}
\tilde{S}(t) &= \exp\{-rt\}S(0)\exp\left\{\mu t - \frac{1}{2}\sigma^2 t + \sigma W(t)\right\} \\
&= S(0)\exp\left\{(\mu - r)t - \frac{1}{2}\sigma^2 t + \sigma W(t)\right\}.
\end{aligned}
$$

To explore situations where this becomes a martingale with respect to the probability P, we compute conditional expectations.

10

Exercise 2.1 Prove that, for $u < t$, $\mathbb{E}(\tilde{S}(t)|\mathcal{F}_u^W) = \tilde{S}(u)\exp\{(\mu - r)t\}$.

Thus the process would be a martingale if the drift parameter μ were equal to the risk-free rate: $\mu = r$. While we cannot simply impose this condition on the expected values of the risky stock price, we may hope to make progress by changing the probability measure to a probability Q with the same null sets as P. (This restriction is relevant since the no-arbitrage condition concerns 'almost sure' properties of strategy values.) The question is how to find such a Q.

We know from [SCF] that for any Wiener process W, $\exp\{-\frac{1}{2}\sigma^2 t + \sigma W(t)\}$ is a martingale, so we try to write the discounted stock prices in a similar form

$$\tilde{S}(t) = S(0)\exp\left\{-\frac{1}{2}\sigma^2 t + \sigma\left(\frac{\mu - r}{\sigma}t + W(t)\right)\right\}.$$

Setting

$$W_Q(t) = \frac{\mu - r}{\sigma}t + W(t)$$

we have

$$\tilde{S}(t) = S(0)\exp\left\{-\frac{1}{2}\sigma^2 t + \sigma W_Q(t)\right\}.$$

If we can construct a probability measure Q under which W_Q is a Wiener process, then $\tilde{S}(t)$ will be a martingale with respect to Q and the natural filtration $\mathcal{F}_t^W = \mathcal{F}_t$ to simplify the notation (since W and W_Q differ by a deterministic constant, which has no impact on the filtration).

Let us examine to what extent W_Q satisfies the conditions for Wiener process. This looks quite promising: W_Q starts from zero, the increments

$$W_Q(t) - W_Q(s) = \frac{\mu - r}{\sigma}(t - s) + W(t) - W(s)$$

have normal distribution with the desired variance $(t - s)$ (the additive constant does not affect variance), and for the same reason the increments are also independent. However, they have non-zero expectations, so our remaining task is summarised in the heading of the next subsection.

Removing the drift

We begin with a heuristic computation which will provide us with a method of guessing the form of the new probability Q. At the risk of seeming pedantic we shall use $\mathbb{E}_P$ instead of $\mathbb{E}$, in order to distinguish it from $\mathbb{E}_Q$. As observed above, the main problem is the expectation of $W_Q(t) - W_Q(s)$. To simplify notation, write $W_Q(t) = bt + W(t)$, where $b = \frac{\mu - r}{\sigma}$. (This quantity is called the market price of risk and it expresses the risk premium $\mu - r$, known from portfolio theory, in the units of risk.) The expectation of $W_Q(t)$ is obviously

$$\mathbb{E}_P(W_Q(t)) = \mathbb{E}_P(bt + W(t)) = bt$$

and this can be written, using the density of the random variable $W(t)$, as follows

$$\mathbb{E}_P(W_Q(t)) = \int_{-\infty}^{\infty}(bt + x)f_{W(t)}(x)dx$$

$$= \int_{-\infty}^{\infty}(bt + x)\frac{1}{\sqrt{2\pi t}}e^{-\frac{x^2}{2t}}dx.$$

In order to obtain zero it is sufficient to change the form of the density: clearly

$$0 = \int_{-\infty}^{\infty}(bt + x)\frac{1}{\sqrt{2\pi t}}e^{-\frac{(x+bt)^2}{2t}}dx$$

since after changing variable to $y = x + bt$, this is the expectation of a zero-mean normal random variable. Multiplying out the square in the exponential gives

$$0 = \int_{-\infty}^{\infty}(bt + x)e^{-\frac{1}{2}b^2t - bx}\frac{1}{\sqrt{2\pi t}}e^{-\frac{x^2}{2t}}dx$$

$$= \int_{-\infty}^{\infty}(bt + x)e^{-\frac{1}{2}b^2t - bx}f_{W(t)}(x)dx$$

$$= \int_{\Omega}(bt + W(t))e^{-\frac{1}{2}b^2t - bW(t)}dP,$$

using two formulations of the expectation.

For $A \subset \Omega$, $A \in \mathcal{F}$, we define a new measure Q by setting

$$Q(A) = \int_A e^{-\frac{1}{2}b^2t - bW(t)}dP$$

so that

$$\int_{\Omega}(bt + W(t))e^{-\frac{1}{2}b^2t - bW(t)}dP = \int_{\Omega}(bt + W(t))dQ.$$

But we have shown that the left-hand side is zero, while $bt + W(t) = W_Q(t)$, and the term on the right is its Q-expectation, so

$$0 = \mathbb{E}_Q(W_Q(t)).$$

Since $\mathbb{E}_P(W_Q(t)e^{-\frac{1}{2}b^2 t - bW(t)}) = \mathbb{E}_Q(W_Q(t))$, the random variable

$$M(t) = e^{-\frac{1}{2}b^2 t - bW(t)}$$

plays the role of a density of Q with respect to P. We should make sure that it can be used in such capacity. It is strictly positive, being an exponential function, and the process $M(t)$ is a martingale so it has constant expectation. For $t = 0$, $M(0) = 1$ so $\mathbb{E}_P(M(t)) = 1$, in other words

$$\int_\Omega e^{-\frac{1}{2}b^2 t - bW(t)} dP = 1$$

for all t. Therefore all $M(t)$ meet the conditions for being a density, and indeed, the measures P and Q are equivalent in the sense that their collections of null sets are the same, since $M(t) > 0$ everywhere. From the perspective of measurability is it natural to take $M(T)$, which has the richest structure.

Girsanov theorem – simple version

We are ready to formulate the main result of this section, which shows that taking care of the expectation of W_Q suffices to make this a Wiener process under Q.

Theorem 2.1
The process $W_Q(t) = bt + W(t)$ is a Wiener process under the probability Q defined by

$$Q(A) = \int_A e^{-\frac{1}{2}b^2 T - bW(T)} dP.$$

Proof We want to prove that the increments of W_Q are independent and have normal distribution of the desired form.

Let $0 = t_0 < t_1 < \cdots < t_n = T$ and $a_1, \ldots, a_n \in \mathbb{R}$. We tackle independence and the form of the cumulative distribution function of increments together, by taking

$$A = \bigcap_{i=1}^n \{W_Q(t_i) - W_Q(t_{i-1}) \le a_i\}$$

and computing

$$Q(A) = \mathbb{E}_Q(\mathbf{1}_A) = \mathbb{E}_P\left(e^{-bW(T) - \frac{1}{2}b^2 T} \mathbf{1}_A\right)$$

since for any random variable Y

$$\int_\Omega Y e^{-\frac{1}{2}b^2 t - bW(t)} dP = \int_\Omega Y dQ.$$

The indicator of the intersection is the product of indicators so we further have

$$Q(A) = \mathbb{E}_P\left(\prod_{i=1}^{n} e^{-b(W(t_i)-W(t_{i-1}))-\frac{1}{2}b^2(t_i-t_{i-1})} \mathbf{1}_{\{W(t_i)-W(t_{i-1})+b(t_i-t_{i-1})\le a_i\}}\right).$$

Since the increments $W(t_i) - W(t_{i-1})$ are independent under P,

$$\cdots = \prod_{i=1}^{n} \mathbb{E}_P\left(e^{-b(W(t_i)-W(t_{i-1}))-\frac{1}{2}b^2(t_i-t_{i-1})} \mathbf{1}_{\{W(t_i)-W(t_{i-1})+b(t_i-t_{i-1})\le a_i\}}\right). \tag{2.1}$$

The increments $W(t_i)-W(t_{i-1})$ have normal distribution $N(0, t_i-t_{i-1})$, which allows us to use the following general fact.

If X is a random variable with normal distribution $N(0, t)$, then

$$\mathbb{E}_P(e^{-bX-\frac{1}{2}b^2 t}\mathbf{1}_{\{X+bt\le a\}}) = \int_{\{x+bt\le a\}} e^{-bx-\frac{1}{2}b^2 t} \frac{1}{\sqrt{2\pi t}} e^{-\frac{x^2}{2t}} dx$$

$$= \int_{\{x+bt\le a\}} \frac{1}{\sqrt{2\pi t}} e^{-\frac{(x+bt)^2}{2t}} dx$$

$$= \int_{\{y\le a\}} \frac{1}{\sqrt{2\pi t}} e^{-\frac{y^2}{2t}} dy$$

$$= P(X \le a).$$

Applied to $X = W(t_i) - W(t_{i-1})$ in each factor of (2.1) this gives

$$\prod_{i=1}^{n} \mathbb{E}_P\left(e^{-b(W(t_i)-W(t_{i-1}))-\frac{1}{2}b^2(t_i-t_{i-1})} \mathbf{1}_{\{W(t_i)-W(t_{i-1})+b(t_i-t_{i-1})\le a_i\}}\right)$$

$$= \prod_{i=1}^{n} P(W(t_i) - W(t_{i-1}) \le a_i).$$

By taking just one increment, it follows, in particular, that for each i,

$$Q\left(W_Q(t_i) - W_Q(t_{i-1}) \le a_i\right) = P(W(t_i) - W(t_{i-1}) \le a_i),$$

so the increments $W_Q(t_i) - W_Q(t_{i-1})$ have normal distribution $N(0, t_i - t_{i-1})$ since the cumulative distribution function has the proper form and it determines the distribution. Moreover, the above computation gives

$$Q\left(\bigcap_{i=1}^{n} \{W_Q(t_i) - W_Q(t_{i-1}) \le a_i\}\right) = \prod_{i=1}^{n} P(W(t_i) - W(t_{i-1}) \le a_i)$$

$$= \prod_{i=1}^{n} Q(W_Q(t_i) - W_Q(t_{i-1}) \le a_i),$$

which means that the increments $W_Q(t_i) - W_Q(t_{i-1})$ for $i = 1, \ldots, n$ are independent under Q. By definition, $W_Q(t)$ is therefore a Wiener process under Q.   □

Remark 2.2
The above theorem is a special case of an important result known as the **Girsanov theorem**, which applies in a general setting when b is a stochastic process and not just a constant. We shall prove the general version in Chapter 6.

In the probability space $(\Omega, \mathcal{F}, Q)$ the stock price dynamics are said to be **risk-neutral**. This means that there is no drift when we work with discounted values, which turns the discounted stock price into a stochastic integral, as the next corollary shows.

Corollary 2.3
The processes of stock prices and discounted stock prices satisfy

$$dS(t) = rS(t)dt + \sigma S(t)dW_Q(t),$$
$$d\tilde{S}(t) = \tilde{S}(t)\sigma dW_Q(t).$$

Proof With $S(t) = S(0)\exp\{rt - \frac{1}{2}\sigma^2 t + \sigma W_Q(t)\}$ the Itô formula gives the first equation (it applies to any Wiener process). To find the stochastic differential for the discounted process we need the formula for the differential of the product (also called the integration-by-parts formula, see [SCF]), which in general reads

$$d(X_1 X_2) = X_1 dX_2 + X_2 dX_1 + b_1 b_2 dt$$

where

$$dX_i = a_i dt + b_i dW, \quad i = 1, 2.$$

We take $X_1(t) = e^{-rt}$, $X_2 = S$, so that $dX_1(t) = -re^{-rt}dt$ and $b_1 = 0$, to obtain

$$\begin{aligned}
d\tilde{S}(t) &= d(e^{-rt}S(t)) \\
&= -re^{-rt}S(t)dt + e^{-rt}dS(t) \\
&= (\mu - r)\tilde{S}(t)dt + \sigma\tilde{S}(t)dW(t) \\
&= \tilde{S}(t)\sigma dW_Q(t).
\end{aligned}$$
    □

Remark 2.4
Since W_Q is a Wiener process, from the point of view of its probability distribution it is indistinguishable from W. In the literature the above equations are frequently given without the subscript Q but with the added comment

that we work in 'a risk-neutral world'. Let us, however, remember that the real world is not risk-neutral; if we look at past data, these are manufactured under P, not Q.

2.2   Self-financing strategies

The notion of a replicating strategy will depend on which assets are of interest to the problem under discussion. Our choice is made from all traded assets but restrictions on this choice become necessary for practical as well as theoretical reasons. For example, to discuss a call option on a certain stock we do not need to consider any other stocks. But to price an option to exchange one stock for another, the underlying market must of course include them both. For now we are restricting our attention to just one stock, with more general cases to follow.

Remark 2.5

In discrete-time models we insisted that our trading strategies should be predictable, e.g. the stock and bond holdings $(x(n), y(n))$ in a single-stock model were assumed to be known (selected) at the previous trading date $n - 1$, and thus $\mathcal{F}_{n-1}$-measurable. In general continuous-time market models the definition of predictability is somewhat more subtle. However, as long as we deal with randomness arising from a Wiener process, which is almost surely path-continuous, in turns out that we may work with adapted strategies instead.

Definition 2.6

A (trading) **strategy** in the underlying (single-stock) market is an adapted process $(x, y) = \{(x(t), y(t) : t \in [0, T]\}$, with $x(t)$ indicating the number of shares of stock and $y(t)$ the numbers of bonds (money-market account units, to be more precise) held at time t.

Definition 2.7

The **value** of the strategy (x, y) is the process $V_{(x,y)} = (V_{(x,y)}(t))_{t \in [0,T]}$ defined by

$$V_{(x,y)}(t) = x(t)S(t) + y(t)A(t).$$

When it is clear which strategy (x, y) is meant, we drop the subscript and write $V(t)$ for ease of notation.

The next definition is motivated by analogy with a similar condition in discrete markets, expressing the idea that no funds are withdrawn from or injected into our investment. In a discrete-time single-stock model (see [DMFM]) the self-financing condition can be reformulated, in terms of the increments $\Delta_k X = X(k) - X(k-1)$ for V, S and A respectively, as

$$\Delta_k V = x(k)\Delta_k S + y(k)\Delta_k A.$$

Such increments are used in building stochastic integrals, so this motivates the next definition.

Definition 2.8
The strategy (x, y) is **self-financing** if

$$dV(t) = x(t)dS(t) + y(t)dA(t).$$

Within the Black–Scholes model for S this means that the value of a strategy is an Itô process with the charateristics as seen in the defining relation. Taking into account the form of differentials involved, we find

$$dV(t) = [\mu x(t)S(t) + ry(t)A(t)]dt + \sigma x(t)S(t)dW(t).$$

Note that we are not assuming that x or y are Itô processes. However, for the stochastic differential equation to make sense (that is, for the stochastic integral to be well-defined) they must be square-integrable P-a.s., in other words, we demand that $\int_0^T x^2(s)ds$ and $\int_0^T y^2(s)ds$ are a.s. finite (see [SCF], Section 4.6). This is no restriction in practice, where any investor's total wealth is finite.

In the discrete model, when using the discounted processes the increment in the risk-free asset vanishes in the self-financing condition:

$$\Delta_k \widetilde{V} = x(k)\Delta_k \widetilde{S}.$$

The point of the next proposition is to derive the same condition in continuous time, which implies that the position in the risk-free asset is irrelevant when we focus on discounted values.

Proposition 2.9
A strategy is self-financing if and only if

$$d\tilde{V}(t) = x(t)d\tilde{S}(t). \tag{2.2}$$

where $\tilde{V}(t) = e^{-rt}V(t)$.

Proof Assume that (x, y) is self-financing. The product rule provides

$$d\tilde{V}(t) = d(e^{-rt}V(t)) = -re^{-rt}V(t)dt + e^{-rt}dV(t).$$

Inserting the definition of V and the self-financing condition, this becomes

$$d\tilde{V}(t) = -re^{-rt}(x(t)S(t) + y(t)A(t))dt + e^{-rt}(x(t)dS(t) + y(t)dA(t))$$
$$= -re^{-rt}x(t)S(t)dt - re^{-rt}y(t)A(t)dt + e^{-rt}x(t)dS(t) + e^{-rt}y(t)dA(t).$$

But $dA(t) = rA(r)dt$ so the terms with y cancel, and

$$d\tilde{V}(t) = x(t)[-re^{-rt}S(t)dt + e^{-rt}dS(t)] = x(t)d(e^{-rt}S(t)) = x(t)d\tilde{S}(t)$$

since $de^{-rt} = -re^{-rt}dt$ implies $d(e^{-rt}S(t)) = -re^{-rt}S(t)dt + e^{-rt}dS(t)$.

Finally, we check that (2.2) implies self-financing.

Assume (2.2), and compute as before

$$dV(t) = d(e^{rt}\tilde{V}(t)) = re^{rt}\tilde{V}(t)dt + e^{rt}d\tilde{V}(t).$$

Then insert (2.2) to get

$$dV(t) = rV(t)dt + e^{rt}x(t)d\tilde{S}(t)$$
$$= ry(t)A(t)dt + rx(t)S(t)dt + e^{rt}x(t)(-re^{-rt}S(t)dt + e^{-rt}dS(t))$$
$$= y(t)dA(t) + x(t)dS(t)$$

again using $d\tilde{S}(t) = -re^{-rt}S(t)dt + e^{-rt}dS(t)$. □

Corollary 2.10
The process $x(t)$ and the number $V(0)$ determine the adapted process $y(t)$ so that $(x(t), y(t))$ is self-financing.

Proof By (2.2), x and $V(0)$ give

$$\tilde{V}(t) = V(0) + \int_0^t x(u)d\tilde{S}(u),$$

but $V(t) = e^{rt}\tilde{V}(t) = x(t)S(t) + y(t)A(t)$, so

$$y(t) = \frac{1}{A(t)}\left(e^{rt}[V(0) + \int_0^t x(u)d\tilde{S}(u)] - x(t)S(t)\right).$$

The measurability of this random variable with respect to $\mathcal{F}_t$ is clear: it is obvious for all terms except the stochastic integral, and here recall that this is a limit of a sequence of approximating sums, all being $\mathcal{F}_t$-measurable, convergence is point-wise (almost surely) and measurability is preserved in the limit (see [SCF]). □

Exercise 2.2 Consider the following strategy: $x(t) = \frac{V(0)}{S(0)}$ for $t \in [0, t_1)$, $x(t) = 2x(0)$ for $t \in [t_1, t_2)$ and $x(t_2) = 0$ with $V(0)$, $S(0)$ known, $0 < t_1 < t_2$ prescribed in advance (so all money is invested in stock at the beginning, then the number of shares is doubled at time t_1 with liquidation of the risky position at time t_2). Choose the process y so that the strategy is self-financing. Within the Black–Scholes model, with given μ, σ, r, what is the probability that $y(t_2) < 0$? Give a numerical example.

2.3 The No Arbitrage Principle

The notion of arbitrage depends on the market chosen since it is formulated by means of the value processes of strategies. In the underlying market, consisting of stock and money market account, it involves strategies based on these two securities alone, which we emphasize by the notation

$$V_{(x,y)}(t) = x(t)S(t) + y(t)A(t).$$

We shall allow strategies that yield arbitrage the freedom to have negative values at some intermediate trading dates, but will demand that these temporary losses remain bounded. In the discrete setting the existence of such arbitrage opportunities allows one to build strategies with non-negative value processes which also yield riskless profit, as we saw in [DMFM]. With continuous trading the situation is more complex, but our assumption will be seen to be necessary for a key result we prove below.

Definition 2.11
We say that $(x(t), y(t))$ is an **arbitrage opportunity** (or simply an arbitrage) if $V_{(x,y)}(0) = 0$, $V_{(x,y)}(t) \geq -L$, for all t and some constant L, and with positive probability $V_{(x,y)}(t') > 0$ for some t'.

We assume that a European derivative security is traded and its price is denoted by $H(t)$, with $H(T) = H$ as a given, $\mathcal{F}_T$-measurable random variable. Adding the derivative security creates an **extended market**, consisting of the assets $S(t), A(t), H(t)$. The **strategy** is now a triple $(x(t), y(t), z(t))$ with value

$$V_{(x,y,z)}(t) = x(t)S(t) + y(t)A(t) + z(t)H(t).$$

We assume that $H(t)$ is an Itô process (and that $\int_0^T z^2(s)ds < \infty$ P-a.s.) to be able to formulate the self-financing condition

$$dV_{(x,y,z)}(t) = x(t)dS(t) + y(t)dA(t) + z(t)dH(t).$$

Remark 2.12

As we shall see below, for pricing and hedging we can often restrict ourselves to constant $z(t)$, in fact $z(t) = 1$ or $z(t) = -1$ will do, so with $z(t) = 1$, for instance, this condition reads:

$$V_{(x,y,z)}(T) - V_{(x,y,z)}(0) = \int_0^T x(t)dS(t) + \int_0^T y(t)dA(t) + H(T) - H(0).$$

Thus the assumption that $H(t)$ is an Itô process is often omitted in the literature. However, it will be crucial for our next theorem, which shows that the replication price is the unique price for H consistent with the key economic assumption we now assert for the extended market.

The definition of arbitrage can be extended in a natural way.

Definition 2.13

We say that $(x(t), y(t), z(t))$ is an **arbitrage** (in the extended market) if $V_{(x,y,z)}(0) = 0$, $V_{(x,y,z)}(t) \geq -L$, for all t and some constant L, and with positive probability $V_{(x,y,z)}(t') > 0$ for some t'.

We make a fundamental assumption, as follows.

Assumption 2.14

Arbitrage opportunities do not exist in the extended market.

Definition 2.15

A strategy (x, y) **replicates** the derivative security with payoff H if $H = V_{(x,y)}(T)$. The market model is **complete** if every $\mathcal{F}_T^S$-measurable random variable H can be replicated.

We emphasise that the replicating strategy uses only the assets in the underlying market, stock and bond. Replication in the extended market would be trivial: $x(t) = y(t) = 0$, $z(t) = 1$ for all t.

The next result shows that, under the assumption that the price processes $S(t)$ and $H(t)$ are Itô processes, the derivative price process $H(t)$ must coincide with the value process $V_{(x,y)}(t)$ of the replicating strategy at all times if arbitrage is to be avoided. In the finance literature the identity of these two processes is often taken without proof as the definition of no-arbitrage prices, without any mention of extended markets.

In discrete time, the identity of these two price processes comes for free as a consequence of the two Fundamental Theorems (see [DMFM,

Theorem 4.40]), although a direct construction of an arbitrage whenever the two prices differ at some intermediate trading date is not difficult to achieve. In general continuous-time pricing models the relationship between the existence of martingale probabilities and the absence of arbitrage is considerably more subtle. Fortunately, under the assumption that the stock and derivative price processes are both Itô processes, a direct construction of an arbitrage, starting out in identical fashion to that used in the discrete case, is again possible. This construction is quite lengthy and is deferred to the end of the chapter – we outline only the basic idea here.

Theorem 2.16

If H is replicated by $(x(t), y(t))$ and its price process $H(t)$ is an Itô process, the No Arbitrage Principle implies that for all t in $[0, T]$, $H(t) = V_{(x,y)}(t)$.[1]

Proof As usual in such proofs, we wish to benefit from the difference between the values of assets that are claimed to be equal. At the earliest time t_0 such a difference appears with positive probability, we buy the cheap and short the expensive asset, investing the difference risk-free. If we can maintain such a position, this difference will give us an arbitrage profit, since, at time T, due to replication the risky positions will offset each other. However, we have to ensure that the value of the strategy, zero at time t_0, remains above $-L$ at all times. To this end we liquidate the risky position once the value falls, to rebuild it if the trend reverses, with some inevitable losses. These actions are taken at a sequence of random times, carefully designed to keep these losses under control so that a positive profit is achieved at time T.

The construction proving the theorem can be found on page 30. $\square$

2.4 Admissible strategies

We first consider examples of trading strategies that lead to unacceptable conclusions and should therefore be excluded from the class of strategies that we allow investors to pursue, the class of admissible strategies.

Example 2.17
Our first example resembles the familiar 'doubling strategy' that can be employed to make a riskless profit in a sequence of games of tossing a

---

[1] M. Capiński and E. Kopp, Derivative pricing methodology in continuous-time models, *Appl. Math. Lett.* (2012), doi:10.1016/j.anl.2012.05.11.

fair coin. We bet £1 in the first game; if we lose we double the bet to £2, etc. So we double the stake each time we lose, and stop as soon as we win a game. If we are able to wait indefinitely, we are sure to have a net gain of £1: if the win occurs at game n, we win 2^n (having staked 2^{n-1} on this game) and up to that time our total stake has been $1 + 2 + \cdots 2^{n-1} = 2^n - 1$. We have probability 1 that n is finite, since losing the first k games in succession has probability 2^{-k} (assuming independence of the games) and so $P(n < \infty) = \sum_{k=1}^{\infty} 2^{-k} = 1$. Of course, in our ideal market we have unrestricted borrowing, so we could equally well have bet £100,000 to begin with! However, we do need to be able to risk unlimited amounts and wait indefinitely for our win.

Example 2.18
We design a similar strategy in the Black–Scholes model. We choose a strategy where rebalancing of portfolios is restricted to a countable set of times t_n, $n = 0, 1, 2, \ldots$, all $t_n < T$, and let $r = 0$ for simplicity.

Assume $V(0) = 1$ and take $x(0) = \frac{1}{S(0)}$, so that $y(0) = 0$ and this position is kept unchanged up to time t_1. At this time we have

$$P(V(t_1) < 2) = P\left(\frac{1}{S(0)} S(t_1) < 2\right)$$

$$= P(\exp\{mt_1 + \sigma W(t_1)\} < 2) \quad \left(\text{here } m = \mu - \frac{1}{2}\sigma^2\right)$$

$$= P\left(W(t_1) < \frac{1}{\sigma}(\ln 2 - mt_1)\right)$$

$$= N\left(\frac{1}{\sigma\sqrt{t_1}}(\ln 2 - mt_1)\right)$$

$$= p, \text{ say.}$$

On the set $V(t_1) < 2$ we continue the game and at time t_1 take $x(t_1)$ such that with probability p we will have $V(t_2) < 2$. The problem boils down to finding $x(t_1)$ since then $y(t_1) = V(t_1) - x(t_1)S(t_1)$. Taking the limiting case $V(t_2) = 2$ we get $2 = x(t_1)S(t_2) + V(t_1) - x(t_1)S(t_1)$ so the proper choice is

$$x(t_1) = \frac{2 - V(t_1)}{S(t_2) - S(t_1)}.$$

The condition on the probability gives the growth factor α between t_1 and t_2:

$$p = P\left(\frac{S(t_2)}{S(t_1)} < \alpha\right) = P(\exp\{m(t_2 - t_1) + \sigma[W(t_2) - W(t_1)]\} < \alpha)$$

and finding the bond position from the self-financing condition we get the portfolio

$$x(t_1) = \frac{2 - V(t_1)}{S(t_1)(\alpha - 1)}$$

$$y(t_1) = V(t_1) - x(t_1)S(t_1) = V(t_1) - \frac{2 - V(t_1)}{\alpha - 1}.$$

Now

$$P(V(t_2) < 2) = P\left(\frac{2 - V(t_1)}{S(t_1)(\alpha - 1)}S(t_2) + V(t_1) - \frac{2 - V(t_1)}{\alpha - 1} < 2\right)$$

$$= P\left(\frac{1}{S(t_1)}S(t_2) < \alpha\right) = p.$$

Continuing in this fashion we have a piece-wise constant processes $x(t)$, $y(t)$ such that probability of never exceeding 2 is 0 (it is $\lim_{n\to\infty} p^n$) so with probability 1 we will double our money.

Exercise 2.3 Design a version of this strategy with positive risk-free rate.

The possibility of continuous changes of the portfolio allows us to simplify the construction.

Example 2.19
For simplicity assume again $r = 0$ so that $dS(t) = \sigma S(t)dW(t)$ in the risk-neutral world. Discrete approximation over a time step of length h would give

$$S(t + h) - S(t) = \sigma S(t)\sqrt{h}\xi$$

with $\xi = \pm 1$, or, in other words

$$S(t + h) = S(t)(1 + \sigma\sqrt{h}\xi).$$

To execute the doubling strategy at some instant t we have to find $x(t)$ so that in the favourable scenario we earn some amount of money $M(t)$ guaranteeing to cover past losses and generating the additional income equal to double the money invested at time 0. In the positive scenario, $\xi = 1$, the price goes up and we earn

$$x(t)[S(t)(1 + \sigma \sqrt{h}) - S(t)] = x(t)\sigma S(t) \sqrt{h}$$

and for this to be $M(t)$ we need

$$x(t) = \frac{M(t)}{\sigma S(t) \sqrt{h}}.$$

As in the previous examples, we can borrow unlimited amounts to build the strategy, we do not care about losses since they will be carried over to the next period.

Take $V(0)$ arbitrary and motivated by the above computation let

$$x(t) = \frac{1}{\sigma \tilde{S}(t) \sqrt{T - t}}.$$

The risk free component can be computed given the initial value and the stock position so that the strategy is self-financing. The risk-free position will be negative if the stock price is low. If the stock price falls then the amount borrowed increases and this increase gets larger as the terminal time approaches.

The next result will show that with probability one we can get as rich as we wish within the specified time limit. We precede it with a lemma of general interest.

Lemma 2.20
If a is deterministic then $Y(t) = \int_0^t a(s)dW(s)$ has normal distribution with variance $\int_0^t a^2(s)ds$. In addition, the process $Y(t)$ is Gaussian.

Proof See page 36. □

Proposition 2.21
For each $M > 0$

$$P(\min\{t : \tilde{V}(t) \geq M\} \leq T) = 1.$$

Proof **Step 1.** We will find the exact form of $\tilde{V}(t)$.

We know that $d\tilde{S}(t) = \sigma\tilde{S}(t)dW_Q(t)$ and then

$$dV(t) = x(t)d\tilde{S}(t)$$

$$= x(t)\sigma\tilde{S}(t)dW_Q(t) = \frac{1}{\sqrt{T-t}}dW_Q(t)$$

with the $x(t)$ inserted. We know that the stochastic integral of a deterministic function is Gaussian, and here we have

$$\tilde{V}(t) = \int_0^t \frac{1}{\sqrt{T-u}}dW_Q(u).$$

Let

$$\gamma(t) = \int_0^t \frac{1}{T-u}du$$

with $\gamma(t) = 0$ for $t \le 0$. Clearly $\gamma(t) \to \infty$ as $t \to T$ since

$$\int_0^t \frac{1}{T-u}du = -\int_T^{T-t} \frac{1}{y}du = \ln y|_{T-t}^T = \ln T - \ln(T-t) \to \infty.$$

Step 2. We claim that $\tilde{V}(t)$ and $W_Q(\gamma(t))$ have the same distribution.

We will compare these processes by examining their covariances. Let $s \le t$,

$$\mathbb{E}_Q(\tilde{V}(t)\tilde{V}(s)) = \mathbb{E}_Q(\mathbb{E}_Q(\tilde{V}(t)\tilde{V}(s)|\mathcal{F}_s))$$

$$= \mathbb{E}_Q(\tilde{V}(s)\mathbb{E}_Q(\tilde{V}(t)|\mathcal{F}_s))$$

$$= \mathbb{E}_Q(\tilde{V}^2(s)) = \gamma(s)$$

so

$$\mathbb{E}_Q(\tilde{V}(t)\tilde{V}(s)) = \min\{\gamma(t), \gamma(s)\}.$$

For the Wiener process W_Q, with $s \le t$ we obtain

$$\mathbb{E}_Q(W_Q(\gamma(t))W_Q(\gamma(s))) = \mathbb{E}_Q(\mathbb{E}_Q(W_Q(\gamma(t))W_Q(\gamma(s))|\mathcal{F}_{\gamma(s)}))$$

$$= \mathbb{E}_Q(W_Q(\gamma(s)\mathbb{E}_Q(W_Q(\gamma(t))|\mathcal{F}_{\gamma(s)}))$$

$$= \mathbb{E}_Q(W_Q^2(\gamma(s))) = \gamma(s)$$

so

$$\mathbb{E}_Q(W_Q(\gamma(t))W_Q(\gamma(s))) = \min\{\gamma(t), \gamma(s)\}.$$

Therefore the process $(t, \omega) \to \tilde{V}(t, \omega), t \in [0, T]$ is a Gaussian process with continuous paths, mean 0 and the same covariances as the process $\{(u, \omega) \to W_Q(u, \omega) : u \ge 0\}$ where we set $u = \gamma(t)$ for $t \in [0, T]$. Hence the two processes have the same distribution.

Step 3. We use a well-known property of the Wiener process (see [SCF]):

$$Q(\max_{u \geq 0} W_Q(u) \leq M) = 0.$$

As Q and P have the same null sets this ensures that we also have

$$P(\max_{u \geq 0} W_Q(u) \leq M) = 0.$$

Since $\tilde{V}(t)$ and $W_Q(\gamma(t))$ have the same distribution we see that $\tilde{V}(t)$ will P-almost surely reach level M in the interval $[0, T)$.

Let

$$\tau = \min\{t : \tilde{V}(t) = M\}$$

and modify our strategy

$$x'(t) = \begin{cases} x(t) \text{ for } t \leq \tau \\ 0 \text{ for } t > \tau. \end{cases}$$

Having reached the target wealth we liquidate our stock position so we put all the money into the risk free asset. The discounted value of the portfolio remains constant. The component y' of the strategy is chosen so that the strategy is self-financing.

As a result we finally have

$$\tilde{V}_{(x',y')}(T) = M. \qquad \qquad \square$$

The conclusion is unacceptable from the point of view of the No Arbitrage Principle. This example also violates market practice, where it is impossible to borrow heavily to gamble on a reversal of one's fortunes. The bank would require a collateral, which in this case would be the shares held by the investor, but if the stock price goes down, this excludes an increase in borrowing. A simple remedy to eliminate such unrealistic strategies is to require that the value of the portfolio be bounded from below by a determinstic constant. The next proposition shows that the above example is no longer possible if such a restiction is imposed.

Proposition 2.22
If (x, y) is self-financing and $V(t)$ is bounded below by a constant, then $\tilde{V}(t)$ is a supermartingale with respect to Q.

Proof   Recall that

$$d\tilde{V}(t) = x(t)d\tilde{S}(t) = x(t)\tilde{S}(t)\sigma dW_Q(t)$$

so $\tilde{V}(t)$ is a local Q-martingale, since we know that a stochastic integral is a local martingale. It is proved in [SCF, Proposition 4.28] that a non-negative local martingale is a supermartingale, and by considering $\tilde{V}(t) + L$ instead of $\tilde{V}(t)$ it is clear that the result extends to this case. □

Corollary 2.23
Doubling strategies contradict the assumption $V(t) \geq -L$.

Proof A supermartingale has decreasing expectation so $\mathbb{E}(\tilde{V}(t)) \leq V(0)$ and this contradicts $\tilde{V}_{(x',y)}(T) = M$ for arbitrary M. □

Another example of an unacceptable strategy is one leading to inevitable bankruptcy (a **suicide** strategy). If we go bankrupt with probability 1, starting with a positive investment, the opposite party will gain a riskless profit, which contradicts the No Arbitrage Principle. For a specific example, let $V(0) = 1$ and as before put

$$x(t) = \frac{1}{\sigma \tilde{S}(t) \sqrt{T - t}}.$$

Then

$$\tau = \min\{t : \tilde{V}_{(x,y)}(t) = M\} \leq T$$

with probability 1 as we noticed above. Let $M = 0$ and modify the strategy in the following way. We begin with positive wealth and we liquidate our position at the moment we go bankrupt. The risk-free position will also be zero then, and so will be the terminal wealth:

$$x'(t) = \begin{cases} x(t) \text{ for } t \leq \tau \\ 0 \text{ for } t > \tau. \end{cases}$$

Then

$$V(t) \geq 0$$
$$V_{(x',y')}(T) = 0 - \text{this is unacceptable.}$$

We suspect that if we can lose money with certainty, one can also gain some money with certainty reversing the strategy, which would violate the No Arbitrage Principle. Let $x'' = -x'$, $y'' = -y' + 1$. Then $V_{(x'',y'')}(0) = 0$, $V_{(x'',y'')}(T) = e^{rT} > 0$, which is an arbitrage:

$$V_{(x'',y'')}(0) = V_{(-x',-y')}(0) + 1 = 0,$$
$$V_{(x'',y'')}(T) = V_{(-x',-y')}(T) + A(T) = e^{rT}.$$

This motivates the next definition.

Definition 2.24

A self-financing strategy (x, y) is called **admissible** if

(1) $V(t) \geq -L$,

(2) $\tilde{V}(t)$ is a Q-martingale.

The second condition can be replaced by the requirement that the expected value of a strategy be constant, since, as we know, a supermartingale with constant expectation is a martingale. Other conditions guaranteeing that martingale condition are also possible, the crucial requirement is to make sure that a local martingale is a martingale.

The two conditions imposed eliminate the above doubling and suicide strategies. We have already explained that insisting that the investor's wealth must stay above some constant (usually negative) level at all times will eliminate doubling strategies. The suicide strategy is not admissible since a martingale has constant expectation, so if we start with positive wealth we cannot have zero with certainty at the terminal time since the expectation would then be zero as well.

Admissible strategies are optimal in a certain sense.

Proposition 2.25

If a derivative security with payoff H can be replicated by a self-financing strategy (x_1, y_1) and by an admissible strategy (x_2, y_2), then

$$V_{(x_2, y_2)}(0) \leq V_{(x_1, y_1)}(0).$$

Proof   The inequality means that the admissible strategies are cheaper. This is intuitively clear since the potential waste of money from the suicidal strategies has been eliminated. We have

$$V_{(x_1, y_1)}(T) = H,$$
$$V_{(x_2, y_2)}(T) = H.$$

The process $\tilde{V}_{(x_2, y_2)}(t)$ is a martingale so

$$V_{(x_2, y_2)}(0) = \mathbb{E}(\tilde{V}_{(x_2, y_2)}(T)).$$

The process $\tilde{V}_{(x_1, y_1)}(t)$ is a supermartingale, the expectation decreases, so

$$V_{(x_1, y_1)}(0) \geq \mathbb{E}(\tilde{V}_{(x_1, y_1)}(T)).$$

The right-hand sides of the last two relations are equal, which proves the claim. $\square$

We noticed before that, as a result of the No Arbitrage Principle, the value of a derivative is the the same as the value of a replicating strategy. Uniqueness of the replicating strategies follows from this fact but it is interesting that the No Arbitrage Principle is not needed explicitly (it is of course implicit in the definition of admissible strategies). Solving the pricing problem now reduces to establishing the existence of a replicating strategy.

Proposition 2.26
If a derivative security H can be replicated by two admissible strategies (x_1, y_1) and (x_2, y_2), then they are the same, that is,

$$x_1(t) = x_2(t),$$
$$y_1(t) = y_2(t).$$

Proof The conditions for replication imply, after applying the discount factor e^{-rT}, that:

$$\tilde{V}_{(x_1,y_1)}(T) = \tilde{H}$$
$$\tilde{V}_{(x_2,y_2)}(T) = \tilde{H}.$$

Next, use the fact that an admissible strategy is a martingale with respect to the martingale probability:

$$\mathbb{E}_Q(\tilde{V}_{(x_1,y_1)}(T)|\mathcal{F}_t) = \tilde{V}_{(x_1,y_1)}(t)$$
$$\mathbb{E}_Q(\tilde{V}_{(x_2,y_2)}(T)|\mathcal{F}_t) = \tilde{V}_{(x_2,y_2)}(t)$$

Now the left-hand sides are equal by the replication and so are the right-hand sides, and after multiplying both sides by e^{rt}, we obtain

$$V_{(x_1,y_1)}(t) = V_{(x_2,y_2)}(t).$$

Both strategies are self-financing, so by definition

$$dV_{(x_1,y_1)}(t) = x_1(t)dS(t) + y_1(t)dA(t)$$
$$dV_{(x_2,y_2)}(t) = x_2(t)dS(t) + y_2(t)dA(t).$$

Write $X(t) = V_{(x_1,y_1)}(t) - V_{(x_2,y_2)}(t) = 0$. We find the Itô differential of X using linearity and the self-financing property of both strategies

$$
\begin{aligned}
dX &= dV_{(x_1,y_1)}(t) - dV_{(x_2,y_2)}(t) \\
&= x_1(t)dS(t) + y_1(t)dA(t) - x_2(t)dS(t) + y_2(t)dA(t) \quad \text{(self-financing)} \\
&= [x_1(t) - x_2(t)]dS(t) + [y_1(t) - y_2(t)]dA(t) \quad \text{(linearity)} \\
&= \{[x_1(t) - x_2(t)]\mu S(t) + [y_1(t) - y_2(t)]rA(t)\}dt \\
&\quad + [x_1(t) - x_2(t)]\sigma S(t)dW(t)
\end{aligned}
$$

after inserting $dS(t) = \mu S(t)dt + \sigma S(t)dW(t)$, and $dA(t) = rA(t)dt$. Since the representation of the Itô process X in the form $dX(t) = a(t)dt + b(t)dW(t)$ is unique (see [SCF]) and here X is the zero process, it follows that both coefficients are 0. Thus $x_1(t) - x_2(t) = 0$ and therefore also $y_1(t) - y_2(t) = 0$ for all t.

□

2.5 Proofs

Theorem 2.16

If H is replicated by $(x(t), y(t))$ and its price process $H(t)$ is an Itô process, the No Arbitrage Principle implies that for all t in $[0, T]$, $H(t) = V_{(x,y)}(t)$.

Proof We assume, without loss of generality, that $A(t) = 1$ for all t, so that for any strategy (x, y),

$$V_{(x,y)}(t) = x(t)S(t) + y(t)$$

for all t. If $(x(t), y(t))$ replicates $H(t)$, then $H = V_{(x,y)}(T)$.

Suppose that for some $t_0 < T$ we have $V_{(x,y)}(t_0, \omega) \neq H(t_0, \omega)$ for $\omega \in B$, $P(B) > 0$. Then B is the union of two disjoint events

$$B_1 = \{\omega : V_{(x,y)}(t_0, \omega) < H(t_0, \omega)\}, \quad B_2 = \{\omega : V_{(x,y)}(t_0, \omega) > H(t_0, \omega)\},$$

and at least one of them has positive probability. We now build an arbitrage strategy x_a, y_a, z_a which contradicts the No Arbitrage Principle.

For $s < t_0$ we do nothing: $x_a(s) = y_a(s) = z_a(s) = 0$, hence $V_{(x_a, y_a, z_a)}(s) = 0$. At any $\omega \notin B$ we keep this zero portfolio until time T.

Step 1. Starting portfolio.

At t_0, only for scenarios ω in B, and depending on which inequality obtains at ω, we buy the cheap asset and sell the expensive one to invest the balance risk-free. So for $\omega \in B_1$ we put $z_a(t_0, \omega) = -1$, $x_a(t_0, \omega) = x(t_0, \omega)$, $y_a(t_0, \omega) = y(t_0, \omega) + H(t_0, \omega) - V_{(x,y)}(t_0, \omega)$ and on B_2 we take $z_a(t_0, \omega) = 1$, $x_a(t_0, \omega) = -x(t_0, \omega)$, $y_a(t_0, \omega) = -y(t_0, \omega) + V_{(x,y)}(t_0, \omega) - H(t_0, \omega)$. We express this in a unified way for ω in B by setting

$$Y(t_0) = |V_{(x,y)}(t_0) - H(t_0)|,$$

since then, at t_0 we have

$$x_a(t_0, \omega) = \mathbf{1}_{B_1}(\omega)x(t_0, \omega) - \mathbf{1}_{B_2}(\omega)x(t_0, \omega),$$
$$y_a(t_0, \omega) = \mathbf{1}_{B_1}(\omega)y(t_0, \omega) - \mathbf{1}_{B_2}(\omega)y(t_0, \omega) + \mathbf{1}_{B_1 \cup B_2}(\omega)Y(t_0, \omega),$$
$$z_a(t_0, \omega) = -\mathbf{1}_{B_1}(\omega) + \mathbf{1}_{B_2}(\omega),$$

with $V_{(x_a, y_b, z_a)}(t_0) = 0$.

If we could keep the analogous portfolio (using $x(t), y(t)$ instead of $x(t_0)$, $y(t_0)$) for all t in the interval $[t_0, T]$ we would earn $Y(t_0, \omega)$ for ω in B, due to replication. However, this is impossible in general since we have to make sure that the strategy satisfies the conditions required for arbitrage; in particular, its value at any $t > t_0$ should not be allowed to go below $-L$.

The construction of the processes $x_a(t), y_a(t), z_a(t)$, for $t > t_0$ will be based on a sequence of stopping times indicating the periods during which we have to withdraw from investing in the replicating strategy $(x(t), y(t))$ to control the losses. The losses may emerge as a result of the difference between $H(t)$ and $V_{(x,y)}(t)$ going the wrong way. We wish to limit the total accumulated loss at any time to $\frac{1}{2}L$ so that our value process remains above $-L$, while on the other hand, we wish to limit our loss to $\frac{1}{2}Y(t_0)$, so that by time T we retain at least the half of the initial gain. So we could modify the construction by setting $Y(t_0) = \min\{L, |V_{(x,y)}(t_0) - H(t_0)|\}$ in the above, but for simplicity we assume instead that $Y(t_0) \leq L$.

Step 2. The first period.

For $t \geq t_0, \omega \in B$, we let

$$x_a(t, \omega) = \mathbf{1}_{B_1}(\omega)x(t, \omega) - \mathbf{1}_{B_2}(\omega)x(t, \omega),$$

$$y_a(t, \omega) = \mathbf{1}_{B_1}(\omega)y(t, \omega) - \mathbf{1}_{B_2}(\omega)y(t, \omega) + \mathbf{1}_{B_1 \cup B_2}(\omega)Y(t_0, \omega),$$

$$z_a(t, \omega) = -\mathbf{1}_{B_1}(\omega) + \mathbf{1}_{B_2}(\omega).$$

We monitor the value of this strategy

$$V_{(x_a, y_b, z_a)}(t) = x_a(t)S(t) + y_a(t) + z_a(t)H(t)$$

as time progresses, ready to react if unwanted losses emerge.

First consider $\omega \in B_1$. If at $t \geq t_0$ the difference $H(t, \omega) - V_{(x,y)}(t, \omega) < Y(t_0(\omega))$, we need do nothing, as $V_{(x_a, y_b, z_a)}(t, \omega) > 0$, and it reaches the value $Y(t_0, \omega)$ at time T. However, if $H(t, \omega) - V_{(x,y)}(t, \omega) > Y(t_0, \omega)$, we suffer temporary losses and we must make sure that our total value does not fall below $-L$. So we construct the first stopping time τ_1 for the action to prevent this. Let

$$\tau_1(\omega) = \inf\left\{s > t_0 : H(s, \omega) - V_{(x,y)}(s, \omega) \geq Y(t_0, \omega)\left(1 + \frac{1}{2}\right)\right\}$$

so that $H(s, \omega) - V_{(x,y)}(s, \omega)$ first hits $Y(t_0, \omega)(1 + \frac{1}{2})$ at time $\tau_1(\omega)$, and putting $\tau_1(\omega) = T$ if this never happens.

Similarly, for $\omega \in B_2$ we define

$$\tau_1(\omega) = \inf\left\{s > t_0 : V_{(x,y)}(s, \omega) - H(s, \omega) \geq Y(t_0, \omega)\left(1 + \frac{1}{2}\right)\right\}$$

and for ω in $\Omega \backslash B$ we set $\tau_1(\omega) = T$. Since $B \in \mathcal{F}_{t_0}$ it clear that τ_1 is a finite $\mathcal{F}_t$-stopping time since the processes H and $V_{(x,y)}$ have continuous paths, so the first hitting time of a closed set is an $\mathcal{F}_t$-stopping time (see Exercise 2.5 below). It is convenient to introduce the process

$$Y(t) = |V_{(x,y)}(t) - H(t)|, \quad t \geq t_0$$

since then for $\omega \in B$

$$\tau_1(\omega) = \inf\left\{s > t_0 : Y(s,\omega) \geq Y(t_0,\omega)\left(1 + \frac{1}{2}\right)\right\} \wedge T$$

with convention $\inf\{\emptyset\} = +\infty$. This covers the actions on both components B_1 and B_2 of B.

If $\omega \in B$ we liquidate our holdings in H and $V_{(x,y)}$ at time $\tau_1(\omega)$ and so

$$z_a(\tau_1) = 0, \quad x_a(\tau_1) = 0, \quad y_a(\tau_1) = -\frac{1}{2}Y(t_0).$$

On B this gives

$$V_{(x_a,y_a,z_a)}(\tau_1) = -\frac{1}{2}Y(t_0) > -L.$$

Clearly this change is performed within the funds available. The loss on risky assets is fully covered by a fraction of $Y(t_0)$, the portfolio value $V_{(x_a,y_a,z_a)}(\tau_1)$ is the same before and after the change, since, almost surely on B, the left-limit

$$V_{(x_a,y_a,z_a)}(\tau_1-,\omega) = \lim_{t \nearrow \tau_1(\omega)} V_{(x_a,y_a,z_a)}(s,\omega) = Y(t_0,\omega) - \lim_{t \nearrow \tau_1(\omega)} Y(t,\omega) = -\frac{1}{2}Y(t_0).$$

Note that this and the fact that value stays fixed after $\tau_1(\omega)$ shows that $V_{(x_a,y_a,z_a)}$ is path-continuous at $\tau_1(\omega)$.

Step 3. The second period.

For $t \geq \tau_1$ we keep the position taken at τ_1 and have constant components

$$z_a(t) = 0, \quad x_a(t) = 0, \quad y_a(t) = -\frac{1}{2}Y(t_0).$$

The next change is aimed at recovering some loss and such a possibility follows from the fact that the difference $H(t) - V_{(x,y)}(t)$ goes to 0 eventually, so there is $\tau_2(\omega)$ at which $Y(t,\omega) = |H(t,\omega) - V_{(x,y)}(t,\omega)|$ crosses $Y(t_0,\omega)(1+\frac{1}{4})$ going downwards. We want the sequence τ_n we construct to converge to T so we require $\tau_2 \geq T - \frac{1}{2}$ (assume $T > 1$ with obvious modification otherwise).

If $H(t) - V_{(x,y)}(t)$ has finite variation, then since it is an Itô propcess, its stochastic part is zero and the dynamics must be the same as that of the risk-free assets (see Exercise 2.4). As a result, it is constant and there is no need to modify our strategy at all. Hence we work under the assumption that $Y(t)$ has infinite variation and so for $\omega \in B$ there exists $s \in (T - \frac{1}{2}, T)$ such that $Y(s) > Y(t_0)(1 + \frac{1}{2})$, while at T this difference is 0, so the stopping time

$$\tau_2(\omega) = \min\left\{s \geq \max\left\{\tau_1, T - \frac{1}{2}\right\} : Y(s, \omega) \leq Y(t_0, \omega)\left(1 + \frac{1}{4}\right)\right\} \wedge T \text{ if } \omega \in B,$$

$$\tau_2(\omega) = T \text{ if } \omega \in \Omega \backslash B, .$$

is well defined. At this random time, for $\omega \in B$, we rebuild our holdings in H and $V_{(x,y)}$ setting

$$x_a(\tau_2, \omega) = \mathbf{1}_{B_1}(\omega)x(\tau_2(\omega), \omega) - \mathbf{1}_{B_2}(\omega)x(\tau_2(\omega), \omega),$$

$$y_a(\tau_2, \omega) = \mathbf{1}_{B_1}(\omega)y(\tau_2(\omega), \omega) - \mathbf{1}_{B_2}(\omega)y(\tau_2(\omega), \omega)$$

$$+ \mathbf{1}_{B_1 \cup B_2}(\omega)[-\frac{1}{2}Y(t_0, \omega) + \frac{1}{4}Y(t_0, \omega)],$$

$$z_a(\tau_2, \omega) = -\mathbf{1}_{B_1}(\omega) + \mathbf{1}_{B_2}(\omega),$$

We have made up some lost ground, since $|H(\tau_2) - (x(\tau_2)S(\tau_2) + y(\tau_2))| = (1 + \frac{1}{4})Y(t_0)$ and the net result of our actions at τ_1 and τ_2 is that our holding of cash at time τ_2 is $\frac{3}{4}Y(t_0)$.

Step 4. General construction.

We continue in this fashion: in general, for $\omega \in B$ we set $\tau_0 = t_0$ and for $n \geq 0$,

$$\tau_{2n+1} = \min\left\{s \geq \tau_{2n} : Y(s, \omega) \geq Y(t_0)\left(1 + \frac{1}{2}\frac{1}{2^n}\right)\right\} \wedge T,$$

$$\tau_{2n+2}$$

$$= \min\left\{s \geq \max\left\{\tau_{2n+1}, T - \frac{1}{2n+2}\right\} : Y(s, \omega) \leq Y(t_0)\left(1 + \frac{1}{2}\frac{1}{2^{n+1}}\right)\right\} \wedge T,$$

with $\tau_k = T$ outside B, keeping the value above $-L$ at all times and losing in total at most half of the initial profit, thus maintaining an arbitrage profit of at least $\frac{1}{2}Y(t_0)$ at time T on all of B. It is routine to check that the τ_k are stopping times.

Next we introduce the sets

$$C_k = \{(t, \omega) : \omega \in B, \ \tau_k(\omega) \leq t < \tau_{k+1}(\omega)\}, \quad k = 0, 1, 2, \ldots$$

and only on sets of the form C_{2n} do our strategies involve positions in H and $V_{(x,y)}$; on C_{2n+1} we have concentrated our holdings in the risk-free asset in order to handle the arbitrage profit, so our total value remains constant, as $A(t) = 1$ for all t. We can write for $\omega \in B = B_1 \cup B_2$

$$x_a(s,\omega) = \sum_{n=0}^{\infty} \mathbf{1}_{C_{2n}}(s,\omega)[\mathbf{1}_{B_1}(\omega) - \mathbf{1}_{B_2}(\omega)]x(s,\omega),$$

$$y_a(s,\omega) = \sum_{n=0}^{\infty} \mathbf{1}_{C_{2n}}(s,\omega)[\mathbf{1}_{B_1}(\omega) - \mathbf{1}_{B_2}(\omega)]y(s,\omega)$$

$$+ \sum_{n=0}^{\infty} \mathbf{1}_{C_{2n} \cup C_{2n+1}}(1 + \frac{1}{2^{n+1}})Y(t_0,\omega),$$

$$z_a(s,\omega) = \sum_{n=0}^{\infty} \mathbf{1}_{C_{2n}}(s,\omega)[-\mathbf{1}_{B_1}(\omega) + \mathbf{1}_{B_2}(\omega)],$$

and outside these sets, x_a, z_a are 0 and y_a is constant.

Step 5. Self-financing condition.

We have assumed that $A(t) = 1$ for all t in $[0, T]$, and the self-financing condition reads

$$V_{(x_a,y_b,z_a)}(t) = \int_{t_0}^{t} x_a(s)dS(s) + \int_{t_0}^{t} z_a(s)dH(s). \qquad (2.3)$$

For $t < t_0$ both sides are zero. Fix $t \in [t_0, T)$, and note that the sequence τ_n converges to T, $\tau_n \geq T - \frac{1}{n}$, so there is a deterministic n_0 such that $\tau_{n_0} \leq t$, $\tau_{n_0+1} > t$ for $\omega \in B$ (with $\tau_n(\omega) = T$ for $\omega \notin B$). So the sums in the definition of x_a, y_a, z_a are finite and so we will have finite sums on both sides above. Therefore it is sufficient to prove the required identity by working on consecutive intervals to see that the corresponding components are equal.

Consider the first interval: $t \in [\tau_0, \tau_1)$. Define $D_0 = \{\omega \in B : t_0 \leq t < \tau_1(\omega)\}$. For all $s \leq t$, for all $(s, \omega) \in C_0$

$$x_a(s,\omega) = \mathbf{1}_{C_0}(s,\omega)\left(\mathbf{1}_{B_1}(\omega)x(s,\omega) - \mathbf{1}_{B_2}(\omega)x(s,\omega)\right),$$

$$y_a(s,\omega) = \mathbf{1}_{C_0}(s,\omega)\left(\mathbf{1}_{B_1}(\omega)y(s,\omega) - \mathbf{1}_{B_2}(\omega)y(s,\omega) + \mathbf{1}_{B_1 \cup B_2}(\omega)Y(s_0,\omega)\right),$$

$$z_a(s,\omega) = \mathbf{1}_{C_0}(s,\omega)\left(-\mathbf{1}_{B_1}(\omega) + \mathbf{1}_{B_2}(\omega)\right).$$

For $\omega \in D_0$ the right-hand side of (2.3) is

$$\int_{t_0}^t \mathbf{1}_{C_0} \left[\mathbf{1}_{B_1} x(s) - \mathbf{1}_{B_2} x(s) \right] dS(s) + \int_{t_0}^t \mathbf{1}_{C_0} \left[-\mathbf{1}_{B_1} + \mathbf{1}_{B_2} \right] dH(s)$$

$$= (\mathbf{1}_{B_1} - \mathbf{1}_{B_2}) \left(\mathbf{1}_{D_0} \int_{t_0}^t x(s) dS(s) - \mathbf{1}_{D_0} (H(t) - H(t_0)) \right)$$

(by Prop. 4.19 of [SCF])

$$= (\mathbf{1}_{B_1} - \mathbf{1}_{B_2}) \left(V_{(x,y)}(t) - V_{(x,y)}(t_0) - (H(t) - H(t_0)) \right)$$

$((x, y)$ is self-financing)

$$= (\mathbf{1}_{B_1} - \mathbf{1}_{B_2}) \left(x(t) S(t) + y(t) - V_{(x,y)}(t_0) - (H(t) - H(t_0)) \right)$$

$$= x_a(t) S(t) + y_a(t) - \mathbf{1}_{B_1 \cup B_2} Y(t_0) + z_a H(t) + (\mathbf{1}_{B_1} - \mathbf{1}_{B_2}) \left[H(t_0) - V_{(x,y)}(t_0) \right]$$

$$= V_{(x_a, y_b, z_a)}(t).$$

(Strictly speaking Proposition 4.19 of [SCF] requires right-closed intervals which can be obtained by considering $\tau_1 - \varepsilon$ instead of τ_1. The generalisation to localisation over intervals $[v, \tau)$ is straightforward; see Exercise 2.6 below.)

For the second interval $[\tau_1, \tau_2) = \{(t, \omega) : \tau_1(\omega) \leq t < \tau_2(\omega)\}$ we note that x_a, z_a are zero here, hence so is $\int_{\tau_1}^t x_a(s) dS(s) + \int_{\tau_1}^t z_a(s) dH(s)$ but due to the construction the value of the strategy remains constant: $V_{(x_a, y_a, z_a)}(\tau_1) = V_{(x_a, y_a, z_a)}(t)$.

For further active periods (non-zero x_a, z_a) we argue in the same way as for $t \in [\tau_0, \tau_1)$, working on the sets C_k for even k, whereas for non-active sets (where x_a, z_a are zero) we note that $V_{(x_a, y_a, z_a)}(t)$ is constant on C_k for odd k. So we have shown that our arbitrage strategy is self-financing. $\square$

Exercise 2.4 Prove that if the value process of an asset $B(t)$ satisfies the equation $dB(t) = g(t) B(t) dt$, where g is a stochastic process, then $g(t) = r$ a.s. for all $t \geq 0$.

Exercise 2.5 Given a filtration $(\mathcal{F}_t)_{t \in [0,T]}$ and an adapted process X with a.s. continuous paths, show that the first hitting of a closed set in $\mathbb{R}$ is an $\mathcal{F}_t$-stopping time.

Exercise 2.6 Prove that if $f, g \in M^2$ and τ_1, τ_2 are stopping times such that $f(s, \omega) = g(s, \omega)$ whenever $\tau_1(\omega) \leq s < \tau_2(\omega)$, then for any $t_1 \leq t_2$

$$\int_{t_1}^{t_2} f(s)dW(s) = \int_{t_1}^{t_2} g(s)dW(s)$$

for almost all ω satisfying $\tau_1(\omega) \leq t_1 \leq t_2 < \tau_2(\omega)$.

Lemma 2.20

If a is deterministic then $Y(t) = \int_0^t a(s)dW(s)$ has normal distribution with variance $\int_0^t a^2(s)ds$. In addition, the process $Y(t)$ is Gaussian.

Proof It suffices to show that the characteristic function of $Y(t)$ has the right form, namely (see [PF]) for any real λ:

$$\mathbb{E}(e^{i\lambda Y(t)}) = \exp\left\{-\frac{1}{2}\lambda^2 \int_0^t a^2(s)ds\right\}.$$

Employ the Itô formula with $F(x) = e^{i\lambda x}$ (we only have it for real functions but working with real and imaginary parts gives this extension easily), so that $F'(x) = i\lambda e^{i\lambda x}$, $F''(x) = \lambda^2 e^{i\lambda x}$); thus

$$e^{i\lambda Y(t)} = 1 + i\lambda \int_0^t e^{i\lambda Y(u)}a(u)dW(u) - \frac{1}{2}\lambda^2 \int_0^t e^{i\lambda Y(u)}a^2(u)du.$$

Since $|e^{i\lambda Y(u)}| \leq 1$, $e^{i\lambda Y(u)} \in M^2$. Take the expectation with respect to P and by Fubini we obtain

$$\mathbb{E}(e^{i\lambda Y(t)}) = 1 - \frac{1}{2}\lambda^2 \int_0^t \mathbb{E}(e^{i\lambda Y(u)})a^2(u)du.$$

Now write $\mathbb{E}(e^{i\lambda Y(t)}) = \psi(t)$, so that ψ satisfies

$$\psi(t) = 1 - \frac{1}{2}\lambda^2 \int_0^t \psi(u)a^2(u)du,$$

$$\psi'(t) = -\frac{1}{2}\lambda^2\psi(t)a^2(t),$$

with $\psi(0) = 1$. But this problem has a unique solution of the required form.

For any $0 = t_0 < t_1 < \cdots < t_n \leq T$, the increments $Y(t_k) - Y(t_{k-1})$, $k = 1, \ldots, n$, are Gaussian, so the vector of the increments $(Y(t_n) - Y(t_{n-1}), \ldots, Y(t_1) - Y(t_0))$ is Gaussian (see [PF], [SCF]). $\qquad \square$

3

Option pricing and hedging

Having fixed the class of admissible trading strategies we can develop techniques for pricing European derivatives. The key concept remains that of replication: we wish to show that a wide class of derivative securities can be replicated in the Black–Scholes model. We first derive and employ a fundamental property of martingales: given a Wiener process W, any square-integrable martingale for its natural filtration $\mathcal{F}_t^W$ can be represented as an Itô integral. This leads to a direct calculation of the price process for any path-independent European derivative, and we illustrate this by finding explicit formulae for the two basic 'vanilla' options: the European put and call. Finally, we show that the Black–Scholes PDE is solved by the formula for the call option and we compare the two approaches.

Let $H(t)$ be the value process of a derivative and suppose for the present that we can replicate it. This means that there exists an admissible strategy $(x(t), y(t))$ such that

$$V_{(x,y)}(t) = H(t).$$

In particular this means that the discounted process $\tilde{H}(t)$ is a martingale with respect to the risk-neutral probability Q and, consequently, for a European claim (henceforth writing $\mathcal{F}_t$ for $\mathcal{F}_t^S = \mathcal{F}_t^W$)

$$\tilde{H}(t) = \mathbb{E}_Q(\tilde{H}(T)|\mathcal{F}_t) = \mathbb{E}_Q(e^{-rT}H|\mathcal{F}_t).$$

On the other hand, as the strategy is self-financing we know that

$$d\tilde{V}(t) = x(t)d\tilde{S}(t) = x(t)\tilde{S}(t)\sigma dW_Q(t),$$

in other words,

$$\tilde{V}_{(x,y)}(t) = V(0) + \int_0^t x(u)\tilde{S}(u)\sigma dW_Q(u).$$

This means that to execute the replication we need $x(t)$ to satisfy

$$\mathbb{E}_Q(e^{-rT}H|\mathcal{F}_t) = V(0) + \int_0^t x(u)\tilde{S}(u)\sigma dW_Q(u).$$

This is therefore an example of a general problem: given a martingale M (such as the process on the left above), find a process f such that $M(t)$ is the stochastic integral of f. The next section is devoted to solving this problem.

3.1   Martingale representation theorem

Recall that if $f \in \mathcal{M}^2$ then

$$M(t) = \int_0^t f(s)dW(s) \tag{3.1}$$

is a martingale, and $M(t) \in L^2(\Omega)$. We will show that the converse is true: any square-integrable martingale $M(t)$ for the filtration $\mathcal{F}_t^W$ generated by a Wiener process can be written as a stochastic integral with respect to W. (An impatient and trusting reader may skip the rest of this section and proceed to the next one where we apply this fact to replicate an option.)

So processes defined by the stochastic integral cover a wide class of martingales. As we have just seen, this will bring us closer to solving the replication problem, where we will work with W_Q. Here we take an arbitrary Wiener process, if only to simplify the notation.

The next proposition finds a representation for some special martingales. This can be regarded as an example, but as we shall see, in fact a lot of ground is covered. Searching for non-trivial examples of martingales, an exponential one springs to mind, and we must be able to decompose it if our general claim is to be valid.

Proposition 3.1

For any bounded deterministic function $g : [0, T] \to \mathbb{R}$ there exists $f_g \in \mathcal{M}^2$ such that

$$\exp\{ \int_0^t g(s)dW(s) - \frac{1}{2} \int_0^t g^2(s)ds \} = 1 + \int_0^t f_g(s)dW(s).$$

Proof The process we are decomposing can be written in the form

$$Z(t) = \exp\{X(t)\},$$

where

$$X(t) = \int_0^t g(s)dW(s) - \frac{1}{2} \int_0^t g^2(s)ds.$$

Apply the Itô formula with $Z(t) = F(X(t))$, $F(x) = e^x = F_x = F_{xx}$ and

$$dX(t) = g(t)dW(t) - \frac{1}{2}g^2(t)dt$$

so that

$$dZ(t) = F_x(X(t))g(t)dW(t) - F_x(X(t))\frac{1}{2}g^2(t)dt + \frac{1}{2}F_{xx}(X(t))g^2(t)dt$$

$$= Z(t)g(t)dW(t).$$

This implies, with $Z(0) = 1$,

$$Z(t) = 1 + \int_0^t Z(s)g(s)dW(s)$$

so we put $f_g(s) = Z(s)g(s)$.

It remains to show that $f_g \in \mathcal{M}^2$. Since g is bounded, $|g| \leq C$, say,

$$\mathbb{E}\left(\int_0^T Z^2(t)g^2(t)dt \right) \leq C^2\mathbb{E}\left(\int_0^T Z^2(t)dt \right)$$

$$= C^2\mathbb{E}\left(\int_0^T \exp\left\{ 2\int_0^t g(s)dW(s) - \int_0^t g^2(s)ds \right\} dt \right)$$

$$= C^2\exp\left\{ -\int_0^t g^2(s)ds \right\}\mathbb{E}\left(\int_0^T \exp\left\{ 2\int_0^t g(s)dW(s) \right\} dt \right).$$

Since the stochastic integral of a deterministic function is a normally distributed random variable, we have

$$\mathbb{E}\left(\exp\left\{ 2\int_0^t g(s)dW(s) \right\} \right) = \exp\left\{ 2\int_0^t g^2(s)ds \right\}$$

and the integral from 0 to T of this function is finite. So Fubini's theorem applies and we conclude that

$$\mathbb{E}\left(\int_0^T \exp\left\{2\int_0^t g(s)dW(s)\right\}dt\right) = \int_0^T \mathbb{E}\left[\exp\left\{2\int_0^t g(s)dW(s)\right\}\right]dt$$

$$= \int_0^T \exp\left\{2\int_0^t g^2(s)ds\right\}dt$$

$$\leq T\exp\{2TC^2\} < \infty. \qquad \Box$$

Exercise 3.1　Find the representation of $M(t) = \left(\int_0^t gdW\right)^2 - \int_0^t g^2 ds$.

Next we show that the task reduces to the seemingly simpler one of representing random variables by stochastic integrals. This reduction is very easy to establish.

Proposition 3.2
Suppose that for any $\mathcal{F}_T$-measurable $X \in L^2(\Omega)$ there exists $f_X \in \mathcal{M}^2$ such that

$$X = \mathbb{E}(X) + \int_0^T f_X(s)dW(s). \qquad (3.2)$$

Then any martingale $M(t) \in L^2(\Omega)$ can be written in the form

$$M(t) = M(0) + \int_0^t f_M(s)dW(s)$$

for some $f_M \in \mathcal{M}^2$.

Proof　Since $M(t) - M(0)$ is a square-integrable martingale if $M(t)$ is, we may take $M(0) = 0$. Let $X = M(T)$, put $f_M = f_X$, so that

$$M(T) = \int_0^T f_M(s)dW(s)$$

and take the conditional expectation $\mathbb{E}(\cdot|\mathcal{F}_t^W)$ on both sides to get

$$\mathbb{E}(M(T)|\mathcal{F}_t^W) = \mathbb{E}\left(\int_0^T f_M(s)dW(s)|\mathcal{F}_t^W\right).$$

The martingale property of M yields

$$\mathbb{E}(M(T)|\mathcal{F}_t^W) = M(t)$$

and the martingale property of the stochastic integral completes the proof, as

$$\mathbb{E}\left(\int_0^T f_M(s)dW(s)|\mathcal{F}_t^W\right) = \int_0^t f_M(s)dW(s). \qquad \square$$

If the decomposition of martingales is going to provide us with replicating strategies, uniqueness is a welcome feature.

Proposition 3.3
An $\mathcal{F}_T$-measurable $X \in L^2(\Omega)$ can be written in the form (3.2) in a unique way, i.e, if there exist $f_1, f_2 \in \mathcal{M}^2$ such that

$$X = \mathbb{E}(X) + \int_0^T f_1(s)dW(s),$$

$$X = \mathbb{E}(X) + \int_0^T f_2(s)dW(s),$$

then $f_1 = f_2$.

Proof   By subtraction we see that

$$\int_0^T (f_1(s) - f_2(s))dW(s) = 0.$$

Clearly

$$\mathbb{E}\left(\int_0^T (f_1(s) - f_2(s))dW(s)\right)^2 = 0$$

so by the Itô isometry,

$$\mathbb{E}\int_0^T (f_1(s) - f_2(s))^2 ds = 0.$$

Zero expectation of a non-negative random variable leaves it with little freedom: for almost all $\omega \in \Omega$

$$\int_0^T (f_1(s, \omega) - f_2(s, \omega))^2 ds = 0.$$

For each such ω we further have $f_1(t, \omega) = f_2(t, \omega)$ almost surely with respect to t. The processes, f_1 and f_2, regarded as elements of the space $\mathcal{M}^2$, which is an L^2 space with respect to (t, ω), are therefore equal in this space. $\qquad \square$

The general idea of the construction is to provide a representation of a general random variable by approximating it by a sequence of random variables of some special form for which the representation result has already been established. Herein lies the reason for restricting our attention to random variables: such an approximation is much easier for random variables than for processes.

By Proposition 3.1 we have a stochastic integral representation for some special random variables

$$X = \exp\left\{\int_0^T g(s)dW(s) - \frac{1}{2}\int_0^T g^2(s)ds\right\}$$

and to use Proposition 3.2 we have to extend the representation to arbitrary X. But we begin with a move in the opposite direction.

Proposition 3.4
Random variables of the form

$$X = \exp\left\{\sum_{k=1}^n c_k(W(t_{k+1}) - W(t_k)\right\}$$

where $t_k \in [0,T]$, $t_k < t_{k+1}$, $c_k \in \mathbb{R}$, admit the representation (3.2). The same holds for their linear combinations with deterministic coefficients.

Proof This reduces to Proposition 3.1 by considering deterministic step functions g: if

$$g(t) = \sum_{k=1}^n c_k \mathbf{1}_{[t_k, t_{k+1})},$$

then

$$\exp\left\{\int_0^T g(s)dW(s) - \frac{1}{2}\int_0^T g^2(s)ds\right\} = 1 + \int_0^T f_X(s)dW(s)$$

so multiplying both sides by $\exp\{\frac{1}{2}\int_0^T g^2(s)ds\}$, a constant which, as we know, is the expectation of $\exp\{\int_0^T g(s)dW(s)\}$, gives the result. The extension to linear combination is obvious by linearity of the stochastic integral. □

For technical reasons we now extend the representation to some complex random variables. Before we do this, some explanation is needed.

For a process $f : [0,T] \times \Omega \to \mathbb{C}$ we can introduce the class $\mathcal{M}_{\mathbb{C}}^2$ by reformulating the integrability condition or, equivalently, requiring that real part f_{Re} and the imaginary part f_{Im} of f are both in $\mathcal{M}^2$. The stochastic integral of a complex process can be defined as

$$\int_0^t f(s)dW(s) = \int_0^t f_{\mathrm{Re}}(s)dW(s) + i \int_0^t f_{\mathrm{Im}}(s)dW(s).$$

We are ready for the complex version of the representation of exponential random variables.

Proposition 3.5
Linear combinations of random variables of the form

$$X = \exp\left\{ i \sum_{k=1}^n c_k(W(t_{k+1}) - W(t_k)) \right\}$$

where $t_k \in [0, T]$, $t_k < t_{k+1}$, $c_k \in \mathbb{R}$, admit the representation (3.2) by means of a complex-valued process $f_X \in \mathcal{M}_{\mathbb{C}}^2$.

Proof For

$$Z(t) = \exp\left\{ i \int_0^t g(s)dW(s) + \frac{1}{2} \int_0^t g^2(s)ds \right\}$$

we will show that

$$Z(t) = 1 + \int_0^t ig(s)Z(s)dW(s) \tag{3.3}$$

and thus we will establish the complex version of Proposition 3.1, where we have $f_g(s) = g(s)Z(s)$, while here we have the same with g replaced by ig. The rest of the argument leading from $Z(t)$ to X is the same as in the real case above.

We will tackle $Z(t)$ by analysing real and imaginary parts

$$Z(t) = \exp\left\{ \frac{1}{2} \int_0^t g^2(s)ds \right\} \cos\left(\int_0^t g(s)dW(s) \right)$$
$$+ i \exp\left\{ \frac{1}{2} \int_0^t g^2(s)ds \right\} \sin\left(\int_0^t g(s)dW(s) \right)$$
$$= Z_{Re}(t) + iZ_{Im}(t).$$

We apply the Itô formula to $Z_{Re}(t)$: $Z_{Re}(t) = f(t, Y(t))$, where $Y(t) = \int_0^t g(s)dW(s)$ and

$$f(t, x) = \exp\left\{\frac{1}{2}\int_0^t g^2(s)ds\right\}\cos x,$$

$$f_t(t, x) = \frac{1}{2}g^2(t)\exp\left\{\frac{1}{2}\int_0^t g^2(s)ds\right\}\cos x,$$

$$f_x(t, x) = -\exp\left\{\frac{1}{2}\int_0^t g^2(s)ds\right\}\sin x,$$

$$f_{xx}(t, x) = -\exp\left\{\frac{1}{2}\int_0^t g^2(s)ds\right\}\cos x,$$

and

$$dY(t) = g(t)dW(t),$$

so that

$$dZ_{Re}(t) = i^2 g(t)\exp\left\{\frac{1}{2}\int_0^t g^2(s)ds\right\}\sin\left(\int_0^t g(s)dW(s)\right).$$

Similarly

$$dZ_{Im}(t) = ig(t)\exp\left\{\frac{1}{2}\int_0^t g^2(s)ds\right\}\cos\left(\int_0^t g(s)dW(s)\right),$$

which proves (3.3). $\qquad\square$

Consider the space of complex-valued square integrable random varibles $L_{\mathbb{C}}^2(\Omega)$. The collection of all exponential random variables will prove to be quite rich. As we said earlier, random variables are easier to handle than processes; but this does not mean easy, as the next lemma shows. This is a technical fact which essentially belongs to functional analysis, so we locate the proof separately at the end of the chapter.

Lemma 3.6
The family $\mathcal{L}$ of all linear combinations of random variables

$$X = \exp\left\{i\sum_{k=1}^n c_k(W(t_{k+1}) - W(t_k))\right\}$$

is dense in $L_{\mathbb{C}}^2(\Omega)$.

Proof See page 75. $\qquad\square$

This approximation enables us to extend the construction of the representation.

Proposition 3.7

For any $\mathcal{F}_T$-measurable real-valued $X \in L^2(\Omega)$ there exists a unique $f_X \in \mathcal{M}^2$ such that

$$X = \mathbb{E}(X) + \int_0^T f_X(s)dW(s).$$

Proof For complex-valued random variables we already know that $X = \lim_{n \to \infty} X_n$ in $L^2_{\mathbb{C}}(\Omega)$ for some $X_n \in \mathcal{L}$. By Proposition 3.5 these random variables admit a stochastic integral representation of the form

$$X_n = \mathbb{E}(X_n) + \int_0^T f_{X_n}(s)dW(s).$$

Convergence in $L^2_{\mathbb{C}}$ implies convergence in $L^1_{\mathbb{C}}$ since the integral is computed with respect to a probability measure, so $\mathbb{E}(X_n) \to \mathbb{E}(X)$. The sequence $X_n - \mathbb{E}(X_n)$ is Cauchy in $L^2_{\mathbb{C}}(\Omega)$ since the sequence X_n converges in $L^2_{\mathbb{C}}$ so $\int_0^T f_{X_n}(s)\,dW(s)$ is Cauchy in $L^2_{\mathbb{C}}(\Omega)$. As a consequence of the Itô isometry, f_{X_n} is Cauchy in $\mathcal{M}^2_{\mathbb{C}}$, so there exists $f_X \in \mathcal{M}^2_{\mathbb{C}}$ such that $f_X = \lim_{n \to \infty} f_{X_n}$ in the $\mathcal{M}^2_{\mathbb{C}}$-norm. Therefore, again by the Itô isometry,

$$\lim_{n \to \infty} \int_0^T f_{X_n}(s)\,dW(s) = \int_0^T f_X(s)\,dW(s)$$

(where the convergence is in $L^2_{\mathbb{C}}(\Omega)$), and finally

$$X = \mathbb{E}(X) + \int_0^T f_X(s)dW(s).$$

We still have to check that the representation of a real random variable is obtained by means of a real-valued process. If X is real, $\mathbb{E}(X) \in \mathbb{R}$, and so $\int_0^T f_X(s)dW \in L^2(\Omega)$, that is, the imaginary part of this integral is zero (we write f_{Im} for the imaginary part of f_X):

$$\int_0^T f_{\text{Im}}(s)dW(s) = 0.$$

By the Itô isometry, $\mathbb{E}(\int_0^T f^2_{\text{Im}}(s)ds) = 0$ so $f_{\text{Im}}(t) = 0$ almost surely on $\Omega \times [0, T]$. $\qquad\square$

We are ready to summarise all the results of this section.

Theorem 3.8

If M is a martingale with respect to the filtration generated by the Wiener process, and such that $M(t) \in L^2(\Omega)$ for all t, then there is a unique process

$f_M \in \mathcal{M}^2$ *such that*

$$M(t) = M(0) + \int_0^t f_M(s)dW(s).$$

Proof   Proposition 3.7 gives f for $X = M(T)$, Proposition 3.2 gives the representation of the process $M(t)$. Uniqueness follows immediately from the uniqueness of Itô process characteristics but was established directly anyway.   □

A surprising consequence of this fact is that the paths of any such martingale are continuous, since the process defined by the stochastic integral has this property. This does not mean that every martingale is continuous in general. The path-continuity proved here results from dealing with quite a special filtration, namely the one generated by the Wiener process.

Example 3.9

Fix a probability space $(\Omega, \mathcal{F}, P)$ and let $\tau : \Omega \to [0, \infty)$ be a random variable with exponential density, i.e. its cumulative distribution function $F_\tau(t) = P(\tau \le t)$ takes the form $F_\tau(t) = \int_0^t \lambda e^{-\lambda s} ds$ for some fixed $\lambda > 0$. Define the process $L : [0, \infty) \times \Omega \to \{0, 1\}$ by setting $L(t, \omega) = 1$ if $\tau(\omega) \le t$ and zero otherwise. Its natural filtration is given by $\mathcal{F}_t = \sigma(L(s) : s \le t)$. Clearly, L is not a martingale for this filtration, since the expectations $\mathbb{E}_P(L(s)) = P(\tau \le t)$ increase with t. However, this suggests that we should consider the process M defined by $M(t) = L(t) - P(\tau \le t)$ instead. For $s \le t$ we will show that

$$\mathbb{E}(M(t) - M(s)|\mathcal{F}_s) = 0.$$

To this end, for any A in $\mathcal{F}_s$ we obtain

$$\int_A (M(t) - M(s))dP$$

$$= \int_A ([L(t) - P(\tau \le t)] - [L(s) - P(\tau \le s)]) \, dP$$

$$= \int_A (L(t) - L(s))dP - P(\{\tau \in (s, t]\} \cap A)$$

$$\text{(since } \{\tau \in (s, t]\} \text{ is independent of } \mathcal{F}_s)$$

$$= \int_A \mathbf{1}_{\{\tau \in (s, t]\}}dP - P(\{\tau \in (s, t]\} \cap A)$$

$$= 0,$$

so M is an example of a discontinuous martingale. This is not a contradiction since the representation theorem requires the fitration generated by W, which is not the case here.

3.2 Completeness of the model

Recall that a path-independent derivative security of **European** type is of the form

$$H = h(S(T))$$

for some real Borel function h. We shall assume throughout that:

- $H \geq 0$,
- $\mathbb{E}(H^{\alpha}) < \infty$ for some $\alpha > 2$.

The general case of H with arbitrary sign can be tackled by decomposing H into positive and negative parts, pricing each component and subtracting the results by the general principle of additivity of value. The purpose of the second condition is to make sure that H is square integrable with respect to the martingale probability. To ensure this we need better regularity under the original measure. In practice this is not a significant restriction.

Recall that Theorem 2.1 applied to the Black–Scholes model with $b(s) = \frac{\mu-r}{\sigma}$ gives the martingale probability Q as

$$Q(A) = \int_A \exp\left\{-bW(T) - \frac{1}{2}Tb^2\right\} dP.$$

Therefore, in particular,

$$\mathbb{E}_Q(H^2) = \mathbb{E}_P\left(H^2 \exp\left\{-bW(T) - \frac{1}{2}Tb^2\right\}\right).$$

We are working in a derivative pricing model, based on a probability space $(\Omega, \mathcal{F}, P)$ and time set $[0, T]$, with a single underlying asset S whose natural filtration $\mathcal{F}_t^S$ satisfies $\mathcal{F}_T^S = \mathcal{F}$. Definition 2.15 states that such a model is complete if each European derivative H can be replicated by a self-financing strategy. To avoid doubling and suicide strategies we should add the requirement that the replicating strategy should be admissible. By narrowing the class of strategies, we make the task of finding a replication harder. Our goal is to show that the Black–Scholes model is complete in this strong sense. We will use the martingale representation theorem with respect to W_Q, which is a Wiener process under Q with the same filtration. This requires square integrability under Q and the following lemma shows that our assumptions guarantee this.

Lemma 3.10
If $\mathbb{E}_P(H^\alpha) < \infty$ *for some* $\alpha > 2$ *then* $\mathbb{E}_Q(H^2) < \infty$, *where* Q *is the martingale measure in the BS model.*

Proof We use the Hölder inequality (see [PF])

$$\mathbb{E}_P(|XY|) \le [\mathbb{E}_P(X^p)]^{\frac{1}{p}}[\mathbb{E}_P(Y^q)]^{\frac{1}{q}}, \quad \frac{1}{p} + \frac{1}{q} = 1, \ p > 1,$$

with $X = H^2$, $Y = \exp\{-bW(T) - \frac{1}{2}Tb^2\}$, $p = \frac{\alpha}{2}$ (hence $q = \frac{\alpha}{\alpha-2}$, and $X^p = H^\alpha$) to obtain

$$\mathbb{E}_P\left(H^2 \exp\left\{-bW(T) - \frac{1}{2}Tb^2\right\}\right)$$

$$\le [\mathbb{E}(H^\alpha)]^{\frac{2}{\alpha}}\left[\mathbb{E}_P\left(\exp\left\{-qbW(T) - \frac{1}{2}qTb^2\right\}\right)\right]^{\frac{1}{q}}$$

$$\le c[\mathbb{E}_P(\exp\{-qbW(T)\})]^{\frac{1}{q}},$$

where $c = [\mathbb{E}_P(H^\alpha)]^{\frac{2}{\alpha}}\exp\{-\frac{1}{2}qTb^2\} < \infty$. Under P the random variable $W(T)$ has normal distribution with zero mean so

$$\mathbb{E}_P(\exp\{-qbW(T)\}) = \exp\left\{\frac{1}{2}q^2b^2T\right\} < \infty. \qquad \square$$

Theorem 3.11
The Black–Scholes model is complete in the following sense: for each $\mathcal{F}_T$*-measurable* $H \ge 0$ *with* $\mathbb{E}(H^\alpha) < \infty$ *for some* $\alpha > 2$, *there is an admissible replicating strategy* (x, y) *such that*

$$V_{(x,y)}(t) = \mathbb{E}_Q(e^{-r(T-t)}H|\mathcal{F}_t).$$

Proof Replication follows from this formula upon taking $t = T$:

$$V_{(x,y)}(T) = \mathbb{E}_Q(H|\mathcal{F}_T) = H,$$

where the last equality follows from the $\mathcal{F}_T$-measurability of H.
Since $A(t) = e^{rt}$,

$$V_{(x,y)}(t) = A(t)\mathbb{E}_Q(e^{-rT}H|\mathcal{F}_t) = A(t)M(t)$$

where $M(t) = \mathbb{E}_Q(e^{-rT}H|\mathcal{F}_t)$.
The process M is defined by conditional expectations of the same square-integrable random variable, $e^{-rT}H$, relative to σ-fields in a filtration, so it

is a square-integrable martingale:

$$
\begin{aligned}
\mathbb{E}_Q(M^2(t)) &= \mathbb{E}_Q([\mathbb{E}_Q(e^{-rT}H|\mathcal{F}_t)]^2) \\
&\le \mathbb{E}_Q(\mathbb{E}_Q(e^{-2rT}H^2|\mathcal{F}_t)) \quad \text{(by the Jensen inequality)} \\
&= e^{-2rT}\mathbb{E}_Q(H^2) < \infty.
\end{aligned}
$$

We seek an admissible strategy (x, y) with value

$$
V_{(x,y)}(t) = A(t)M(t). \tag{3.4}
$$

The assumptions of the representation theorem are satisfied so we can write M as a stochastic integral with respect to the Wiener process W_Q. Therefore we can find the unique adapted process $f(t)$ such that

$$
M(t) = M(0) + \int_0^t f(s)dW_Q(s)
$$

so

$$
dM(t) = f(t)dW_Q(t).
$$

We compute the differential of both sides of (3.4). On the left we apply the self-financing condition:

$$
\begin{aligned}
dV_{(x,y)}(t) &= x(t)dS(t) + y(t)dA(t) \\
&= x(t)rS(t)dt + x(t)\sigma S(t)dW_Q(t) + ry(t)A(t)dt
\end{aligned}
$$

since $dS(t) = rS(t)dt + \sigma S(t)dW_Q(t)$. On the right, integration by parts gives, since $A(t)$ is deterministic,

$$
\begin{aligned}
d(A(t)M(t)) &= A(t)dM(t) + M(t)dA(t) \\
&= A(t)f(t)dW_Q(t) + rA(t)M(t)dt.
\end{aligned}
$$

We are searching for the form of the replicating strategy. Equating the differentials provides us with a candidate, since for $V_{(x,y)}(t) = A(t)M(t)$ to hold, their differentials should be equal

$$
x(t)rS(t)dt + x(t)\sigma S(t)dW_Q(t) + ry(t)A(t)dt = A(t)f(t)dW_Q(t) + rA(t)M(t)dt.
$$

Rearranging we have:

$$
\begin{aligned}
0 = {} & [x(t)rS(t) + ry(t)A(t) - rA(t)M(t)]\, dt \\
& + [x(t)\sigma S(t) - A(t)f(t)]\, dW_Q(t).
\end{aligned}
$$

Again we use the fact that the differential representation of an Itô process is unique:

$$x(t)rS(t) + ry(t)A(t) - rA(t)M(t) = 0,$$
$$x(t)\sigma S(t) - A(t)f(t) = 0.$$

From the second equality

$$x(t) = \frac{A(t)f(t)}{\sigma S(t)},$$

which inserted in the first gives

$$\frac{A(t)f(t)}{\sigma S(t)}rS(t) + ry(t)A(t) - rA(t)M(t) = 0$$

so that

$$y(t) = M(t) - \frac{f(t)}{\sigma}.$$

The strategy (x, y) thus obtained is a candidate for the admissible replicating strategy we seek. We check that it satisfies all our conditions.

For replication use the definition $V_{(x,y)}(t) = x(t)S(t) + y(t)A(t)$ to see that

$$
\begin{aligned}
V_{(x,y)}(t) &= \frac{A(t)f(t)}{\sigma S(t)}S(t) + (M(t) - \frac{f(t)}{\sigma})A(t) \\
&= \frac{f(t)}{\sigma}A(t) + M(t)A(t) - \frac{f(t)}{\sigma}A(t) \\
&= M(t)e^{rt} \\
&= \mathbb{E}_Q(e^{-r(T-t)}H|\mathcal{F}_t),
\end{aligned}
$$

since $M(t) = \mathbb{E}_Q(e^{-rT}H|\mathcal{F}_t)$ by definition. Using this identity at T shows that the strategy replicates H.

For admissibility note that $\tilde{V}_{(x,y)}(t) = V_{(x,y)}(t)A^{-1}(t) = M(t)$ is a martingale with respect to Q.

To verify the self-financing condition, compute, using the formula for x:

$$f(t) = \sigma x(t)S(t)A^{-1}(t) = \sigma x(t)S(t)e^{-rt}$$

so

$$
\begin{aligned}
d\tilde{V}_{(x,y)}(t) &= dM(t) = f(t)dW_Q(t) \\
&= \sigma x(t)\tilde{S}(t)dW_Q(t) \\
&= x(t)d\tilde{S}(t).
\end{aligned}
$$

This condition is equivalent to the self-financing condition as was proved in Proposition 2.9.

Finally, $H \geq 0$ so for all $t \leq T$, $V_{(x,y)}(t) = \mathbb{E}_Q(e^{-r(T-t)}H|\mathcal{F}_t) \geq 0$. $\square$

3.3 Derivative pricing

One of our principal objectives is to derive prices for derivative securities in the Black–Scholes model. We first derive a general formula for any European path-independent derivative and then provide concrete computations of the prices of put and call options.

Recall that in the Black–Scholes model there exists at least one probability Q such that the discounted price process $\tilde{S}$ is a martingale. First we consider the question whether the model can support martingale probabilities other than Q. If Q_1 is some other martingale probability, the discounted price process, and therefore the discounted value process under any admissible strategy is a Q_1-martingale with final value $\tilde{H} = e^{-rT}H$. In other words, $\tilde{V}(t) = \mathbb{E}_{Q_1}(e^{-rT}H|\mathcal{F}_t^W)$ for every $t \leq T$. This leads at once to the following important result.

Theorem 3.12
The martingale probability Q in the Black–Scholes model is unique.

Proof Take $B \in \mathcal{F}_T^S = \mathcal{F}$ and let $H = \mathbf{1}_B$. This bounded random variable can be taken as the payoff of a derivative security. Using discounted values we have, for any martingale probability Q_1, by definition of H,

$$
\begin{aligned}
e^{-rT}Q_1(B) &= \mathbb{E}_{Q_1}(\tilde{H}) \\
&= \mathbb{E}_{Q_1}(\tilde{V}(T)) \quad \text{(replication)} \\
&= \mathbb{E}_{Q_1}(V(0)) \quad (Q_1 \text{ is a martingale probability}) \\
&= V(0) \\
&= e^{-rT}\mathbb{E}_Q(H) \quad (Q \text{ is a martingale probability}) \\
&= e^{-rT}Q(B).
\end{aligned}
$$

As B is arbitrary, the two martingale probabilities coincide, so Q is the unique martingale probability for the model. □

We have shown that in the Black–Scholes model there is no ambiguity, either about the admissible replicating strategy or about the martingale probability: both are uniquely defined and constructed explicitly in this model.

General derivative securities

Now consider a general path-independent European derivative security $H = h(S(T))$ where the stock price process S satisfies

$$
S(T) = S(t) \exp\left\{\left(r - \frac{1}{2}\sigma^2\right)(T - t) + \sigma(W_Q(T) - W_Q(t))\right\}.
$$

We wish to compute

$$H(t) = e^{-r(T-t)}\mathbb{E}_Q(h(S(T))|\mathcal{F}_t)$$

$$= \mathbb{E}_Q\left(e^{-r(T-t)}h\left(S(t)\exp\left\{\left(r - \frac{1}{2}\sigma^2\right)(T-t) + \sigma(W_Q(T) - W_Q(t))\right\}\right)|\mathcal{F}_t\right).$$
$$(3.5)$$

Here the independence of the increments of the Wiener process W_Q under Q comes to our rescue. The following lemma, which describes a general property of conditional expectations, does the trick (see [PF] for a proof).

Lemma 3.13
Let G be a sub-σ-field of $\mathcal{F}$ and assume that Y is independent of G while Z is G-measurable. Given a bounded Borel function $\Psi(y, z)$, define the function $\psi(z) = \mathbb{E}(\Psi(Y, z))$. Then

$$\mathbb{E}(\Psi(Y, Z)|G) = \psi(Z).$$

We can now compute the conditional expectation in (3.5) for bounded h (note that this holds for the put option but not for the call). The lemma is applied to the martingale probability Q, with $\mathbb{E}_Q$ in place of $\mathbb{E}$, and setting

$$G = \mathcal{F}_t,$$
$$Y = W_Q(T) - W_Q(t),$$
$$Z = S(t),$$
$$\Psi(y, z) = e^{-r(T-t)}h\left(z\exp\left\{\left(r - \frac{1}{2}\sigma^2\right)(T-t) + \sigma y\right\}\right).$$

We have to find the form of ψ. The function Ψ depends on t and so does ψ and we highlight this fact in our notation:

$$\psi(t, z) = \mathbb{E}_Q(\Psi(t, z, Y)|\mathcal{F}_t)$$

$$= \mathbb{E}_Q(e^{-r(T-t)}h\left(z\exp\left\{\left(r - \frac{1}{2}\sigma^2\right)(T-t) + \sigma(W_Q(T) - W_Q(t))\right\}\right),$$

where the final step uses the fact that $W_Q(T) - W_Q(t)$ is independent of $\mathcal{F}_t$. Moreover, $W_Q(T) - W_Q(t) \sim \sqrt{T-t}Y_1$, where Y_1 is standard normal, so the expectation on the right equals

$$e^{-r(T-t)}\mathbb{E}_Q\left(h\left(z\exp\left\{\left(r - \frac{1}{2}\sigma^2\right)(T-t) + \sigma\sqrt{T-t}Y_1\right\}\right)\right),$$

which becomes

$$e^{-r(T-t)}\int_{\mathbb{R}} f_{Y_1}(y)h\left(z\exp\left\{\left(r - \frac{1}{2}\sigma^2\right)(T-t) + \sigma\sqrt{T-t}y\right\}\right)dy$$

with $f_{Y_1}(y) = \frac{1}{\sqrt{2\pi}} e^{-\frac{y^2}{2}}$ as the density of Y_1. Thus, finally, we have

$$\psi(t,z) = e^{-r(T-t)} \int_{\mathbb{R}} \frac{1}{\sqrt{2\pi}} e^{-\frac{y^2}{2}} h\left(z \exp\left\{\left(r - \frac{1}{2}\sigma^2\right)(T-t) + \sigma\sqrt{T-t}\,y\right\}\right) dy.$$

$$(3.6)$$

We are ready to realise the first of our main objectives in this chapter, namely to find the explicit formulae for the prices of the vanilla options.

Put options

To obtain the famous Black–Scholes option pricing formula for the European put we must compute $\psi(t,z)$ in (3.6) when $h(z) = (K - z)^+$. We must check that the integrability condition $\mathbb{E}_P(H^\alpha) < \infty$ is satisfied so that these options fit the above general scheme. For the put option this is obvious since the payoff is bounded:

$$0 \le \max\{0, (K - S(T))\} \le K$$

hence integrable to any power.

Recall that in (3.6) we established a general formula for the auxiliary function for the price, which now becomes

$$\psi(t,z) = e^{-r(T-t)} \int_{\mathbb{R}} \frac{1}{\sqrt{2\pi}} e^{-\frac{y^2}{2}} \left(K - z e^{(r-\frac{1}{2}\sigma^2)(T-t)+\sigma y\sqrt{T-t}}\right)^+ dy.$$

Our goal is to find a concrete form of this function.

First we reduce the range of integration, which will allow us to tackle nonlinearity of the payoff function.

As $a^+ = 0$ for $a \le 0$, the function under the integral is non-zero only if

$$K - z e^{(r-\frac{1}{2}\sigma^2)(T-t)+\sigma y\sqrt{T-t}} \ge 0.$$

Solving this yields

$$\left(r - \frac{1}{2}\sigma^2\right)(T-t) + \sigma y\sqrt{T-t} \le \ln\frac{K}{z},$$

$$y\sigma\sqrt{T-t} \le \ln\frac{K}{z} - \left(r - \frac{1}{2}\sigma^2\right)(T-t),$$

and finally

$$y \le d(t,z) = \frac{\ln\frac{K}{z} - \left(r - \frac{1}{2}\sigma^2\right)(T-t)}{\sigma\sqrt{T-t}}.$$

In the restricted range of integration the positive part of the expression is equal to the the the expression itself, so

$$\psi(t, z) = e^{-r(T-t)} \int_{-\infty}^{d(t,z)} \frac{1}{\sqrt{2\pi}} e^{-\frac{y^2}{2}} \left(K - z e^{(r-\frac{1}{2}\sigma^2)(T-t)+\sigma y \sqrt{T-t}} \right) dy.$$

Removing the positive part allows us to apply the additivity of the integral:

$$\psi(t, z) = e^{-r(T-t)} \int_{-\infty}^{d(t,z)} \frac{1}{\sqrt{2\pi}} e^{-\frac{y^2}{2}} K dy$$

$$- e^{-r(T-t)} \int_{-\infty}^{d(t,z)} \frac{1}{\sqrt{2\pi}} e^{-\frac{y^2}{2}} \left(z e^{(r-\frac{1}{2}\sigma^2)(T-t)+\sigma y \sqrt{T-t}} \right) dy.$$

The first term is

$$K e^{-r(T-t)} N(d(t, z)),$$

where N denotes the standard normal cumulative distribution function,

$$N(d) = \frac{1}{\sqrt{2\pi}} \int_{-\infty}^{d} e^{-\frac{1}{2}y^2} dy.$$

The second term can be written as

$$e^{-r(T-t)} e^{(r-\frac{1}{2}\sigma^2)(T-t)} z \int_{-\infty}^{d(t,z)} \frac{1}{\sqrt{2\pi}} e^{-\frac{y^2}{2}+\sigma y \sqrt{T-t}} dy,$$

and now the integral can be found easily. We have

$$\frac{1}{\sqrt{2\pi}} \int_{-\infty}^{d(t,z)} e^{-\frac{1}{2}y^2+y\sigma\sqrt{T-t}} dy = \frac{1}{\sqrt{2\pi}} \int_{-\infty}^{d(t,z)} e^{-\frac{1}{2}(y^2-2y\sigma\sqrt{T-t}+\sigma^2(T-t))+\frac{1}{2}\sigma^2(T-t)} dy$$

$$= \frac{1}{\sqrt{2\pi}} \int_{-\infty}^{d(t,z)} e^{-\frac{1}{2}(y-\sigma\sqrt{T-t})^2+\frac{1}{2}\sigma^2(T-t)} dy.$$

The change of variables $v = y - \sigma \sqrt{T-t}$, $dv = dy$ turns this into

$$e^{\frac{1}{2}\sigma^2(T-t)} \int_{-\infty}^{d(t,z)-\sigma\sqrt{T-t}} \frac{1}{\sqrt{2\pi}} e^{-\frac{1}{2}v^2} dv = e^{\frac{1}{2}\sigma^2(T-t)} N\left(d(t, z) - \sigma \sqrt{T-t} \right),$$

since if $y = d(t, z)$, then $v = d(t, z) - \sigma \sqrt{T-t}$. Here we recognise the cumulative standard normal distribution function as in the first term. The only difference is the point at which it is computed. This means that

$$e^{-r(T-t)} e^{(r-\frac{1}{2}\sigma^2)(T-t)} z \int_{-\infty}^{d(t,z)} \frac{1}{\sqrt{2\pi}} e^{-\frac{y^2}{2}+\sigma y \sqrt{T-t}} dy = z N\left(d(t, z) - \sigma \sqrt{T-t} \right).$$

Corollary 3.14

The above computation shows that for $t \leq T$

$$\mathbb{E}_Q(\mathbf{1}_{\{S(T) \leq K\}}|\mathcal{F}_t) = N(d(t, S(t))),$$

$$\mathbb{E}_Q(S(T)\mathbf{1}_{\{S(T) \leq K\}}|\mathcal{F}_t) = e^{r(T-t)}S(t)N\left(d\left(t, S(t) - \sigma\sqrt{T-t}\right)\right).$$

Proof By restricting to the set where $\{S(T) \leq K\}$ the put price can be written as

$$
\begin{aligned}
P(t) &= \mathbb{E}_Q\left(e^{-r(T-t)}(K - S(T))^+|\mathcal{F}_t\right) \\
&= \mathbb{E}_Q\left(e^{-r(T-t)}(K - S(T))\mathbf{1}_{\{S(T) \leq K\}}|\mathcal{F}_t\right) \\
&= \mathbb{E}_Q\left(e^{-r(T-t)}K\mathbf{1}_{\{S(T) \leq K\}}|\mathcal{F}_t\right) - \mathbb{E}_Q\left(e^{-r(T-t)}S(T)\mathbf{1}_{\{S(T)-K\}}|\mathcal{F}_t\right)
\end{aligned}
$$

and in our calculation we dealt separately with these two terms to obtain the above identities. □

Recall that:

$$P(t) = e^{-r(T-t)}\mathbb{E}_Q(h(S(T))|\mathcal{F}_t) = \psi(t, S(t))$$

since, by Lemma 3.13, the conditional expectation reduces to inserting the stock price into the function ψ. So we have proved the following theorem.

Theorem 3.15

The price, at time $t \leq T$, of the European put option with strike K is

$$P(t) = Ke^{-r(T-t)}N(d(t, S(t))) - S(t)N\left(d(t, S(t)) - \sigma\sqrt{T-t}\right),$$

where

$$d(t, z) = \frac{\ln\frac{K}{z} - r(T-t) + \frac{1}{2}\sigma^2(T-t)}{\sigma\sqrt{T-t}}.$$

Call options

A similar formula for a call results from the well-known call-put parity relation between call and put prices which we now derive (see also [DMFM]).

We begin by noting that the call payoff can be replicated. For this we need $\max\{0, (S(T) - K)\}$ to be in $L^\alpha(P)$ for some $\alpha > 2$. Note first that we can find c_1, c_2 such that

$$\mathbb{E}_P((S(T) - K)^\alpha) \leq c_1\mathbb{E}_P(S^\alpha(T)) + c_2$$

and then using the expression for the stock price

$$S(T) = S(0) \exp\left\{\mu T - \frac{\sigma^2}{2}T + \sigma W(T)\right\}$$

we have, for all α,

$$\mathbb{E}_P\left[\exp\left\{\mu T - \frac{\sigma^2}{2}T + \sigma W(T)\right\}^\alpha\right] \le \exp\left\{\alpha\mu T - \frac{\alpha}{2}\sigma^2 T\right\} \mathbb{E}_P[\exp\{\alpha\sigma W(T)\}]$$

$$= \exp\left\{\alpha\mu T - \frac{\alpha}{2}\sigma^2 T + \frac{1}{2}\alpha^2\sigma^2 T\right\} < \infty,$$

where we again employed the formula $\mathbb{E}(\exp\{X\}) = \exp\{\frac{1}{2}\text{Var}(X)\}$ for centred normal X; here with $X = \alpha\sigma W(T)$, so that $\text{Var}(X) = \alpha^2\sigma^2 T$.

As a result, the process $C(t)$ of prices of a call is equal to the process of values of the replicating strategy and, as such, is a Q-martingale after discounting, a fact we need below.

Theorem 3.16
Denote the prices at time t of the European call and put with strike K and exercise date T by C(t) and P(t) respectively. Then

$$C(t) - P(t) = S(t) - Ke^{-r(T-t)}$$

Proof   We analyse the relation between the payoffs: If $S(T) - K \ge 0$, then

$$S(T) - (S(T) - K)^+ + (K - S(T))^+ = S(T) - (S(T) - K) + 0 = K,$$

and if $S(T) - K \le 0$, then

$$S(T) - (S(T) - K)^+ + (K - S(T))^+ = S(T) - 0 + (K - S(T)) = K.$$

As a result we get

$$S(T) - C(T) + P(T) = S(T) - (S(T) - K)^+ + (K - S(T))^+ = K.$$

After multiplying both sides by e^{-rT} this becomes

$$\tilde{S}(T) - \tilde{C}(T) + \tilde{P}(T) = Ke^{-rT}.$$

We know that $\tilde{S}(t)$, $\tilde{C}(t)$, $\tilde{P}(t)$ are Q-martingales so

$$\mathbb{E}_Q(\tilde{S}(T) - \tilde{C}(T) + \tilde{P}(T)|\mathcal{F}_t) = \tilde{S}(t) - \tilde{C}(t) + \tilde{P}(t) = Ke^{-rT}.$$

The result now follows once we multiply both sides by e^{rt}.   □

This gives the Black–Scholes formula for the price of a call option:

$$
\begin{aligned}
C(t) &= S(t) + P(t) - Ke^{-r(T-t)} \quad \text{(by call-put parity)}\\
&= S(t) + Ke^{-r(T-t)}N(d(t, S(t)))\\
&\quad - S(t)N\left(d(t, S(t)) - \sigma\sqrt{T-t}\right) - Ke^{-r(T-t)}\\
&= S(t)\left(1 - N\left(d(t, S(t)) - \sigma\sqrt{T-t}\right)\right) - Ke^{-r(T-t)}(1 - N(d(t, S(t))))\\
&= S(t)N\left(-d(t, S(t)) + \sigma\sqrt{T-t}\right) - Ke^{-r(T-t)}N(-d(t, S(t))).
\end{aligned}
$$

We record this result as the next theorem.

Theorem 3.17
The price, at time $t \le T$, of the European call option with strike K is

$$
C(t) = S(t)N\left(-d(t, S(t)) + \sigma\sqrt{T-t}\right) - Ke^{-r(T-t)}N(-d(t, S(t))),
$$

where

$$
d(t, z) = \frac{\ln\frac{K}{z} - r(T-t) + \frac{1}{2}\sigma^2(T-t)}{\sigma\sqrt{T-t}}.
$$

Exercise 3.2 Show that, similarly to Corollary 3.14, the above calculations imply

$$
\begin{aligned}
\mathbb{E}_Q(\mathbf{1}_{\{S(T)\ge K\}}|\mathcal{F}_t) &= N\left(-d(t, S(t)) + \sigma\sqrt{T-t}\right),\\
\mathbb{E}_Q(S(T)\mathbf{1}_{\{S(T)\ge K\}}|\mathcal{F}_t) &= e^{r(T-t)}S(t)N(-d(t, S(t))).
\end{aligned}
$$

Finally, we make a simple notational change, requiring only basic algebra, to convert the above formula to the form found in most textbooks. This is done purely to ease comparison. Write

$$
d_+(t, z) = \frac{\ln\frac{z}{K} + \left(r + \frac{1}{2}\sigma^2\right)(T-t)}{\sigma\sqrt{T-t}},
$$

$$
d_-(t, z) = \frac{\ln\frac{z}{K} + \left(r - \frac{1}{2}\sigma^2\right)(T-t)}{\sigma\sqrt{T-t}}.
$$

Then

$$d(t, z) = \frac{\ln \frac{K}{z} - r(T - t) + \frac{1}{2}\sigma^2(T - t)}{\sigma \sqrt{T - t}}$$

$$= -\frac{\ln \frac{z}{K} + r(T - t) - \frac{1}{2}\sigma^2(T - t)}{\sigma \sqrt{T - t}}$$

$$= -d_-(t, z)$$

and

$$d(t, z) - \sigma \sqrt{T - t} = \frac{\ln \frac{K}{z} - r(T - t) + \frac{1}{2}\sigma^2(T - t)}{\sigma \sqrt{T - t}} - \frac{\sigma^2(T - t)}{\sigma \sqrt{T - t}}$$

$$= \frac{\ln \frac{K}{z} - r(T - t) - \frac{1}{2}\sigma^2(T - t)}{\sigma \sqrt{T - t}}$$

$$= -\frac{\ln \frac{z}{K} + r(T - t) + \frac{1}{2}\sigma^2(T - t)}{\sigma \sqrt{T - t}}$$

$$= -d_+(t, z).$$

Theorem 3.18 (Black–Scholes formula)
The European call and put prices take the form

$$C(t) = S(t)N(d_+(t, S(t))) - Ke^{-r(T-t)}N(d_-(t, S(t))).$$
$$P(t) = -S(t)N(-d_+(t, S(t))) + Ke^{-(T-t)}N(-d_-(t, S(t))).$$

where

$$d_+(t, z) = \frac{\ln \frac{z}{K} + \left(r + \frac{1}{2}\sigma^2\right)(T - t)}{\sigma \sqrt{T - t}},$$

$$d_-(t, z) = \frac{\ln \frac{z}{K} + \left(r - \frac{1}{2}\sigma^2\right)(T - t)}{\sigma \sqrt{T - t}}.$$

Proof   We have shown that

$$C(t) = S(t)N\left(-d(t, S(t)) + \sigma \sqrt{T - t}\right) - Ke^{-r(T-t)}N(-d(t, S(t)))$$
$$P(t) = Ke^{-r(T-t)}N(d(t, S(t))) - S(t)N\left(d(t, S(t)) - \sigma \sqrt{T - t}\right)$$

and with the indicated notational change the result follows, since

$$d(t, z) = -d_-(t, z),$$
$$d(t, z) - \sigma \sqrt{T - t} = -d_+(t, z).$$

□

A special case is worth mentioning since it is frequently used: we simply insert zero to the above formulae. We emphasise the factors on which the option prices depend. Here we have the interest rate which is a factor concerned with the risk-free part of the market, independently of the stock. The exercise time and price specify the option payoff. They are decided by the party selling the option. The current stock price is of course known. The most important factor is σ, the volatility of stock prices. The Black–Scholes model assumes that it is constant and for pricing in actual markets it must be estimated; below we indicate briefly how this might be done. To stress the dependence of option prices on the various parameters we list them in the notation for the option premium in the next result.

Theorem 3.19 (Black–Scholes premium)
The call and put option prices at time $t = 0$ are:

$$C(r, T, K, S(0), \sigma) = S(0)N(d_+(S(0))) - Ke^{-rT}N(d_-(S(0))),$$
$$P(r, T, K, S(0), \sigma) = -S(0)N(-d_+(S(0))) + Ke^{-rT}N(-d_-(S(0))),$$

where

$$d_+(z) = \frac{\ln\frac{z}{K} + \left(r + \frac{1}{2}\sigma^2\right)T}{\sigma\sqrt{T}},$$
$$d_-(z) = \frac{\ln\frac{z}{K} + \left(r - \frac{1}{2}\sigma^2\right)T}{\sigma\sqrt{T}}.$$

In the new notation the identities in Corollary 3.14 and Exercise 3.2 take a slightly simpler form

Corollary 3.20
For any $K > 0$ and $t \le T$ the stock price process S satisfies the following identities

$$\mathbb{E}_Q(\mathbf{1}_{\{S(T)\le K\}}|\mathcal{F}_t) = N(-d_-(t, S(t)))$$
$$\mathbb{E}_Q(S(T)\mathbf{1}_{\{S(T)\le K\}}|\mathcal{F}_t) = e^{r(T-t)}S(t)N(-d_+(t, S(t)))$$

and

$$\mathbb{E}_Q(\mathbf{1}_{\{S(T)\ge K\}}|\mathcal{F}_t) = N(d_-(t, S(t))) \tag{3.7}$$
$$\mathbb{E}_Q(S(T)\mathbf{1}_{\{S(T)\ge K\}}|\mathcal{F}_t) = e^{r(T-t)}S(t)N(d_+(t, S(t))). \tag{3.8}$$

Exercise 3.3 Find the prices for a call and a put, and the probabilities (both risk-neutral and physical) of these options being in the money, if $S(0) = 100$, $K = 110$, $T = 0.5$, $r = 5\%$, $\mu = 8\%$, $\sigma = 35\%$.

The function

$$\sigma \to C(r, T, K, S(0), \sigma)$$

is strictly increasing when $r, T, K, S(0)$ are kept fixed. To prove this we need to compute the derivative with respect to σ and show that it is positive. We will perform this calculation later and at the moment we take this for granted.

Exercise 3.4 Sketch the graph of $\sigma \to C(T, K, r, S(0), \sigma)$.

A strictly increasing function can always be inverted. However, one often cannot derive an explicit form for the inverse function, so in practice the values of σ corresponding to call prices have to be found numerically.

The inverse function

$$C \to \sigma(T, K, r, S(0), C)$$

is called the **implied volatility**. This function can be used if we know the market prices of some options and apply the Black–Scholes formula to them to find the corresponding σ. We know that there is a one-to-one correspondence between the volatility and the option price, so if the Black–Scholes formula accurately reflects market practice, different option prices should yield the same σ. However, in real markets it turns out that the resulting σ's are not equal, contrary to the assumptions of the Black–Scholes model. For relatively small and large call prices the σ's are larger than for the intermediate prices. The graph of σ against the option price is U-shaped, hence it is called the 'volatility smile'.

Exercise 3.5 Sketch the graph of the function $k \mapsto \sigma(T, K, r, S(0), C)$, where $S(0) = 100$, $T = 0.5$, $r = 5\%$ and the prices are as below.

K	85	90	95	100	105	110	115
C	21.59	18.3	14.67	10.97	7.74	6.01	5.46

> **Exercise 3.6** Consider the Bachelier model, i.e. assume $S(t) = S(0) + \mu t + \sigma W(t)$. Assume $r = 0$ and find a formula for the call price.

3.4 The Black–Scholes PDE

We now concentrate attention on the European call option. By Theorem 3.18 the Black–Scholes formula for the call option can be written in the form

$$C(t) = u(t, S(t)),$$

where

$$u(t, z) = zN(d_+(t, z)) - Ke^{-r(T-t)}N(d_-(t, z)),$$

using the notation of Theorem 3.18. We now show that u satisfies the partial differential equation derived informally in Chapter 1 by computing its partial derivatives u_t, u_z and u_{zz}.

Proposition 3.21
The function u satisfies

$$u_t + rzu_z + \frac{1}{2}\sigma^2 z^2 u_{zz} = ru, \quad t < T, z > 0,$$
$$u(T, z) = (z - K)^+.$$

Proof At exercise the option price equals to the payoff, which implies the final condition:

$$u(T, S(T, \omega)) = C(T, \omega) = (S(T, \omega) - K)^+ \quad \text{for all } \omega \in \Omega.$$

Since $W(T)$ is normally distributed, it takes all real values so the set of numbers $\{S(T, \omega) : \omega \in \Omega\}$ covers the whole interval $(0, \infty)$ and u is well-defined for all positive z.

The derivation of the equation is technical and lengthy but elementary. All we have to do is to compute the derivatives to see that the equation is satisfied.

Step 1. First we prove that

$$Ke^{-r(T-t)}n(d_-(t, z)) = zn(d_+(t, z))$$

with the standard normal density $n(d) = N'(d) = \frac{1}{\sqrt{2\pi}} e^{-\frac{d^2}{2}}$ for any real d, and where the notation $d_+(t, z)$, $d_-(t, z)$ includes the dependence on $z = S(t, \omega)$ for given $\omega \in \Omega$. Thus we wish to verify that

$$Ke^{-r(T-t)} e^{-\frac{1}{2}d_-^2(t,z)} = ze^{-\frac{1}{2}d_+^2(t,z)}, \tag{3.9}$$

which reduces to

$$\frac{z}{K} = e^{-\frac{1}{2}d_-^2(t,z) - r(T-t) + \frac{1}{2}d_+^2(t,z)} = e^{\frac{1}{2}\left(d_+^2(t,z) - d_-^2(t,z)\right) - r(T-t)}.$$

We tackle the exponentials, which requires elementary algebra: first compute

$$d_+(t, z) - d_-(t, z) = \frac{\ln\frac{z}{K} + \left(r + \frac{1}{2}\sigma^2\right)(T-t)}{\sigma\sqrt{T-t}} - \frac{\ln\frac{z}{K} + \left(r - \frac{1}{2}\sigma^2\right)(T-t)}{\sigma\sqrt{T-t}}$$

$$= \sigma\sqrt{T-t} \tag{3.10}$$

and

$$d_+(t, z) + d_-(t, z) = \frac{\ln\frac{z}{K} + \left(r + \frac{1}{2}\sigma^2\right)(T-t)}{\sigma\sqrt{T-t}} + \frac{\ln\frac{z}{K} + \left(r - \frac{1}{2}\sigma^2\right)(T-t)}{\sigma\sqrt{T-t}}$$

$$= 2\frac{\ln\frac{z}{K} + r(T-t)}{\sigma\sqrt{T-t}}$$

to see that

$$\frac{1}{2}\left(d_+^2(t, z) - d_-^2(t, z)\right) - r(T-t) = \frac{1}{2}2\frac{\ln\frac{z}{K} + r(T-t)}{\sigma\sqrt{T-t}}\sigma\sqrt{T-t} - r(T-t)$$

$$= \ln\frac{z}{K}$$

as required.

Step 2. The next step is the computation of the time derivative. We claim that

$$u_t(t, z) = \frac{\partial}{\partial t}u(t, z) = -Kre^{-r(T-t)}N(d_-(t, z)) - zn(d_+(t, z))\frac{\sigma}{2\sqrt{T-t}}.$$

We compute the derivatives using elementary calculus and (3.9)

$$\frac{\partial}{\partial t}u(t,z) = zn(d_+(t,z))\frac{\partial}{\partial t}d_+(t,z)$$
$$- Kre^{-r(T-t)}N(d_-(t,z))$$
$$- Ke^{-r(T-t)}n(d_-(t,z))\frac{\partial}{\partial t}d_-(t,z)$$
$$= zn(d_+(t,z))\frac{\partial}{\partial t}d_+(t,z)$$
$$- Kre^{-r(T-t)}N(d_-(t,z)) - zn(d_+(t,z))\frac{\partial}{\partial t}d_-(t,z)$$
$$= -Kre^{-r(T-t)}N(d_-(t,z)) + zn(d_+(t,z))\left(\frac{\partial}{\partial t}d_+(t,z) - \frac{\partial}{\partial t}d_-(t,z)\right)$$

and the final touch is, by (3.10),

$$\frac{\partial}{\partial t}(d_+(t,z) - d_-(t,z)) = \frac{d}{dt}\sigma\sqrt{T-t} = -\frac{\sigma}{2\sqrt{T-t}},$$

which completes the computation of the time derivative.

Step 3. For the derivative with respect to z we claim that

$$\frac{\partial}{\partial z}u(t,z) = N(d_+(t,z)).$$

It is worth noting that the final result is surprisingly simple bearing in mind the fact that the variable z occurs in the formula for u in three places. First we note that

$$\frac{\partial}{\partial z}d_+(t,z) = \frac{\partial}{\partial z}d_-(t,z)$$

hence

$$\frac{\partial}{\partial z}u(t,z) = zn(d_+(t,z))\frac{\partial}{\partial z}d_+(t,z) + N(d_+(t,z)) - Ke^{-r(T-t)}n(d_-(t,z))\frac{\partial}{\partial z}d_-(t,z)$$
$$= zn(d_+(t,z))\frac{\partial}{\partial z}d_+(t,z) + N(d_+(t,z)) - zn(d_+(t,z))\frac{\partial}{\partial z}d_+(t,z).$$

since (3.9) implies

$$Ke^{-r(T-t)}n(d_-(t,z)) = zn(d_+(t,z)).$$

Therefore

$$u_z(t,z) = \frac{\partial}{\partial z}u(t,z) = N(d_+(t,z)) \tag{3.11}$$

as we claimed.

Step 4. Finally we compute the second order derivative u_{zz}, which is simply

$$u_{zz}(t,z) = \frac{\partial^2}{\partial z^2} u(t,z) = \frac{\partial}{\partial z} N(d_+(t,z)) = n(d_+(t,z)) \frac{1}{\sigma z \sqrt{T-t}}$$

since

$$\frac{\partial}{\partial z} d_+(t,z) = \frac{\partial}{\partial z} \left(\frac{\ln z - \ln K + \left(r + \frac{1}{2}\sigma^2(T-t)\right)}{\sigma \sqrt{T-t}} \right) = \frac{1}{\sigma \sqrt{T-t}} \frac{1}{z}.$$

Putting all the pieces together we find out that u indeed satisfies the equation. □

The PDE we have found for the call option is known as the **Black–Scholes PDE**. In a later section we shall give a replication argument which shows that this PDE arises in the pricing of a much wider class of European derivative securities, provided their payoff functions satisfy suitable growth conditions.

Exercise 3.7 Derive the version of the above PDE for the Bachelier model $(S(t) = S(0) + \mu t + \sigma W(t))$.

From Black–Scholes PDE to option price

At present, however, we remain with the call option and investigate if we can invert the above procedure: whether starting from the Black–Scholes PDE we can derive the option price at any time $t \le T$.

Remark 3.22

One may prefer to formulate this as the usual initial-value problem and this is straightforward with time change $s = T - t$, $v(s,z) = u(T - s, z)$ hence

$$v_s(s,z) = \frac{1}{2}\sigma^2 z^2 v_{zz}(s,z) + rz v_z(s,z) - rv(s,z) \quad \text{for } s > 0,$$
$$v(0,z) = h(z).$$

We need to describe the stock price dynamics with the martingale probability Q, since the solution of the pricing problem was obtained using this probability. Under Q, the drift coefficient in the Black–Scholes SDE is the risk-free rate, r. As a first step we show that the 'discounted' version of $u(t, S(t))$ is a Q-martingale for any sufficiently smooth function $u(t,z)$ satifying the Black–Scholes PDE.

Lemma 3.23

Let $u(t,z)$ be a function of class $C^{1,2}$ from $\mathbb{R}^2_+$ to $\mathbb{R}$, and let $S(t)$ satisfy

$$dS(t) = rS(t)dt + \sigma S(t)dW_Q(t).$$

If $u(t,z)$ has bounded derivative u_z and

$$u_t + rzu_z + \frac{1}{2}\sigma^2 z^2 u_{zz} = ru,$$

then $e^{-rt}u(t, S(t))$ is a Q-martingale.

Proof We apply the Itô formula after first using integration by parts and then inserting the above form of $dz = d(S(t))$:

$$d\left[e^{-rt}u(t, S(t))\right] = -re^{-rt}u(t, S(t))dt + e^{-rt}d[u(t, S(t))]$$

$$= -re^{-rt}udt$$

$$+ e^{-rt}\left(u_t dt + u_z rS(t)dt + u_z \sigma S(t)dW_Q(t) + \frac{1}{2}u_{zz}\sigma^2 S^2(t)dt\right)$$

$$= e^{-rt}\left(u_t + rS(t)u_z + \frac{1}{2}\sigma^2 S^2(t)u_{zz} - ru\right)dt$$

$$+ e^{-rt}\sigma S(t)u_z dW_Q(t).$$

If $u(t,z)$ satisfies the equation, then the term in the brackets is zero, so that

$$d\left[e^{-rt}u(t, S(t))\right] = e^{-rt}\sigma S(t)u_z dW_Q(t). \tag{3.12}$$

We know that a stochastic integral produces a local martingale. The martingale property requires additional regularity of the function under the stochastic integral. With our assumptions u_z is bounded and $S(t) \in M^2_{[0,T]}$ since, using the fact that $S(t) = S(0)\exp\left(r - \frac{1}{2}\sigma^2\right)t + \sigma W_Q(t)$:

$$\mathbb{E}_Q\left[\int_0^T S^2(t)dt\right] = S^2(0)\int_0^T \mathbb{E}_Q \exp\left\{2\left(\mu - \frac{1}{2}\sigma^2\right)t + 2\sigma W(t)\right\}dt$$

$$= S^2(0)\int_0^T \exp\left\{2\left(\mu - \frac{1}{2}\sigma^2\right)t + \sigma^2 t\right\}dt < \infty$$

hence $e^{-rt}\sigma S(t)u_z \in M^2_{[0,T]}$, so $e^{-rt}u(t, S(t))$ is a Q-martingale. $\square$

The Lemma applies to the call option, since the solution for the call price has bounded partial derivative u_z: our computation in (3.11) of this derivative as $N(d_+(t,z))$ showed that it is the value of a cumulative distribution function, so its values lie in $[0, 1]$. Now we can demonstrate that the Black–Scholes PDE yields the price process of the call option. We state and prove the result for a general European derivative security H with (non-negative) payoff $H(T) \in L^2(Q)$.

Theorem 3.24
If $H(T) = h(S(T)) \geq 0$ is in $L^2(Q)$, and if $u(t, z)$ solves

$$u_t + rzu_z + \frac{1}{2}\sigma^2 z^2 u_{zz} = ru,$$

$$u(T, z) = h(z)$$

with bounded u_z, then for all $t \in [0, T]$,

$$H(t) = u(t, S(t)).$$

Proof   By the terminal condition $u(T, z) = h(z)$ we have

$$u(T, S(T)) = H(T).$$

We know that for the discounted values we have

$$\tilde{H}(t) = \mathbb{E}_Q(\tilde{H}(T)|\mathcal{F}_t).$$

We also know that $e^{-rt}u(t, S(t))$ is a Q-martingale (by the previous lemma) so

$$\begin{aligned}
H(t) &= e^{rt}\mathbb{E}_Q\left(e^{-rT}u(T, S(T))|\mathcal{F}_t\right) \\
&= e^{rt}e^{-rt}u(t, S(t)) \\
&= u(t, S(t)).
\end{aligned} \qquad \square$$

Remark 3.25
With some experience in the theory of partial differential equations one can see that the boundedness assumption on u_z is redundant: the result remains valid as long as the function h in the terminal condition has linear growth in z.

Remark 3.26
The above considerations show a deep relationship between solutions to stochastic differential equations and solutions to partial differential equations. The main idea is best seen in a simple case, so consider a version of Lemma 3.23 with $S(t + u) = x + \sigma W(u)$, so that $S(t) = x$, and suppose that u is a solution of

$$u_t + \frac{1}{2}\sigma^2 u_{zz} = 0, \quad s < T, \tag{3.13}$$

$$u(T, z) = h(z).$$

Then $u(t, x + \sigma W(T - t))$ is a martingale and

$$u(t, x) = \mathbb{E}(h(x + \sigma W(T - t))), \qquad (3.14)$$

which is a particular case of the famous Feynman–Kac formula. This provides a method to obtain approximate solutions of PDEs by Monte-Carlo simulation: run many copies of the Wiener process, compute the values of h at the terminal times and average. For such a simple equation there is no point of doing this but in more genereal non-linear cases this may by a valuable method. The heart of this lies in the fact that the density of $W(t)$ solves a certain second-order PDE (the heat equation).

Exercise 3.8 Give a detailed justification of the claims of this remark.

Exercise 3.9 Show that the function defined by (3.14) is sufficiently regular and solves (3.13).

The replicating strategy

The martingale representation theorem enabled us to prove completeness of the Black–Scholes model. Although this fact proves the existence of replicating strategies for the derivative securities of interest to us, it remains unsatisfactory. For practical purposes we would like to have some specific formula or at least a method of finding such a strategy explicitly. An advantage of the next theorem is that it provides a simple prescription for computing a replicating strategy provided we can solve the equation involved. Again we consider a general European derivative.

Theorem 3.27
If $H(T) = h(S(T)) \geq 0$ is L^2 with respect to Q and if $u(t, z)$ solves

$$u_t + rzu_z + \frac{1}{2}\sigma^2 z^2 u_{xx} = ru,$$
$$u(T, z) = h(z)$$

with bounded u_z, then

$$x(t) = u_z(t, S(t)),$$
$$y(t) = \frac{u(t, S(t)) - x(t)S(t)}{A(t)}$$

is an admissible strategy that replicates the payoff $H(T)$.

Proof   The above choices of $x(t), y(t)$ guarantee that

$$V_{(x,y)}(t) = x(t)S(t) + y(t)A(t) = u(t, S(t)).$$

By Theorem 3.24 we know that $u(t, S(t)) = H(t)$, the price of the derivative security, so we have

$$V_{(x,y)}(T) = u(T, S(T)) = H(T).$$

Since $H(t) \geq 0$ this implies $u(t, S(t)) \geq 0$ which implies the first condition for admissibility: we have shown that the value process of the strategy is bounded below for all $t \in [0, T]$.

Since $u(t, S(t)) = H(t)$ and $\tilde{H}(t) = \mathbb{E}_Q(\tilde{H}(T)|\mathcal{F}_t)$ is a martingale, it follows that $\tilde{V}_{(x,y)}(t)$ is a martingale.

The self-financing property of (x, y) follows from the relation (3.12) proved in Lemma 3.23

$$\begin{aligned} d\tilde{V}_{(x,y)}(t) &= d\left[e^{-rt}u(t, S(t))\right] \\ &= e^{-rt}\sigma S(t)u_z(t, S(t))dW_Q(t) \\ &= x(t)d\tilde{S}_t, \end{aligned}$$

which is equivalent to the self-financing property, as we saw in Proposition 2.9.   □

Remark 3.28
By Proposition 2.26, the strategy (x, y) found in Theorem 3.27 is the unique admissible strategy replicating H, and it is minimal (or 'best possible') in the sense that any self-financing strategy (x', y') with non-negative value process has initial value $V_{(x',y')}(0) \geq V_{(x,y)}(0)$, as was shown in Proposition 2.25.

3.5   The Greeks

Replication gives a way of protecting a short position in an option by constructing a strategy which guarantees us the money we will need to fulfil the obligation. Insuring a position against this risk is called **hedging**. The practical difficulty lies in the fact that we have to adjust our position according to the changing circumstances. Thus we consider the dynamical behaviour of the option price (which equals the value process of the replicating strategy) relative to each of the parameters that occur in the BS formula.

The first factor to discuss is the stock price. For this reason we introduce the notation which highlights the dependence of the value on stock price.

We wish to consider this in isolation, so we assume for the purpose that the other parameters, e.g., the riskless interest rate r or the volatility σ, remain unchanged.

Take a portfolio (x, y, z) in the extended market, where the letter z denotes the position in a derivative security. For fixed t write $V_{(x,y,z)}(t) = V(S)$.

Sensitivity of the value with respect to S is measured by the derivative, usually called the **delta** of the portfolio:

$$\text{delta}_V = \frac{\partial}{\partial S} V(S).$$

If

$$\frac{\partial}{\partial S} V(S) = 0,$$
$$V(S + \varepsilon) \approx V(S),$$

so that, informally, the value function is close to being constant if the prices do not change too much.

For example, let $z = -1$ (position in the call option) which is the position of a trader who has written and sold one call option.

The problem is to find (x, y) so that $\frac{\partial}{\partial S} V(S) = 0$ which is called **delta hedging**. We have

$$\frac{\partial}{\partial S} V = \frac{\partial}{\partial S}(xS + yA + zC)$$

since the derivative is a linear operation. In the first term the S-derivative is x. The money market account does not depend on the stock price so the derivative is zero. The only non-trivial case is in the third term where we have the option, which depends on the stock price is a complicated way. However, we know that derivative is relatively simple:

$$\frac{\partial}{\partial S} V = x \frac{\partial}{\partial S} S + y \frac{\partial}{\partial S} A + z \frac{\partial}{\partial S} C$$
$$= x + z \times \text{delta}_C$$
$$= x - N(d_+)$$

so the solution is

$$x = N(d_+).$$

In the above spirit, we consider the dependence on the other variables in the Black–Scholes formula. We also consider how $\frac{\partial V}{\partial S}$ itself changes with changes in S.

For a general portfolio whose value depends on the factors describing the dynamics of the assets and the maturity of options involved, $V = V(T, r, S, \sigma)$, we write

$$\text{delta}_V = \frac{\partial V}{\partial S},$$

$$\text{gamma}_V = \frac{\partial^2 V}{\partial S^2},$$

$$\text{theta}_V = \frac{\partial V}{\partial T},$$

$$\text{vega}_V = \frac{\partial V}{\partial \sigma},$$

$$\text{rho}_V = \frac{\partial V}{\partial r}.$$

Exercise 3.10   Given an European call C and put P, both with strike K and expiry T, show that $\text{delta}_C - \text{delta}_P = 1$. Deduce that $\text{delta}_P = -N(-d_+)$ and that $\text{gamma}_P = \text{gamma}_C$.

Delta hedging gives protection against small changes of the stock prices. A more effective strategy is based on analysing the second derivative in S as well, since it allows us to assess how rapidly we need to change the stock holdings. To take into account the other parameters we introduce the corresponding partial derivatives. For example, the goal might be to make them all zero. This means that five conditions are imposed so to find a portfolio we need five variables. Therefore the portfolio built to hedge one option must include some other derivatives.

For the call option we obtain, here restricting attention to values at time $t = 0$,

$$\text{delta}_C = N(d_+),$$

$$\text{gamma}_C = \frac{1}{S\sigma\sqrt{T}} n(d_+), \qquad \text{where } n(x) = \frac{1}{\sqrt{2\pi}} e^{-\frac{1}{2}x^2}$$

$$\text{theta}_C = -\frac{S\sigma}{2\sqrt{T}} n(d_+) - rKe^{-rT} N(d_-),$$

$$\text{vega}_C = S\sqrt{T} n(d_+),$$

$$\text{rho}_C = TKe^{-rT} N(d_-)$$

We proved the first three expressions in the proof of Proposition 3.21. To complete the story we verify the remaining two. Recall that

$$C(r, T, K, S(0), \sigma) = S(0)N(d_+) - Ke^{-rT}N(d_-)$$

where

$$d_+ = \frac{\ln \frac{S(0)}{K} + \left(r + \frac{1}{2}\sigma^2\right)T}{\sigma\sqrt{T}},$$

$$d_- = \frac{\ln \frac{S(0)}{K} + \left(r - \frac{1}{2}\sigma^2\right)T}{\sigma\sqrt{T}}.$$

The formula (3.9) is also useful here, with n as the standard normal density:

$$Ke^{-r(T-t)}n(d_-(t, x)) = xn(d_+(t, x)).$$

The computation is easy, requiring only elementary calculus and applying the above formula at $(t, x) = (0, S(0))$:

$$\frac{\partial C}{\partial \sigma} = S(0)n(d_+)\frac{\partial d_+}{\partial \sigma} - Ke^{-rT}n(d_-)\frac{\partial d_-}{\partial \sigma}$$

$$= S(0)n(d_+)\frac{\sigma T\sigma\sqrt{T} - \left(\ln \frac{S(0)}{K} + \left(r + \frac{1}{2}\sigma^2\right)T\right)\sqrt{T}}{\sigma^2 T}$$

$$- S(0)n(d_+)\frac{-\sigma T\sigma\sqrt{T} - \left(\ln \frac{S(0)}{K} + \left(r - \frac{1}{2}\sigma^2\right)T\right)\sqrt{T}}{\sigma^2 T}$$

so

$$\frac{\partial C}{\partial \sigma} = S(0)n(d_+)\frac{2\sigma^2 T\sqrt{T} - \sigma^2 T\sqrt{T}}{\sigma^2 T}$$

$$= S(0)n(d_+)\sqrt{T} > 0.$$

To find the derivative of call price with respect to r we proceed in a similar way

$$\frac{\partial C}{\partial r} = S(0)n(d_+)\frac{\partial d_+}{\partial r} - Ke^{-rT}n(d_-)\frac{\partial d_-}{\partial r} + TKe^{-rT}N(d_-)$$

$$= S(0)n(d_+)\frac{\sqrt{T}}{\sigma} - S(0)n(d_+)\frac{\sqrt{T}}{\sigma} + TKe^{-rT}N(d_-)$$

$$= TKe^{-rT}N(d_-).$$

Exercise 3.11 Show that analogous calculations, with T replaced by the **time to expiry** $T - t$, and with $d_\pm(t)$ replacing $d_\pm$, apply to give the Greeks evaluated at time $t < T$.

Remark 3.29

The origin of the terminology of the 'Greeks' is a little obscure. Obviously the intention was to use letters from the Greek alphabet, but 'vega' is not among those. At one stage the (genuinely Greek) letter κ was used to describe the dependence of V upon the volatility, σ, but this was soon superseded by the current convention, and the use of 'vega' has now become universal – arguably revealing a disturbing weakness in the classical education of market participants!

We draw some immediate practical conclusions from the above expressions describing the Greeks.

- gamma$_V$ measures the sensitivity of delta$_V$ (i.e. of our stock holding) against changes in the price of the underlying, so if gamma$_V$ is close to 0 we can reduce transaction costs of our hedging strategy by not having to trade very often or in large amounts.
- gamma$_C$ > 0 means that the call and put option prices are strictly convex functions of the price of the underlying.
- theta$_V$ is sometimes called the **time decay** of the option, since for call C we have theta$_C$ < 0. Theta is often computed in terms of the time to expiry, $(T - t)$. If we assume constant volatility and riskless rates, the option value dynamics are determined by delta and theta.

Exercise 3.12 Verify that theta$_P$ = theta$_C$ + $rKe^{-r(T-t)}$, where C and P are a call and a put respectively, with the same strike K and expiry T. Deduce a formula for theta$_P$.

- rho$_C$ > 0, and by call-put parity again, rho$_C$ − rho$_P$ = TKe^{-rT}, so rho$_P$ < 0. In other words, if the riskless rate rises, then puts become cheaper and calls more expensive. In other words, the market expects stock prices to rise in such circumstances.
- the same use of the parity relation as in the last two Exercises shows immediately that vega$_P$ = vega$_C$. In fact, direct calculation from the BS formula for the put shows that vega$_P$ = $S\sqrt{T}n(-d_+)$, and of course the

standard normal density is symmetric, so that we have $n(-d) = n(d)$ for any real d.

3.6 Risk and return

An application of the Itô formula to the value process of the call option at time t enables us to compare the volatility of the call C with that of the underlying, S. We know that at time $t < T$ the call C has value

$$C(t) = u(t, S(t)) = S(t)N(d_+(t)) - e^{-r(T-t)}KN(d_-(t)),$$

using the notation of Theorem 3.18. Working with the market probability P, so that $dS = \mu S\,dt + \sigma S\,dW$, the Itô formula, applied to $u(t, z)$, provides

$$du = \left(u_t + \mu S u_z + \frac{1}{2}\sigma^2 S^2 u_{zz}\right) dt + \sigma S u_z dW. \qquad (3.15)$$

To compare the performance of the two risky assets, S and C, we seek to establish the 'Black–Scholes dynamics' of the option, by writing (3.15) in the form

$$\frac{du}{u} = \mu_C dt + \sigma_C dW.$$

Comparing this with (3.15), i.e. setting

$$\left(u_t + \mu S u_z + \frac{1}{2}\sigma^2 S^2 u_{zz}\right) dt + \sigma S u_z dW = u(\mu_C dt + \sigma_C dW)$$

we obtain

$$\mu_C = \frac{1}{u}\left(u_t + \mu S u_z + \frac{1}{2}\sigma^2 S^2 u_{zz}\right),$$

$$\sigma_C = \frac{\sigma S u_z}{u}.$$

The volatility of the call is the coefficient of the stochastic term of the ratio $\frac{du}{u}$. Thus we have found the volatility of the call as

$$\sigma_C = \frac{\sigma S}{u} u_z.$$

Applying this with $u(t, S(t)) = C(t)$ so that $u_z(t, S(t)) = N(d_+(t))$, the ratio of the two volatilities is

$$\beta_C(t) = \frac{\sigma_C(t)}{\sigma} = \frac{S(t)}{C(t)}N(d_+(t)) = \frac{S(t)N(d_+(t))}{S(t)N(d_+(t)) - e^{-r(T-t)}KN(d_-(t))} > 1.$$

So the call option has higher volatility (i.e. is 'riskier') than the underlying, as one might expect.

Now consider μ_C: since the value process $C(t) = u(t, S(t))$ of the call option is given by a function that satisfies the Black–Scholes PDE, we know that for our u we have

$$ru = u_t + rS\,u_z + \frac{1}{2}\sigma^2 S^2 u_{zz}$$

$$= u_t + (r - \mu)S\,u_z + \mu S\,u_z + \frac{1}{2}\sigma^2 S^2 u_{zz}$$

$$= u\mu_C + (r - \mu)S\,u_z$$

which gives

$$\mu_C = \frac{1}{u}(ru + (\mu - r)S\,u_z)$$

$$= \frac{S}{u}u_z(\mu - r) + r.$$

With $u(t, S(t)) = C(t)$ and

$$u_z(t, S(t)) = N(d_+(t)),$$

$$\beta_C = \frac{S(t)}{C(t)}N(d_+(t))$$

we therefore have

$$\mu_C - r = \beta_C(\mu - r).$$

In other words, the excess return (over what is expected from riskless investment) of the option is proportional to that of the underlying, and the constant of proportionality (the beta) of the option is greater than 1. These results mirror what is found in the simple one-period binomial model (see [DMFM]).

3.7 Proofs

Lemma 3.6
The family $\mathcal{L}$ of all linear combinations of random variables

$$X = \exp\left\{i\sum_{k=1}^{n} c_k(W(t_{k+1}) - W(t_k))\right\}$$

is dense in $L^2_{\mathbb{C}}(\Omega)$.

Proof   First introduce an intermediate space between $\mathcal{L}$ and L^2 : let

$$\mathcal{R} = \{g(W(t_1), W(t_2) - W(t_1), \ldots, W(t_n) - W(t_{n-1})) :$$
$$n \in \mathbb{N}, 0 \le t_1 < \cdots < t_n \le T, g : \mathbb{R}^n \to \mathbb{C} \text{ bounded Borel}\}.$$

We clearly have the following inclusions of vector spaces

$$\mathcal{L} \subset \mathcal{R} \subset L^2.$$

The claim will follow from two properties: $\mathcal{R}$ is dense in L^2 and $\mathcal{L}$ is dense in $\mathcal{R}$, and we will tackle them below.

Step 1. $\mathcal{R}$ is dense in L^2.

Let $\{s_n\}$ be a countable set of time instants, dense in $[0, T]$. Let

$$\mathcal{F}_n = \sigma\{W(s_1), W(s_2) - W(s_1), \ldots, W(s_n) - W(s_{n-1})\}$$

and clearly

$$\mathcal{F}_n \subset \mathcal{F}_{n+1}.$$

We claim that

$$\mathcal{F}_T = \sigma\left(\bigcup_{n=1}^{\infty} \mathcal{F}_n\right).$$

The inclusion $\supset$ is obvious by the definition of $\mathcal{F}_T$ as the σ-field generated by all $W(s)$, $s \le T$. For the converse, it is sufficient to show that each $W(s)$ is $\sigma(\bigcup \mathcal{F}_n)$-measurable. By the density of $\{s_n\}$ we can find a sequence $s_k \to s$ and clearly $W(s_k) \to W(s)$ almost surely (the convergence is obvious in L^2 so at least a subsequence converges pointwise). Each $W(s_k)$ is $\sigma(\bigcup \mathcal{F}_n)$-measurable and so is the limit.

Take a random variable $X \in L^2(\Omega)$ and consider the sequence

$$M(n) = \mathbb{E}(X|\mathcal{F}_n),$$

which is a martingale. It is L^2-bounded, so we have convergence a.s.(P) and in L^2-norm of $M(n)$ to some Y in L^2 (see [SCF]). In fact, since $Y(\omega) = \lim_n M(n, \omega)$ almost surely, we may define $Y(\omega) = \limsup_n M(n, \omega)$ for every ω in Ω, so that Y is measurable with respect to $\sigma(\bigcup_{n=1}^{\infty} \mathcal{F}_n) = \mathcal{F}_T$.

Finally, we check that

$$\mathbb{E}(X|\mathcal{F}_T) = Y$$

since then (by the convergence in L^2)

$$X = \lim_{n\to\infty} M(n).$$

So far we have shown that $\mathbb{E}(X|\mathcal{F}_n) = \mathbb{E}(Y|\mathcal{F}_n)$ for all n. Hence for $n \geq 1$ and $A \in \mathcal{F}_n$ we have, by definition of conditional expectation, that

$$\int_A XdP = \int_A YdP.$$

Define probabilities Q_1, Q_2 on $\mathcal{F}_T$ by setting

$$Q_1(A) = \int_A \mathbb{E}(X|\mathcal{F}_T)dP$$

$$Q_2(A) = \int_A YdP$$

for $A \in \mathcal{F}_T$. These probabilities agree on the π-system $\bigcup_n \mathcal{F}_n$, hence they agree on $\mathcal{F}_T$. But both $\mathbb{E}(X|\mathcal{F}_T)$ and Y are $\mathcal{F}_T$-measurable, so they must be equal: the set $A = \{Y > \mathbb{E}(X|\mathcal{F}_T)\}$ is in $\mathcal{F}_T$ and $\int_A (Y - \mathbb{E}(X|\mathcal{F}_T))dP = 0$, hence $P(A) = 0$, and similarly for $\{Y < \mathbb{E}(X|\mathcal{F}_T)\}$. We have now shown that $\mathbb{E}(X|\mathcal{F}_T) = Y$.

To conclude the proof of Step 1 it is sufficient to note that $M(n)$ is $\mathcal{F}_n$-measurable so it is in the form

$$M(n) = g(W(t_1), W(t_2) - W(t_1), \ldots, W(t_n) - W(t_{n-1}))$$

(see [PF]).

Step 2. $\mathcal{L}$ is dense in $\mathcal{R}$.

Suppose an element X of $\mathcal{R}$ is orthogonal to any element Y of $\mathcal{L}$, i.e.

$$\langle X, Y \rangle_{L^2(\Omega)} = \mathbb{E}(XY) = 0,$$

where

$$X = g(W(t_1), W(t_2) - W(t_1), \ldots, W(t_n) - W(t_{n-1})),$$
$$Y = \exp\{i \sum a_k[W(t_{k+1}) - W(t_k)]\}.$$

We have to show that $X = 0$, i.e. $g = 0$.

The equality $\mathbb{E}(XY) = 0$ gives

$$\int_{\mathbb{R}^n} g(x_1, \ldots, x_n) \exp\left\{i \sum a_k x_k\right\} f(x_1, \ldots, x_n)d\mathbf{x} = 0,$$

where f is the density of the vector $(W(t_1), W(t_2) - W(t_1), \ldots, W(t_n) - W(t_{n-1}))$. Writing $\phi = (2\pi)^{n/2}gf$ we have

$$h(a_1, \ldots, a_n) = (2\pi)^{-n/2} \int_{\mathbb{R}^n} \phi(x_1, x_2, \ldots, x_n) \exp\left\{i \sum a_k x_k\right\} d\mathbf{x} = 0$$

(in other words, h is the so-called Fourier transform of ϕ).

We will prove that $\phi = 0$ but since $f \neq 0$, this will prove $g = 0$ and conclude the argument.

Obviously

$$\int_{\mathbb{R}^n} h(y_1, \ldots, y_n) \exp\left\{i \sum y_k x_k\right\} dy = 0.$$

Write

$$\psi(x_1, \ldots, x_n) = \exp\left\{-\frac{1}{2}|\mathbf{x}|^2\right\}$$

and consider $\psi(\varepsilon\mathbf{x})$ for $\varepsilon > 0$.

Auxiliary formula.

We will show that

$$\int_{\mathbb{R}^n} \psi(\varepsilon\mathbf{y})h(\mathbf{y}) \exp\left\{i \sum y_k x_k\right\} dy = \int_{\mathbb{R}^n} \int_{\mathbb{R}^n} \psi(\mathbf{z})\phi(\mathbf{x}+\varepsilon\mathbf{y}) \exp\left\{i \sum y_k x_k\right\} d\mathbf{z}dy,$$

$$(3.16)$$

which is just an exercise in applying the Fubini theorem:

$$\int_{\mathbb{R}^n} \psi(\mathbf{y})h(\mathbf{y}) \exp\left\{i \sum y_k x_k\right\} dy$$

$$= \int_{\mathbb{R}^n} \psi(\mathbf{y}) \int_{\mathbb{R}^n} \phi(\mathbf{z}) \exp\left\{-i \sum y_k z_k\right\} d\mathbf{z} \exp\left\{i \sum y_k x_k\right\} dy \quad (h \text{ inserted})$$

$$= \int_{\mathbb{R}^n} \phi(\mathbf{z}) \int_{\mathbb{R}^n} \psi(\mathbf{y}) \exp\left\{i \sum y_k(z_k - x_k)\right\} dyd\mathbf{z}$$

$$= \int_{\mathbb{R}^n} \phi(\mathbf{x} + \mathbf{u}) \int_{\mathbb{R}^n} \psi(\mathbf{y}) \exp\left\{i \sum y_k u_k\right\} dyd\mathbf{u}$$

and then the change of variable: $\mathbf{u} = \varepsilon\mathbf{y}$ completes the argument.

Convergence of the sides of (3.16) as $\varepsilon \to 0$.

LHS. If $\varepsilon \to 0$ then $\psi(\varepsilon\mathbf{x}) \to 1$ and by the dominated convergence theorem

$$\int_{\mathbb{R}^n} \psi(\varepsilon\mathbf{y})h(\mathbf{y}) \exp\left\{i \sum y_k x_k\right\} dy \to \int_{\mathbb{R}^n} h(\mathbf{y}) \exp\left\{i \sum y_k x_k\right\} dy = 0$$

so the left-hand side of (3.16) converges to zero.

RHS. The right-hand side of (3.16) obviously converges to

$$\int_{\mathbb{R}^n} \int_{\mathbb{R}^n} \psi(\mathbf{z})\phi(\mathbf{x}) \exp\left\{i \sum y_k x_k\right\} d\mathbf{z}dy$$

and now we can pull out $\phi(\mathbf{x})$, which is no longer involved in the integration:

$$\text{RHS}(3.16) \to \phi(\mathbf{x}) \int_{\mathbb{R}^n} \int_{\mathbb{R}^n} \psi(\mathbf{z}) \exp\left\{i \sum y_k x_k\right\} d\mathbf{z}dy.$$

Next we compute both integrals (an exercise in calculus); the inner integral is

$$\int_{\mathbb{R}^n} \psi(\mathbf{z}) \exp\left\{i \sum y_k x_k\right\} d\mathbf{z} = \psi(\mathbf{y}),$$

and then

$$\int_{\mathbb{R}^n} \psi(\mathbf{y}) d\mathbf{y} = 1$$

so the right-hand side of (3.16) converges to ϕ.

We can conlude that $\phi = 0$, which completes the proof. $\square$

4

Extensions and applications

4.1   Options on foreign currency

We shall treat foreign currency in the same way as was done for a stock. This can be justified by observing that the price of foreign currency fluctuates randomly: we shall assume that the dynamics are of the same form as we have previously assumed for stocks. In practice, however, the drift term is usually very small; it is related to the movement of risk-free rates in both countries. If they are the same, then the drift term is usually taken to be zero. The volatility coefficient is also typically smaller than for a stock, reflecting the observed reality that, in practice, unexpected large shifts in currency values are fairly exceptional.

So our primary securities are:

$A(t)$, representing the money market account in the home currency,

$S(t)$, representing the price of one unit of foreign currency,

and these are assumed to satisfy the following (familiar) equations

$$dA(t) = rA(t)dt,$$

$$dS(t) = \mu S(t)dt + \sigma S(t)dW(t).$$

We should regard this foreign currency as the balance of a bank account, rather than as a banknote. Then we earn the appropriate rate of interest if we hold some position in this asset. This position increases the level of the account so we add a suitable growth factor to the number of units held, using the foreign risk-free interest rate δ for continuous compounding.

The value of a strategy (x, y) at time t is then equal to

$$V(t) = x(t)e^{\delta t}S(t) + y(t)A(t),$$

where we take account of the fact that the currency earns interest, so our position as in the bank statement will grow. We introduce notation to include the additional units held: $x^{\delta}(t) = x(t)e^{\delta t}$, so that

$$V(t) = x^{\delta}(t)S(t) + y(t)A(t).$$

This describes the position as reflected in the two (home and foreign) bank statements. If we hold 1000 units of foreign currency (euros, say) and interest paid turns this into 1050 euros (one euro being worth $S(t)$ at time t) then the euro bank statement records our holding as 1050 units.

However, it is mathematically convenient to attach the growth factor to the price $S(t)$ of the foreign currency instead, so that we can keep the number of units held unchanged. This auxiliary asset, denoted by

$$S^{\delta}(t) = S(t)e^{\delta t},$$

is a mathematical object only, but it will prove very useful. The value process now reads

$$V(t) = x(t)S^{\delta}(t) + y(t)A(t).$$

We discuss the equation satisfied by this auxiliary asset S^{δ}. First note that $d(e^{\delta t}S(t)) = S(t)d(e^{\delta t}) + e^{\delta t}dS(t)$ and $de^{\delta t} = \delta e^{\delta t}dt$ so that

$$\begin{aligned}
dS^{\delta}(t) &= d(e^{\delta t}S(t)) \\
&= \delta e^{\delta t}S(t)dt + e^{\delta t}dS(t) \\
&= \delta e^{\delta t}S(t)dt + \mu e^{\delta t}S(t)dt + \sigma e^{\delta t}S(t)dW(t) \\
&= (\mu + \delta)S^{\delta}(t)dt + \sigma S^{\delta}(t)dW(t).
\end{aligned}$$

The self-financing condition reads

$$\begin{aligned}
dV(t) &= x(t)dS^{\delta}(t) + y(t)dA(t) \\
&= x(t)d(e^{\delta t}S(t)) + y(t)dA(t) \\
&= x(t)e^{\delta t}dS(t) + \delta x(t)e^{\delta t}S(t)dt + y(t)dA(t) \\
&= x^{\delta}(t)dS(t) + y(t)dA(t) + \delta x^{\delta}(t)S(t)dt.
\end{aligned}$$

The additional term in the modified position is easily explained heuristically. At annual rate δ, the rate for the period dt is $\delta \times dt$, which, multiplied by the price, is the interest earned on each unit held.

For pricing purposes, the discounted value of strategy should be a martingale. This condition was taken as one of the ingredients of the concept of admissibility of the strategy, as it eliminates the suicide strategies which lead to arbitrage opportunities. Take the discounted value

$$\tilde{V}(t) = e^{-rt} V(t)$$

and apply the Itô formula:

$$
\begin{aligned}
d\tilde{V}(t) &= d[e^{-rt} V(t)] \\
&= -re^{-rt} V(t) dt + e^{-rt} dV(t) \ (\text{since } d[e^{-rt} V(t)] = V(t) de^{-rt} + e^{-rt} dV(t)) \\
&= -re^{-rt} V(t) dt + e^{-rt} (x(t) dS^\delta(t) + y(t) dA(t)) \\
&\quad (\text{inserting } dV(t) = x(t) dS^\delta(t) + y(t) dA(t)) \\
&= -re^{-rt} x(t) S^\delta(t) dt - re^{-rt} y(t) A(t) dt \quad (\text{using the form of } dS^\delta(t)) \\
&\quad + (\mu + \delta) e^{-rt} x(t) S^\delta(t) dt + \sigma e^{-rt} x(t) S^\delta(t) dW(t) + re^{-rt} y(t) A(t) dt \\
&= e^{-rt} S^\delta(t) x(t) [(\mu + \delta - r) dt + \sigma dW(t)].
\end{aligned}
$$

Observe that, as in the single-stock model, the holdings in the risk-free asset A do not appear in this formula. This shows a way forward. By converting the expression in the square bracket into the differential of some Wiener process, we at least have a local martingale.

Let

$$W_{Q^\delta}(t) = \frac{\mu + \delta - r}{\sigma} t + W(t).$$

This definition of W_{Q^δ} gives the local martingale property for the discounted value of a strategy after we convert W into a Wiener process: since $\tilde{S}^\delta(t) = e^{-rt} S^\delta(t)$ we obtain

$$d\tilde{V}(t) = \sigma x(t) \tilde{S}^\delta(t) dW_{Q^\delta}(t).$$

For W_{Q^δ} to become a martingale we apply the simplified Girsanov theorem (Theorem 2.1) with

$$u^\delta = \frac{\mu + \delta - r}{\sigma}$$

to obtain the probability Q^δ under which $W(t)$ is a Wiener process:

$$Q^\delta(A) = \mathbb{E}\left(\mathbf{1}_A \exp\left\{-\frac{1}{2}\left(u^\delta\right)^2 T - u^\delta W(T)\right\}\right).$$

We analyse the dynamics of S^δ under W

$$dS^\delta(t) = (\mu + \delta)S^\delta(t)dt + \sigma S^\delta(t)dW(t)$$

$$= (\mu + \delta)S^\delta(t)dt + \sigma S^\delta(t)dW_{Q^\delta}(t) - \sigma S^\delta(t)\frac{\mu + \delta - r}{\sigma}dt$$

(by definition of $W^\delta_Q(t)$)

$$= rS^\delta(t)dt + \sigma S^\delta(t)dW_{Q^\delta}(t)$$

after some cancellation. This explains the significance of S^δ: its drift term uses the interest rate in the home market, which plays the role of the riskless rate. For the discounted values we therefore have

$$d\tilde{S}^\delta(t) = d(e^{-rt}S^\delta(t))$$

$$= -re^{-rt}S^\delta(t)dt + e^{-rt}dS^\delta(t)$$

$$= -re^{-rt}S^\delta(t)dt + e^{-rt}rS^\delta(t)dt + e^{-rt}\sigma S^\delta(t)dW_Q(t)$$

(since $dS^\delta(t) = rS^\delta(t)dt + \sigma S^\delta(t)dW_Q(t)$)

$$= \sigma\tilde{S}^\delta(t)dW_Q(t).$$

As a result we have the martingale property for the discounted modified asset. It is a martingale since the equation can be solved and the martingale property can be established directly, as we did in Exercise 2.1.

Exercise 4.1   Derive the equation satisfied by the futures price assuming that the interest rate is constant. Find the version in the risk-neutral world.

We can draw the conclusion that

$$d\tilde{V}(t) = \sigma x(t)\tilde{S}^\delta(t)dW_{Q^\delta}(t)$$

so $\tilde{V}(t)$ is a local martingale under Q^δ. The discounted value of the modified asset is a martingale as we noticed above, since we can solve the equation. However, we cannot say this about the discounted V without additional information on the process x. As before, we restrict the class of strategies.

Definition 4.1

A strategy (x, y) is admissible if its value process V satisfies
   (1) $dV(t) = x(t)dS^\delta(t) + y(t)dA(t)$,
   (2) $V(t) \geq -L$, for some $L \geq 0$,
   (3) $\tilde{V}(t)$ is Q^δ-martingale.

The point here is that the self-financing condition is the same as before if the modified asset is used.

For the purpose of replication consider a derivative with payoff H and postulate

$$V(T) = H.$$

Recall that the No Arbitrage Principle implies $H(t) = V(t)$, where

$$H(t) = \mathbb{E}_{Q^\delta}(e^{-r(T-t)}H|\mathcal{F}_t)$$

since the analysis performed before applies here. The only difference is that we have S^δ instead of S. All we have to do next is to compute the conditional expectation. To summarise, note that before we had the equation

$$dS(t) = rS(t)dt + \sigma S(t)dW_Q(t)$$

and now we have (with S^δ and Q^δ in the roles of S and Q)

$$dS^\delta(t) = rS^\delta(t)dt + \sigma S^\delta(t)dW_{Q^\delta}(t).$$

For the option value we had, for S and Q,

$$\begin{aligned}H(t) &= e^{-r(T-t)}\mathbb{E}_Q(h(S(T))|\mathcal{F}_t)\\ &= e^{-r(T-t)}\mathbb{E}_Q\left(h(S(t)e^{(r-\frac{1}{2}\sigma^2)(T-t)+\sigma(W_Q(T)-W_Q(t))})|\mathcal{F}_t\right),\end{aligned}$$

which now takes the following form, where the general formula is the same (apart from using Q^δ instead of Q), since the payoff function is concerned with the original asset S rather than with S^δ. So

$$\begin{aligned}H(t) &= e^{-r(T-t)}\mathbb{E}_{Q^\delta}(h(S(T))|\mathcal{F}_t)\\ &= e^{-r(T-t)}\mathbb{E}_{Q^\delta}(h(e^{-\delta T}S^\delta(T))|\mathcal{F}_t)\\ &= e^{-r(T-t)}\mathbb{E}_{Q^\delta}\left(h(e^{-\delta T}S^\delta(t)e^{(r-\frac{1}{2}\sigma^2)(T-t)+\sigma(W_{Q^\delta}(T)-W_{Q^\delta}(t))})|\mathcal{F}_t\right)\\ &= e^{-r(T-t)}\mathbb{E}_{Q^\delta}\left(h(e^{-\delta(T-t)}S(t)e^{(r-\frac{1}{2}\sigma^2)(T-t)+\sigma(W_{Q^\delta}(T)-W_{Q^\delta}(t))})|\mathcal{F}_t\right)\\ &= e^{-r(T-t)}\mathbb{E}_{Q^\delta}\left(h(S(t)e^{(r-\delta-\frac{1}{2}\sigma^2)(T-t)+\sigma(W_{Q^\delta}(T)-W_{Q^\delta}(t))})|\mathcal{F}_t\right).\end{aligned}$$

Our goal is to obtain a formula depending on the price of the underlying asset at some future time t. At this time the price of the asset will be known and will be inserted into the formula. For this purpose we prefer to go to the original asset since its prices will be observed in the market.

The final formula is similar to that obtained earlier. The only difference is the presence of δ. In effect, from now on we proceed as before, replacing r by $r - \delta$. This simply means that the difference between the riskless interest rates in the two markets serves as the effective riskless rate in this model.

We examine the case of a European put option on the foreign currency S, so that the payoff function h has the form $h(z) = (K - z)^+$. To compute the above conditional expectation we first find an auxiliary function and inserting the asset price gives the result. This auxiliary function is obtained explicitly via the ordinary expectation of a function of a random variable with normal distribution, which again reduces to computing an integral:

$$\psi(x, t) = e^{-r(T-t)} \int_{\mathbb{R}} \frac{1}{\sqrt{2\pi}} e^{-\frac{z^2}{2}} \left(K - x e^{(r-\delta-\frac{1}{2}\sigma^2)(T-t)+\sigma z \sqrt{T-t}} \right)^+ dz.$$

We find the interval where the payoff is non-zero, which reduces the range of integration to $(-\infty, d^\delta(t, x))$, where

$$d^\delta(t, x) = \frac{\ln \frac{K}{x} - \left(r - \delta - \frac{1}{2}\sigma^2 \right)(T - t)}{\sigma \sqrt{T - t}}$$

The integration proceeds as for the ordinary European put option; the only difference comes from the presence of δ:

$$\psi(x, t) = e^{-r(T-t)} \int_{-\infty}^{d^\delta(t,x)} \frac{1}{\sqrt{2\pi}} e^{-\frac{z^2}{2}} K dz$$

$$- e^{-r(T-t)} \int_{-\infty}^{d^\delta(t,x)} \frac{1}{\sqrt{2\pi}} e^{-\frac{z^2}{2}} x e^{(r-\delta-\frac{1}{2}\sigma^2)(T-t)+\sigma z \sqrt{T-t}} dz$$

$$= K e^{-rT} N(d^\delta(t, x))$$

$$- \frac{1}{\sqrt{2\pi}} e^{-\delta(T-t)} \int_{-\infty}^{d^\delta(t,x)} e^{-\frac{1}{2}z^2+z\sigma\sqrt{T-t}} dz$$

$$= K e^{-r(T-t)} N(d^\delta(t, x)) - e^{-\delta(T-t)} x N \left(d^\delta(t, x) - \sigma \sqrt{T - t} \right).$$

Exactly as before, this leads to the Black–Scholes formula

$$C(t) = e^{-\delta(T-t)} S(t) N \left(d_+^\delta(t, S(t)) \right) - K e^{-r(T-t)} N \left(d_-^\delta(t, S(t)) \right),$$

$$P(t) = -e^{\delta(T-t)} S(t) N \left(-d_+^\delta(t, S(t)) \right) + K e^{-(T-t)} N \left(-d_-^\delta(t, S(t)) \right),$$

where

$$d_\pm^\delta(t, x) = \frac{\ln \frac{x}{K} + \left(r - \delta \pm \frac{1}{2}\sigma^2 \right)(T - t)}{\sigma \sqrt{T - t}} = \frac{\ln \frac{x e^{-\delta(T-t)}}{K} + \left(r \pm \frac{1}{2}\sigma^2 \right)(T - t)}{\sigma \sqrt{T - t}}.$$

We can see that the formula is identical to the Black–Scholes formula with the stock price replaced by the price discounted by means of the rate δ. In particular, the Black-Scholes formula at $t = 0$ takes the form

$$C(r, T, K, S(0), \sigma) = e^{-\delta T} S(0) N(d_+^\delta) - K e^{-rT} N(d_-^\delta),$$
$$P(r, T, K, S(0), \sigma) = -e^{-\delta T} S(0) N(-d_+^\delta) + K e^{-rT} N(-d_-^\delta),$$

where

$$d_+^\delta = \frac{\ln \frac{S(0)}{K} + \left(r - \delta + \frac{1}{2}\sigma^2\right) T}{\sigma \sqrt{T}},$$

$$d_-^\delta = \frac{\ln \frac{S(0)}{K} + \left(r - \delta - \frac{1}{2}\sigma^2\right) T}{\sigma \sqrt{T}}.$$

Exercise 4.2 Derive a formula for the price of an option written on futures, assuming that the interest rate is constant.

We turn to the problem of hedging a derivative security.

The Black–Scholes formula gives the representation of the price of a derivative security as a deterministic function of the price of the underlying asset. Consider a European call option with price

$$C(t) = u(t, S(t)),$$

which is given via the deterministic function

$$u(t, z) = e^{-\delta(T-t)} z N\left(\frac{\ln \frac{z}{K} + \left(r - \delta + \frac{1}{2}\sigma^2\right)(T - t)}{\sigma \sqrt{T - t}}\right)$$
$$- K e^{-r(T-t)} N\left(\frac{\ln \frac{z}{K} + \left(r - \delta - \frac{1}{2}\sigma^2\right)(T - t)}{\sigma \sqrt{T - t}}\right).$$

The function representing the price satisfies the Black–Scholes partial differential equation. It differs from the equation we had before only by the presence of the parameter δ.

Proposition 4.2
The function u satifies

$$u_t + (r - \delta) z u_z + \frac{1}{2}\sigma^2 z^2 u_{zz} = ru, \quad t < T, z > 0$$
$$u(T, z) = (z - K)^+$$

Proof Exactly as in Proposition 3.21 with r replaced by $r - \delta$. $\qquad \square$

Exercise 4.3 Construct an alternative proof of Proposition 4.2 by observing that the function v, defined by $v(t, z) = e^{\delta(T-t)}u(t, z)$, satisfies

$$v_t + \rho z v_z + \frac{1}{2}\sigma^2 z^2 v_{zz} = \rho v, \quad v(T, z) = (K - z)^+.$$

where $\rho = r - \delta$.

The function u gives an exact form of the replicating strategy, which is constructed in the same way as before. The strategy

$$x(t) = u_z(t, S(t)),$$

$$y(t) = \frac{u(t, S(t)) - x(t)S(t)}{A(t)},$$

replicates the claim:

$$V_{(x,y)}(t) = x(t)S(t) + y(t)A(t) = u(t, S(t)) = C(t).$$

It is self-financing: applying the Itô formula to $u(t, z)$ we have

$$dV(t) = d[u(t, z)] = u_t dt + u_z dz + \frac{1}{2}z^2 u_{zz} dt$$

and, using $z = S(t) = e^{-\delta t}S^\delta(t)$ and $dS^\sigma(t) = rS^\delta(t)dt + \sigma S^\delta(t)dW_{Q^\delta}(t)$ we obtain

$$dz = dS(t) = (r - \delta)S(t)dt + \sigma S(t)dW_{Q^\delta}(t)$$

so that, substituting from the PDE satisfied by u,

$$d[u(t, S(t)] = u_t dt + u_z \left((r - \delta)S(t)dt + \sigma S(t)dW_{Q^\delta}(t)\right) + \frac{1}{2}\sigma^2 S^2(t)u_{zz}dt$$

$$= rudt + \sigma S(t)u_z dW_{Q^\delta}(t)$$

$$= rudt + \sigma S(t)u_z \left(\frac{\mu + \delta - r}{\sigma}dt + dW(t)\right)$$

$$= r(u - S(t)u_z)dt + u_z(\mu S(t)dt + \sigma S(t)dW(t)) + \delta u_z S(t)dt$$

$$= ry(t)A(t)dt + x(t)dS(t) + \delta x(t)S(t)dt$$

$$= x(t)dS(t) + y(t)dA(t) + \delta x(t)S(t)dt.$$

We know that the strategy replicates the option price and this price is the conditional expectation of a non-negative random variable, so the value of the strategy must be non-negative and it is admissible: in addition to being self-financing it satisfies $V_{(x,y)}(t) \geq 0$ and $\tilde{V}_{(x,y)}(t)$ is a Q^δ-martingale:

$$\tilde{V}_{(x,y)}(t) = \tilde{H}(t) = e^{-rT}\mathbb{E}_{Q^\delta}(h(S(T))|\mathcal{F}_t).$$

Dividend paying stock

The above results also apply to options on dividend-paying stock.

Stock dividends generate cash flow in a similar way as foreign currency. We are assuming that the dividend is paid continuously, which is not realistic in the case of a single stock. For a diversified portfolio, containing many stocks, where dividend payments occur frequently for some or other stock in the portfolio, this assumption may adequately approximate reality. In particular, it applies quite well to derivative securities which have a stock index as the underlying asset.

We can view this from two angles and we assume that dividend is paid continuously at the rate δ.

(1) The dividend increases the value of the strategy.

In a time interval of length h, we have a dividend rate for the interval δh, so a positive cash flow of $\delta h S(t)$ per share is generated, that is, we treat the dividend as an additional cash flow which increases the value of a strategy:

$$dV(t) = x(t)dS(t) + y(t)dA(t) + \delta x(t)S(t)dt.$$

(2) The dividend is invested in stock.

We reinvest the dividend immediately by purchasing additional shares, which corresponds to the creation of an auxiliary modified asset reflecting this action, with dynamics

$$
\begin{aligned}
dS^{\delta}(t) &= d(e^{\delta t}S(t))\\
&= \delta e^{\delta t}S(t)dt + e^{\delta t}dS(t) \quad \text{(integration by parts)}\\
&= \delta e^{\delta t}S(t)dt + \mu e^{\delta t}S(t)dt + \sigma e^{\delta t}S(t)dW(t)\\
&= (\mu + \delta)S^{\delta}(t)dt + \sigma S^{\delta}(t)dW(t).
\end{aligned}
$$

With our position in the modified asset denoted by $x^{\delta}(t)$ we have

$$
\begin{aligned}
V(t) &= x^{\delta}(t)S^{\delta}(t) + y(t)A(t)\\
&= x^{\delta}(t)e^{\delta t}S(t) + y(t)A(t).
\end{aligned}
$$

Hence $x^{\delta}(t) = e^{-\delta t}x(t)$. The analysis of foreign currency options therefore applies directly to these situations.

4.2   Structural model of credit risk

Consider a company with assets worth $V(t)$ at time t. The simplest example of a company is an investment fund, where the assets are financial securities. In such a case the assets are liquid and can be converted to cash. In general, this applies only partially, since companies typically have some assets (buildings, equipment, etc.) that are not tradable.

The purchase of the assets was partially financed by a bank loan or a corporate bond issue. For simplicity, we assume that this is done by using a zero-coupon bond. So the company has a debt: suppose the amount D is due at time T, with no intermediate payments.

If $V(T) \leq D$ the company goes bankrupt, debt holders receive $V(T)$, while equity holders receive 0. We assume that the company has limited liability so the shareholders are not required to cover the remaining debt from their own funds.

If $V(T) > D$ the debt is repaid, debt holders get D, equity holders $V(T) - D$. (Here we assume for simplicity that the assets are liquid and can be used to pay the debt.)

Denote the equity by $E(t)$, so the payoff to shareholders at time T is

$$E(T) = \begin{cases} V(T) - D \text{ if } V(T) > D \\ 0 \text{ if } V(T) \leq D \end{cases} = (V(T) - D)^+.$$

We notice that the payoff to the equity holders is the same as the payoff of a call option. In this sense, holding equity confers the right to buy the company, which sounds paradoxical but is logical. The debt liability means that the equity holders do not have full ownership and the company assets can be regarded as collateral for the debt. Full ownership is regained only after the debt has been repaid in full.

We can see the following correspondence:
- stock S – company value V,
- strike price K – face value of debt D,
- call option $C(t)$ – equity $E(t)$.

Assume that the company's value has stock-like dynamics, that is,

$$dV = \mu_V V(t)dt + \sigma_V V(t)dW(t)$$
$$= rV(t)dt + \sigma_V V(t)dW_Q(t)$$

hence the current vaue of the equity can be computed as

$$E(0) = e^{-rT}\mathbb{E}_Q((V(T) - D)^+),$$

which is the Black–Scholes formula. The assumption about the dynamics of company value is strong and difficult to verify since typically the assets are not traded. It is also difficult, if not impossible, to calibrate the model. In addition, it remains questionable whether the Black–Scholes formula can be used: we cannot replicate the option in any meaningful sense, as the underlying asset, the company value, is not traded.

We need to find two unknown parameters: $V(0), \sigma_V$.

We know T, D, r and also assume that $E(0)$, the equity value, is known at time 0. This is true if the stock is traded. In that case the volatility σ_E of the stock price can be estimated on the basis of historical data or as the implied volatility, so we also assume that σ_E is known and constant.

We consider the relationship between σ_E and the volatility σ_V of the company value used in describing the dynamics of V. We know that within the Black–Scholes model we can represent a derivative security as a function of the underlying asset. Here we assume that the prices of the derivative follow an Itô process with constant coefficients, so with

$$E(t) = u(t, V(t))$$

we assume

$$dE(t) = \mu_E E(t)dt + \sigma_E E(t)dW(t).$$

On the other hand, by the Itô formula

$$dE(t) = u_t dt + u_z \mu_V V(t)dt + u_z \sigma_V V(t)dW(t) + \frac{1}{2}u_{zz}\sigma_V^2 V^2(t)dt.$$

We also know that $u_z(t, V(t)) = N(d_+(t))$. The representation of an Itô process as a sum of ordinary and stochastic integrals is unique. So it follows that the coefficients in two representations are the same. We are only concerned with the stochastic part, involving volatility:

$$\sigma_E E(t) = N(d_+(t))\sigma_V V(t).$$

Finally, we find $V(0)$ and σ_V solving (numerically)

$$E(0) = V(0)N(d_+) - De^{-rT}N(d_-),$$

$$\sigma_E = \frac{N(d_+)\sigma_V V(0)}{E(0)},$$

where

$$d_\pm = \frac{\ln\frac{V(0)}{D} + \left(r \pm \frac{1}{2}\sigma_V^2\right)T}{\sigma_V\sqrt{T}}.$$

The equations are complicated and impossible to solve by means of a closed formula. The fact that a unique solution exists follows because the partial derivatives of the call with respect to the parameters are strictly positive.

4.3 Compound options

In the previous section we saw that equity, in the form of a share of stock in a company, can be regarded as a call option on an underlying asset, namely the company value. So, in that setting, an option written on the stock is in fact an option with another option being the underlying security. More generally, options on options, so-called compound options, are widely traded. We now examine how one may find a pricing formula for such a compound option in the European case.

Here by options we mean plain vanillas, so we just consider calls and puts. Even this restriction gives four different possibilities; call on call, call on put, put on call amd put on put. We restrict our attention to the first case.

Suppose a European call option with strike K_2 and exercise time T_2 is traded. Since it will be considered as the 'underlying' for a derivative security, we treat these parameters as fixed and will not highlight the dependence af various quantities on them. The call option price at time t is denoted by $C(t)$.

Consider a new call option (described as a call on call) with exercise time T_1 prior to T_2, $T_1 \leq T_2$ (the underlying option should be alive) and a strike price K_1. The payoff of the call on call is of the form

$$H = \max\{C(T_1) - K_1, 0\}.$$

The idea is to formulate this payoff, contingent on $C(t)$, as a payoff with stock as the underlying security, which can easily be done by employing the Black–Scholes formula. For, as we know

$$C(t) = u(t, S(t))$$

where

$$u(t, z) = zN(d_+(t, z)) - K_2 e^{-r(T_2 - t)} N(d_-(t, z))$$

and the functions d_+ and d_- involve the parameters of the underlying option:

$$d_\pm(t, z) = \frac{\ln \frac{z}{K_2} + \left(r \pm \frac{1}{2}\sigma^2\right)(T_2 - t)}{\sigma \sqrt{T_2 - t}}.$$

So

$$
\begin{aligned}
C(T_1) &= u(T_1, S(T_1)) \\
&= S(T_1)N(d_+(T_1, S(T_1))) - K_2 e^{-r(T_2 - T_1)} N(d_-(T_1, S(T_1))). \quad (4.1)
\end{aligned}
$$

The payoff H can be replicated by a strategy whose discounted value process follows a martingale with respect to the risk neutral probability Q with W_Q as the driver.

For simplicity of notation, we drop the subscript Q in this section since we use the risk-neutral set-up only.

So the no-arbitrage price of the call on call is

$$CC(t) = \mathbb{E}\left(e^{-r(T_1-t)}H|\mathcal{F}_t\right)$$
$$= e^{-r(T_1-t)}\mathbb{E}(\max\{u(T_1, S(T_1)) - K_1, 0\}|\mathcal{F}_t).$$

For simplicity let us just find the price for $t = 0$:

$$CC(0) = e^{-rT_1}\mathbb{E}(\max\{u(T_1, S(T_1)) - K_1, 0\}). \tag{4.2}$$

To get an operational formula we have to employ the representation of the stock price at a fixed time by means of a random variable with standard normal distribution. Recall that

$$S(T_1) = S(0)\exp\left\{\left(r - \frac{1}{2}\sigma^2\right)T_1 + \sigma W(T_1)\right\}$$
$$= F(T_1, X_1),$$

where

$$F(t, x) = S(0)\exp\left\{\left(r - \frac{1}{2}\sigma^2\right)t + \sigma\sqrt{t}x\right\} \tag{4.3}$$

and $X_1 \sim N(0, 1)$ is given by

$$X_1 = \frac{1}{\sqrt{T_1}}W(T_1).$$

Inserting this into (4.2) we have

$$CC(0) = e^{-rT_1}\mathbb{E}(\max\{u(T_1, F(T_1, X_1)) - K_1, 0\}).$$

Procceding as in the derivation of the classical Black–Scholes formula, we employ the density of X_1

$$CC(0) = e^{-rT_1}\int_{\mathbb{R}} \max\{u(T_1, F(T_1, x)) - K_1, 0\}\frac{1}{\sqrt{2\pi}}e^{-\frac{x^2}{2}}dx$$

and next we find the interval where the integrand is non-zero to reduce the range of integration and dispose of the nonlinearity created by the max function.

The functions $x \mapsto F(T_1, x)$ and $z \mapsto u(T_1, z)$ have strictly positive derivatives, so they are strictly increasing, hence invertible. For brevity, denote their composition by

$$\phi(x) = u(T_1, F(T_1, x)),$$

which is again invertible. We find the critical value of the variable x, determining the in-the-money region for the compound option:

$$\phi(x) \geq K_1 \quad \text{iff} \quad x \geq \phi^{-1}(K_1) = x_1, \quad \text{say}. \tag{4.4}$$

The number x_1 has to be found numerically owing to the complexity of the function ϕ.

Consequently

$$CC(0) = e^{-rT_1} \int_{x_1}^{\infty} (u(T_1, F(T_1, x)) - K_1) \frac{1}{\sqrt{2\pi}} e^{-\frac{x^2}{2}} dx$$

$$= e^{-rT_1} \int_{x_1}^{\infty} u(T_1, F(T_1, x)) \frac{1}{\sqrt{2\pi}} e^{-\frac{x^2}{2}} dx - e^{-rT_1} \int_{x_1}^{\infty} K_1 \frac{1}{\sqrt{2\pi}} e^{-\frac{x^2}{2}} dx$$

$$= e^{-rT_1} \int_{x_1}^{\infty} u(T_1, F(T_1, x)) \frac{1}{\sqrt{2\pi}} e^{-\frac{x^2}{2}} dx - e^{-rT_1} K_1 (1 - N(x_1)).$$

To compute the integral on the right, we insert the form of u (see (4.1)) to obtain the following.

Theorem 4.3
The price of a T_1, K_1-call option written on a T_2, K_2-call with $T_1 < T_2$ is given by

$$CC(0) = e^{-rT_1} \int_{x_1}^{\infty} F(T_1, x) N(d_+(T_1, F(T_1, x))) \frac{1}{\sqrt{2\pi}} e^{-\frac{x^2}{2}} dx \tag{4.5}$$

$$- e^{-rT_2} K_2 \int_{x_1}^{\infty} N(d_-(T_1, F(T_1, x))) \frac{1}{\sqrt{2\pi}} e^{-\frac{x^2}{2}} dx \tag{4.6}$$

$$- e^{-rT_1} K_1 (1 - N(x_1)),$$

where $x_1 = \phi^{-1}(K_1)$.

With the formulae for F, d_+ and d_- available, this is could be classified as a closed-form expression with one technical difficulty involved, namely that of finding x_1. However, the task of computing the first two components does not look attractive. We will transform them to more user-friendly forms.

We deal first with the somewhat simpler **second term** (4.6). The integral part of this term in the above formula can be written, since $x \mapsto F(T_1, x)$ is increasing, as

$$= \int_{\mathbb{R}} \mathbf{1}_{\{x \geq x_1\}} N(d_-(T_1, F(T_1, x))) \frac{1}{\sqrt{2\pi}} e^{-\frac{x^2}{2}} dx$$

$$= \int_{\mathbb{R}} \mathbf{1}_{\{F(T_1, x) \geq F(T_1, x_1)\}} N(d_-(T_1, F(T_1, x))) \frac{1}{\sqrt{2\pi}} e^{-\frac{x^2}{2}} dx$$

$$= \mathbb{E}[\mathbf{1}_{\{S(T_1) \geq F(T_1, x_1)\}} N(d_-(T_1, S(T_1)))]$$

$$= \cdots$$

Now recall that (3.7) provides, with $t = T_1$, $T = T_2$ and $K = K_2$, that

$$N(d_-(T_1, S(T_1))) = \mathbb{E}\left(\mathbf{1}_{\{S(T_2) \geq K_2\}} | \mathcal{F}_{T_1}\right).$$

The identity is here used in reverse, in the proof of the Black–Scholes formula we evaluated the expectation on the right to arrive at the expression on the left.

Going back to our main computation, we insert this and continue

$$\cdots = \mathbb{E}\left[\mathbf{1}_{\{S(T_1) \geq F(T_1, x_1)\}} \mathbb{E}(\mathbf{1}_{\{S(T_2) \geq K_2\}} | \mathcal{F}_{T_1})\right]$$

$$= \mathbb{E}\left[\mathbb{E}(\mathbf{1}_{\{S(T_1) \geq F(T_1, x_1)\}} \mathbf{1}_{\{S(T_2) \geq K_2\}}) | \mathcal{F}_{T_1})\right] \quad \text{(since } S(T_1) \text{ is } \mathcal{F}_{T_1}\text{-measurable)}$$

$$= \mathbb{E}\left[\mathbf{1}_{\{S(T_1) \geq F(T_1, x_1)\}} \mathbf{1}_{\{S(T_2) \geq K_2\}}\right] \quad \text{(since } \mathbb{E}[\mathbb{E}(X|\mathcal{G})] = \mathbb{E}(X) \text{ for any } X, \mathcal{G})$$

$$= \cdots$$

Using the form of the stock prices, $S(T_1) = F(T_1, X_1)$, we have

$$\{\omega : S(T_1, \omega) \geq F(T_1, x_1)\} = \{\omega : F(T_1, X_1(\omega)) \geq F(T_1, x_1)\}$$

$$= \{\omega : X_1(\omega) \geq x_1\} \quad \text{(monotonicity of } F(t, \cdot)).$$

Now, by (4.3) we know that $S(T_2) = F(T_2, X_2)$, where $X_2 \sim N(0, 1)$ is given by

$$X_2 = \frac{1}{\sqrt{T_2}} W(T_2),$$

and

$$\{\omega : S(T_2, \omega) \geq K_2\} = \{\omega : F(T_2, X_2(\omega)) \geq K_2\}$$

$$= \{\omega : X_2(\omega) \geq x_2\},$$

where x_2 is the end point of the in-the-money interval for the underlying option. Unlike x_1, this is easy to find: we solve $F(T_2, x_2) = K_2$ to obtain

$$x_2 = \frac{\ln \frac{K_2}{S(0)} - \left(r - \frac{1}{2}\sigma^2\right) T_2}{\sigma \sqrt{T_2}}. \tag{4.7}$$

Going back to the main thread of identities, we have reduced our integral to

$$\int_{x_1}^{\infty} N(d_-(T_1, F(T_1, x))) \frac{1}{\sqrt{2\pi}} e^{-\frac{x^2}{2}} dx = \mathbb{E}\left(\mathbf{1}_{\{X_1 \geq x_1\}} \mathbf{1}_{\{X_2 \geq x_2\}}\right),$$

where both X_1 and X_2 are standard normal, but since, for $i = 1, 2$,

$$X_i = \frac{1}{\sqrt{T_i}} W(T_i)$$

they are correlated with

$$\rho = \mathrm{Cov}(\frac{1}{\sqrt{T_1}} W(T_1), \frac{1}{\sqrt{T_2}} W(T_2)) = \frac{1}{\sqrt{T_1 T_2}} \mathrm{Cov}(W(T_1), W(T_2))$$

$$= \frac{T_1}{\sqrt{T_1 T_2}} = \sqrt{\frac{T_1}{T_2}},$$

since for any Wiener process $\mathrm{Cov}(W(s), W(t)) = \min\{s, t\}$. Denote the density of the bivariate normal vector (X_1, X_2) by $f_{X_1 X_2}$ and we can conclude

$$\int_{x_1}^{\infty} N(d_-(T_1, F(T_1, x))) \frac{1}{\sqrt{2\pi}} e^{-\frac{x^2}{2}} dx = \int_{x_1}^{\infty} \int_{x_2}^{\infty} f_{X_1 X_2}(x, y) dx dy$$

where, with $\rho = \sqrt{\frac{T_1}{T_2}}$, the joint density is given by

$$f_{X_1 X_2}(x, y) = \frac{1}{2\pi} \frac{1}{\sqrt{1 - \rho^2}} \exp\left\{-\frac{x^2 - 2\rho xy + y^2}{2(1 - \rho^2)}\right\}. \tag{4.8}$$

The first term (4.5) in the formula for $CC(0)$ is slightly more complicated but can be computed along the same lines: this time we use (3.8)

$$e^{-r(T-t)} \mathbb{E}\left(S(T) \mathbf{1}_{\{S(T) \geq K\}} | \mathcal{F}_t\right) = S(t) N(d_+(t, S(t)))$$

and obtain

$$\int_{x_1}^{\infty} F(T_1, x) N(d_+(T_1, F(T_1, x))) \frac{1}{\sqrt{2\pi}} e^{-\frac{x^2}{2}} dx$$

$$= \mathbb{E}\left[\mathbf{1}_{\{X_1 \geq x_1\}} F(T_1, X_1) N(d_+(T_1, F(T_1, X_1)))\right]$$

$$= \mathbb{E}\left[\mathbf{1}_{\{X_1 \geq x_1\}} S(T_1) N(d_+(T_1, S(T_1)))\right]$$

$$= e^{-r(T_2 - T_1)} \mathbb{E}\left[\mathbf{1}_{\{X_1 \geq x_1\}} \mathbb{E}\left[S(T_2) \mathbf{1}_{\{S(T_2) \geq K_2\}} | \mathcal{F}_{T_1}\right]\right] \quad \text{(by (3.8))}$$

$$= e^{-r(T_2 - T_1)} \mathbb{E}\left[\mathbb{E}\left[\mathbf{1}_{\{X_1 \geq x_1\}} S(T_2) \mathbf{1}_{\{S(T_2) \geq K_2\}} | \mathcal{F}_{T_1}\right]\right] \quad \text{(since } \{X_1 \geq x_1\} \in \mathcal{F}_{T_1})$$

$$= e^{-r(T_2 - T_1)} \mathbb{E}\left[\mathbf{1}_{\{X_1 \geq x_1\}} S(T_2) \mathbf{1}_{\{S(T_2) \geq K_2\}}\right]$$

$$= S(0) e^{-r(T_2 - T_1)} \mathbb{E}\left[\mathbf{1}_{\{X_1 \geq x_1\}} e^{(r - \frac{1}{2}\sigma^2)T_2 + \sigma\sqrt{T_2} X_2} \mathbf{1}_{\{X_2 \geq x_2\}}\right]$$

$$= S(0) e^{(r - \frac{1}{2}\sigma^2)T_2} e^{-r(T_2 - T_1)} \int_{x_1}^{\infty} \int_{x_2}^{\infty} e^{\sigma\sqrt{T_2} y} f_{X_1, X_2}(x, y) dx dy$$

$$= S(0) e^{rT_1} \int_{x_1}^{\infty} \int_{x_2}^{\infty} \exp\left(-\frac{1}{2}\sigma^2 T_2 + \sigma y \sqrt{T_2}\right) \frac{1}{2\pi} \left(\frac{\sqrt{T_2}}{\sqrt{T_2 - T_1}}\right)$$

$$\times \exp\left(-\frac{1}{2}\left(\frac{T_2}{T_2 - T_1}\right)\left(x^2 - 2\frac{\sqrt{T_1}}{\sqrt{T_2}} xy + y^2\right)\right) dx dy.$$

Simplifying this expression boils down to considering the two exponentials. Let us change the variables first: set $x' = x - \sigma\sqrt{T_1}$ and $y' = y - \sigma\sqrt{T_2}$. Then $dx' = dx$ and $dy' = dy$, and the integrals in x', y' start at $x_1 - \sigma\sqrt{T_1}$ and $x_2 - \sigma\sqrt{T_2}$ respectively. We need to describe the exponential in terms of x', y'. Combining the first terms in each of the products

$$\left(x' + \sigma\sqrt{T_1}\right)^2 = (x')^2 + 2x'\sigma\sqrt{T_1} + \sigma^2 T_1,$$

$$\left(y' + \sigma\sqrt{T_2}\right)^2 = (y')^2 + 2y'\sigma\sqrt{T_2} + \sigma^2 T_2$$

$$-2\frac{\sqrt{T_1}}{\sqrt{T_2}}\left(x' + \sigma\sqrt{T_1}\right)\left(y' + \sigma\sqrt{T_2}\right) = -2\frac{\sqrt{T_1}}{\sqrt{T_2}}\left[x'y' + x'\sigma\sqrt{T_2} + y'\sigma\sqrt{T_1}\right]$$
$$-2\sigma^2 T_1$$

we obtain $\left((x')^2 - 2\frac{\sqrt{T_1}}{\sqrt{T_2}} x'y' + (y')^2\right)$, which is in the form we want, and it will suffice to show that the other terms in the second exponential cancel with those in the first. For this, note that the linear terms add to

$$2x'\sigma\sqrt{T_1} + 2y'\sigma\sqrt{T_2} - 2x'\sigma\sqrt{T_1} - 2y'\sigma\frac{T_1}{\sqrt{T_2}} = 2y'\sigma\frac{T_2 - T_1}{\sqrt{T_2}}$$

so when multiplied by $-\frac{1}{2}\left(\frac{T_2}{T_2 - T_1}\right)$ this is $-\sigma y'\sqrt{T_2}$, while the final terms become $-\frac{1}{2}\left(\frac{T_2}{T_2 - T_1}\right)\sigma^2(T_2 - T_1) = -\frac{1}{2}\sigma^2 T_2$. Hence, together these terms cancel the other exponential, which, in terms of y', is $\sigma\left(y' + \sigma\sqrt{T_2}\right)\sqrt{T_2} - \frac{1}{2}\sigma^2 T_2 = \sigma y'\sqrt{T_2} + \frac{1}{2}\sigma^2\sqrt{T_2}$

We are left with

$$\int_{x_1-\sigma\sqrt{T_1}}^{\infty}\int_{x_2-\sigma\sqrt{T_2}}^{\infty} f_{X_1X_2}(x',y')dx'dy'.$$

Putting all the pieces together we have now proved the following

The price of a T_1, K_1-call option written on a T_2, K_2-call with $T_1 < T_2$ is given by

$$CC(0) = S(0)\int_{x_1-\sigma\sqrt{T_1}}^{\infty}\int_{x_2-\sigma\sqrt{T_2}}^{\infty} f_{X_1X_2}(x,y)dxdy$$

$$-e^{-rT_2}K_2\int_{x_1}^{\infty}\int_{x_2}^{\infty} f_{X_1X_2}(x,y)dxdy$$

$$-e^{-rT_1}K_1(1-N(x_1))$$

where f_{X_1,X_2} denotes the standard bivariate normal density with correlation coefficient $\rho = \sqrt{\frac{T_1}{T_2}}$ and x_1, x_2 are given by (4.4) and (4.7) respectively.

Exercise 4.4 Show that, with N_2 as the standard bivariate normal,

$$CC(0) = S(0)N_2(d_+T_1, S^*), d_+(T_2, K_2); \rho)$$
$$-K_2e^{-rT_2}N_2(d_-T_1, S^*), d_-(T_2, K_2); \rho) - K_1e^{-rT_1}N_1(d_-(T_1, S^*(T_1)),$$

where $\rho = \sqrt{\frac{T_1}{T_2}}$ and S^* is the solution of the equation $u(T_1, z) = S(T_1)$.

4.4 American call options

Recall from [DMFM] that, in discrete time, for stocks that do not pay dividends is it never optimal to exercise the American call option before expiry, and therefore the price processes of the American and European call options are the same. We now show that the same situation obtains in the Black–Scholes model. First we need a simple bound on the European call price. We continue to work only with the risk-neutral probability Q and write $\mathbb{E}$ instead of $\mathbb{E}_Q$ for ease of notation.

Theorem 4.4
Let $C(t)$ be the price of a European call. For all $t \in [0,T]$

$$(S(t) - K)^+ \le C(t).$$

Proof We have $\tilde{C}(t) = \tilde{V}_{(x,y)}(t)$ for an admissible replicating strategy, so $\tilde{C}(t)$ is a Q-martingale for the unique risk-neutral probability Q. Next

$$
\begin{aligned}
C(t) &= e^{rt}\tilde{C}(t) \\
&= e^{rt}\mathbb{E}(\tilde{C}(T)|\mathcal{F}_t) \quad \text{(martingale property)} \\
&= e^{rt}\mathbb{E}(e^{-rT}(S(T) - K)^+|\mathcal{F}_t) \\
&\geq e^{rt}\mathbb{E}(e^{-rT}(S(T) - K)|\mathcal{F}_t) \quad \text{(since } x^+ = \max\{x, 0\} \geq x) \\
&= e^{rt}\mathbb{E}(\tilde{S}(T)|\mathcal{F}_t) - e^{-r(T-t)}K \\
&= e^{rt}\tilde{S}(t) - e^{-r(T-t)}K \quad \text{(martingale property)} \\
&\geq S(t) - K \quad \text{(since } - e^{-r(T-t)}K \geq -K).
\end{aligned}
$$

Moreover, for any t in $[0, T]$ we know that $C(t) \geq 0$, since the final payoff is non-negative, so the result follows. $\qquad \square$

Corollary 4.5
The prices of American and European call are equal.

Proof The holder of American option will never exercise it before time T. This follows from the fact that exercising gives the payoff which brings less than the money obtained from selling the option, as the above theorem shows. Therefore an American option is in fact a European option since it will be only exercised at maturity and consequently the prices must be equal. $\qquad \square$

The situation is different for American puts. Let $P(t)$ be the price of a European put, so we have $\tilde{P}(t) = \tilde{V}_{(x,y)}(t)$ for some admissible replicating strategy, and $\tilde{P}(t)$ is a martingale

$$
\begin{aligned}
P(t) &= e^{rt}\tilde{P}(t) \\
&= e^{rt}\mathbb{E}(\tilde{P}(T)|\mathcal{F}_t) \\
&= e^{rt}\mathbb{E}(e^{-rT}(K - S(T))^+|\mathcal{F}_t) \\
&\geq e^{rt}\mathbb{E}(e^{-rT}(K - S(T))|\mathcal{F}_t) \\
&= e^{-r(T-t)}K - e^{rt}\mathbb{E}(\tilde{S}(T)|\mathcal{F}_t) \\
&= e^{-r(T-t)}K - e^{rt}\tilde{S}(t)
\end{aligned}
$$

(up to here the analysis is the same as for the call)

$$
< K - S(t)
$$

The last inequality is in the opposite direction and we cannot draw the same conclusion as before. So

$$
P(t) \not\geq (K - S(t))^+,
$$

which implies that (just as in the discrete case) there are situations where early exercise of an American put is optimal. This again requires an analysis of optimal stopping times and the construction of an analogue of the Snell envelope (see [DMFM]) which is considerably more subtle in continuous time. In general it is impossible to arrive at closed-form expressions of the put price.

4.5　Variable coefficients

Consider a generalised model where the coefficients are time-dependent, but deterministic, i.e. the stock prices satisfy the following equation:

$$dS(t) = \mu(t)S(t)dt + \sigma(t)S(t)dW(t)$$

and we assume that the coefficients defined on $[0, T]$ are bounded and measurable. This equation has a unique solution of the form

$$S(t) = S(0)\exp\left\{\int_0^t \left[\mu(s) - \frac{1}{2}\sigma^2(s)\right]ds + \int_0^t \sigma(s)dW(s)\right\}.$$

Exercise 4.5 Prove the last claim.

For option pricing, we first investigate the possibility of finding a risk-neutral probability by a natural extension of the method applied before. Recall that the density of Q with respect to P was of the form $M(T) = \exp\{-\frac{1}{2}b^2 T - bW(T)\}$ with $b = \frac{\mu - r}{\sigma}$. If $\sigma(t) \neq 0$ for all t we could use the same idea but an alternative is to take a bounded function $b(t)$ such that

$$\mu(t) - r = \sigma(t)b(t)$$

and define

$$M(t) = \exp\left\{-\frac{1}{2}\int_0^t b^2(s)ds - \int_0^t b(s)dW(s)\right\}.$$

Exercise 4.6 Show that $M(t)$ is a martingale.

Let $Q(A) = \mathbb{E}(\mathbf{1}_A M(T))$,

$$W_Q(t) = W(t) + \int_0^t b(s)ds.$$

The fact that W_Q is a Wiener process under Q can be proved by modyfying the proof of Theorem 2.1, but it is better to wait for the general version of the Girsanov theorem proved in Chapter 6. Then the discounted stock prices follow a martingale and

$$S(t) = S(0) \exp\left\{ rt - \int_0^t \frac{1}{2}\sigma^2(s)ds + \int_0^t \sigma(s)dW_Q(s) \right\}.$$

Exercise 4.7 Prove the last claim.

The analysis perfomed in the previous chapter applies and for a derivative security with payoff H we have the same formula $H(0) = e^{-rT}\mathbb{E}_Q(H)$. Consider a European put option $H = (K - S(T))^+$, then the expectation has the familiar form $H(0) = e^{-rT}\mathbb{E}_Q((K - S(T))^+)$.The random variable $\int_0^T \sigma(s)dW(s)$ has normal distribution with zero expectation and variance equal to $\int_0^T \sigma^2(s)ds = T\bar{\sigma}^2$, say, (see [SCF]), and so can be written in the form

$$\int_0^T \sigma(s)dW(s) = T\bar{\sigma}Y,$$

for Y standard normal. We insert this into the formula for $S(T)$ to see

$$\mathbb{E}_Q((K - S(T))^+) = \int_{\mathbb{R}} \frac{1}{\sqrt{2\pi}} e^{-\frac{y^2}{2}} \left(K - ze^{(r-\frac{1}{2}\bar{\sigma}^2)T+\bar{\sigma}y\sqrt{T}} \right)^+ dy.$$

The final conclusion is immediate: the rest of the derivation is as before for both put and call options: the Black–Scholes formula applies with σ replaced by

$$\bar{\sigma} = \frac{1}{T}\int_0^T \sigma^2(s)ds.$$

Exercise 4.8 Find a PDE for the function $u(t, z)$ generating the option pricess by the formula $H(t) = u(t, S(t))$ for $H = h(S(T))$.

4.6 Growth optimal portfolios

Finally, we briefly describe an alternative approach to option pricing which avoids the use of risk-neutral probabilities, but works directly with the original probability P. The difference is that our discounting is done not by using the riskless rate, but rather by means of a special portfolio whose value process provides a benchmark investment. It is known as the growth optimal portfolio, since it is designed to yield a trading strategy with constant relative weights of investment in stock and bond, chosen to produce the maximum expected logarithmic return, as described below. We begin by finding this portfolio and showing how the resulting trading strategy should be adjusted at each trading date.

In the market

$$dS(t) = \mu S(t)dt + \sigma S(t)dW(t),$$
$$dA(t) = rA(t)dt,$$

consider an investment described by means of time-independent weights w_S, w_A, $w_S + w_A = 1$. Our goal is to find the weights with the highest expected logarithmic return on the value of the portfolio.

Given $V(0)$ we have the inital positions

$$x(0) = \frac{w_S V(0)}{S(0)}, \quad y(0) = \frac{w_A V(0)}{A(0)}$$

and, to keep the constant percentage split, the processes x, y must depend on time. If the strategy is to be self-financing we need

$$dV(t) = x(t)dS(t) + y(t)dA(t)$$

and we wish to have

$$\frac{x(t)S(t)}{V(t)} = w_S, \quad \frac{y(t)A(t)}{V(t)} = w_A,$$

the latter following from $w_S + w_A = 1$. After inserting the form of $x(t)S(t)$, $y(t)A(t)$, we have an equation for V :

$$dV(t) = x(t)\mu S(t)dt + x(t)\sigma S(t)dW(t) + y(t)rA(t)dt$$
$$= \mu w_S V(t)dt + \sigma w_S V(t)dW(t) + rw_A V(t)dt$$
$$= [w_S\mu + w_A r] V(t)dt + w_S \sigma V(t)dW(t).$$

This can be solved (assume $V(0) = 1$ without loss of generality) to obtain

$$V(t) = \exp\left\{ [w_S\mu + w_A r]t - \frac{1}{2}w_S^2\sigma^2 t + w_S \sigma W(t) \right\}.$$

The (annualised) expected logarithmic return is given by

$$\frac{1}{t}\mathbb{E}\left(\ln\left(\frac{V(t)}{V(0)} \right) \right),$$

and here we have $V(0) = 1$ and

$$\ln V(t) = [w_S \mu + w_A r]\, t - \frac{1}{2} w_S^2 \sigma^2 t + w_S \sigma W(t)$$

so that

$$\mathbb{E}(\ln V(t)) = [w_S \mu + w_A r]\, t - \frac{1}{2} w_S^2 \sigma^2 t.$$

This should be annualised, so we divide both sides by t, which gives the following form of the expected return m expressed it terms of a single weight: $w_S = w$, $w_A = 1 - w$

$$m(w) = [w\mu + (1 - w)r] - \frac{1}{2} w^2 \sigma^2.$$

At the maximum value of $m(w)$, its derivative is zero, so we solve

$$m'(w) = \mu - r - w\sigma^2 = 0,$$

which yields

$$w = \frac{\mu - r}{\sigma^2}.$$

The resulting portfolio is the growth optimal portfolio. Inserting this weight into the formula for $V(t)$ we find

$$V(t) = \exp\left\{ \left[\frac{\mu - r}{\sigma^2} \mu + (1 - \frac{\mu - r}{\sigma^2})r \right] t - \frac{1}{2} \left(\frac{\mu - r}{\sigma^2} \right)^2 \sigma^2 t + \frac{\mu - r}{\sigma^2} \sigma W(t) \right\}$$

$$= \exp\left\{ \frac{1}{\sigma^2} \left[r + \frac{1}{2} \left(\frac{\mu - r}{\sigma} \right)^2 \right] t + \frac{\mu - r}{\sigma} W(t) \right\}$$

after a little algebra. As a result we have

$$V(t) = V(0) \exp(at + bW(t)),$$

where

$$b = \frac{\mu - r}{\sigma}$$

$$a = r + \frac{1}{2} b^2.$$

The process V solves the stochastic differential equation

$$dV(t) = \left(a + \frac{1}{2} b^2 \right) V dt + bV dW(t)$$

$$= \left(r + b^2 \right) V dt + bV dW(t).$$

So the volatility of V is the market price of risk for S. Finally, discounting by the riskless rate r gives

$$\tilde{V}(t) = V(0) \exp\left(\frac{1}{2}b^2 t + bW(t)\right),$$

which is a submartingale.

We will employ the process V as the so-called **numeraire**, that is, a reference process representing a benchmark alternative investment (in general, any strictly positive process can be chosen as a numeraire). The idea of comparing with a benchmark is to consider the ratio, with the numeraire in the denominator and the process evaluated in the numerator – which is pretty confusing from the point of view of terminology. But here our options are to revolutionise a widely accepted convention, or just grumble, and we adopt the latter approach.

So far we have used the money market account A as numeraire and then we had the martingale properties of the processess $\frac{S}{A}$, $\frac{C}{A}$ with respect to the risk-neutral probability Q. The growth optimal portfolio $V(t)$ has some intriguing properties.

Proposition 4.6
Each of the following processes is a martingale with respect to the original (physical) probability, P
   (i) $\frac{A(t)}{V(t)}$,
   (ii) $\frac{S(t)}{V(t)}$,
   (iii) $\frac{C(t)}{V(t)}$ *where $C(t)$ is the process of call prices in the Black–Scholes model.*

Proof   For (i), note that

$$\frac{A(t)}{V(t)} = \frac{1}{V(0)} \exp\left(-\frac{1}{2}b^2 t - bW(t)\right)$$

is an exponential martingale – here we assume $A(0) = 1$ but a constant has no impact on the martingale property. Note that negative volatility is irrelevant: if we change $-b$ to b then the process remains the same due to the symmetry of W (more precisely, the symmetry of the increments of W).

For (ii), with $S(t) = S(0) \exp\left(\left[\mu - \frac{1}{2}\sigma^2\right]t + \sigma W(t)\right)$, recall that $V(t) = V(0) \exp((r + \frac{1}{2}b^2)t + bW(t))$, with $b = \frac{\mu - r}{\sigma}$, so we again have an exponential martingale

$$
\begin{aligned}
\frac{S(t)}{V(t)} &= \frac{S(0)}{V(0)} \exp\left(\left[\mu - r - \frac{1}{2}(\sigma^2 + b^2)\right]t + (\sigma - b)W(t)\right) \\
&= \frac{S(0)}{V(0)} \exp\left(-\frac{1}{2}(\sigma - b)^2 t + (\sigma - b)W(t)\right)
\end{aligned}
$$

since $\mu - r = \sigma b$.

The proof of (iii) is a little more involved. We first write $C(t) = u(t, S(t))$, where $u(t, z)$ is given by the Black–Scholes formula with T, σ, K, r fixed (and so omitted), so that

$$
dC(t) = \left(u_t + \mu S u_z + \frac{1}{2}\sigma^2 S^2 u_{zz}\right)dt + \sigma S u_z dW.
$$

Recall that V satisfies

$$
dV = \left(r + b^2\right)Vdt + bVdW(t), \quad \text{where } b = \frac{\mu - r}{\sigma}.
$$

We know from [SCF] that if

$$
dX = a_X X dt + b_X X dW(t)
$$

then

$$
d\left(\frac{1}{X}\right) = -\frac{1}{X}a_X dt - \frac{1}{X}b_X dW(t) + \frac{1}{X}b_X^2 dt,
$$

so here

$$
d\left(\frac{1}{V(t)}\right) = -r\frac{1}{V(t)}dt - b\frac{1}{V(t)}dW(t).
$$

By the formula for the differential of the product

$$d\left(\frac{C(t)}{V(t)}\right) = C(t)d\left(\frac{1}{V(t)}\right) + \frac{1}{V(t)}dC(t) - \sigma S u_z b \frac{1}{V(t)}dt$$

$$= -r\frac{C(t)}{V(t)}dt - b\frac{C(t)}{V(t)}dW(t)$$

$$+ \frac{1}{V(t)}\left(u_t + \mu S u_z + \frac{1}{2}\sigma^2 S^2 u_{zz}\right)dt$$

$$+ \frac{1}{V(t)}\sigma S u_z dW - \sigma S u_z b \frac{1}{V(t)}dt$$

$$= \frac{1}{V(t)}\left[-ru + \left(u_t + \mu S u_z + \frac{1}{2}\sigma^2 S^2 u_{zz}\right) - \sigma S u_z \frac{\mu - r}{\sigma}\right]dt$$

$$- b\frac{u}{V(t)}dW(t) + \frac{1}{V(t)}\sigma S u_z dW$$

$$= \frac{1}{V(t)}\left[-ru + \left(u_t + rS u_z + \frac{1}{2}\sigma^2 S^2 u_{zz}\right)\right]dt$$

$$+ \frac{1}{V(t)}\left[-bu + \sigma S u_z\right]dW,$$

where we used the form of b and the fact that $C(t) = u(t, S(t)) = u$ here. We also know from the analysis of the 'Greek' coefficients that

$$u_t + \mu S u_z + \frac{1}{2}\sigma^2 S^2 u_{zz} - ru = 0,$$

$$d\left(\frac{C(t)}{V(t)}\right) = \frac{1}{V(t)}\left[-bu + \sigma S u_z\right]dW.$$

It remains for us to show that, in the Itô integral $\frac{C(t)}{V(t)}$, the integrand $\frac{1}{V(t)}\left[-bu + \sigma S u_z\right] \in \mathcal{M}^2_{[0,T]}$: we find reals α, β such that

$$|-bu + \sigma S u_z| \le b|C| + \sigma|S N(d_+(t))| \le \alpha S + \beta \quad \text{for } t \in [0, T].$$

Using the formulae for S and V

$$V(t) = V(0)\exp\left(\left[r + \frac{1}{2}b^2\right]t + bW(t)\right),$$

$$S(t) = S(0)\exp\left(\left[r - \frac{1}{2}\sigma^2\right]t + \sigma W(t)\right),$$

we obtain

$$\left|\frac{1}{V(t)}\left[-bu + \sigma S u_z\right]\right| \le \alpha \exp\left(\frac{1}{2}(\sigma^2 + b^2)t + (\sigma - b)W(t)\right) + \beta,$$

which belongs to $\mathcal{M}^2$. $\qquad\square$

Corollary 4.7

The no-arbitrage benchmarked prices of derivative securities are given by the expectations with respect to the original probability

$$\frac{H(t)}{V(t)} = \mathbb{E}\left(\frac{H}{V(T)}|\mathcal{F}_t\right).$$

Proof We know that

$$H(t)e^{-rt} = \mathbb{E}_Q\left(He^{-rT}|\mathcal{F}_t\right),$$

so for any $A \in \mathcal{F}_t$

$$\int_A He^{-rT}dQ = \int_A H(t)e^{-rt}dQ. \tag{4.9}$$

Recall the form of the density of Q with respect to P :

$$Q(A) = \int_A e^{-\frac{1}{2}b^2T - bW(T)}dP$$

with $b = \frac{\mu - r}{\sigma}$ as above. The left-hand side of (4.9) gives

$$\int_A He^{-rT}dQ = \int_A He^{-rT}e^{-\frac{1}{2}b^2T - bW(T)}dP$$

$$= \int_A \frac{H}{V(T)}dP,$$

while the right-hand side takes the form

$$\int_A H(t)e^{-rt}dQ = \int_A H(t)e^{-rt - \frac{1}{2}b^2T - bW(T)}dP$$

$$= \int_A H(t)e^{-rt - \frac{1}{2}b^2t - bW(t)}e^{-\frac{1}{2}b^2(T-t) - b[W(T) - W(t)]}dP$$

$$= \mathbb{E}\left(\mathbf{1}_A H(t)e^{-rt - \frac{1}{2}b^2T - bW(t)}e^{-b(W(T) - W(t))}\right)$$

$$= \mathbb{E}\left(\mathbf{1}_A H(t)e^{-rt - \frac{1}{2}b^2T - bW(t)}\mathbb{E}\left(e^{-b[W(T) - W(t)]}|\mathcal{F}_t\right)\right)$$

$$= \mathbb{E}\left(\mathbf{1}_A H(t)e^{-rt - \frac{1}{2}b^2T - bW(t)}\mathbb{E}\left(e^{-b[W(T) - W(t)]}\right)\right)$$

$$= \mathbb{E}\left(\mathbf{1}_A H(t)e^{-rt - \frac{1}{2}b^2T - bW(t)}e^{\frac{1}{2}b^2(T-t)}\right)$$

$$= \int_A \frac{H(t)}{V(t)}dP.$$

Hence

$$\int_A \frac{H}{V(T)}dP = \int_A \frac{H(t)}{V(t)}dP$$

as claimed. □

Remark 4.8

The emerging alternative pricing method may seem attractive since it does not involve the mysterious risk-neutral probability. However, the benefit is more apparent than real: in principle, to apply this method we have to know the value of market price of risk, while the classical method requires the volatility, which is easier to estimate. To find the market price of risk using the volatility one has to estimate μ, which is very difficult.

Exercise 4.9 Show that benchmarked pricing of plain vanilla options gives the well-known Black–Scholes formula.

5

Path-dependent options

Classical call and put options are examples of derivatives whose payoff depends on the stock price at exercise. We now present examples of options where payoff depends on the path. These are among the so-called exotic options. Instruments of this kind have become ever more prevalent in the markets in the past two decades. For our first class of such options we can still derive explicit closed-form pricing formulae, but such neat outcomes will become ever rarer as the complexity of the options increases, and one is forced, more and more, to rely on numerical approximation techniques. We remain in the Black–Scholes option pricing model, so our previous results apply here.

5.1   Barrier options

Barrier options have payoff functions that are simple modifications of the payoff of a call or put option: the call or put payoff has a cut-off point or barrier that depends on the maximum or minimum of the values of the underlying throughout the interval $[0, T]$. Its calculation involves analysis of the whole path, making barrier options **path-dependent.**

Since we can consider either a call or a put, the maximum or minimum of the stock price, and use the barrier L as a means either of 'creating' or 'killing' the payoff, there are eight types of option to consider. Fortunately, call-put parity reduces our pricing task by half, and we will also be able to price the remaining four options in pairs.

We consider put options, which has the mathematical advantage that the payoff remains bounded in all cases.

Definition 5.1

We say that a put option with strike price K, barrier L and expiry time T is

- **Up-and-Out** if

$$P_{\mathrm{UO}}(T) = (K - S(T))^+ \mathbf{1}_{\{\max_{t \in [0,T]} S(t) \leq L\}},$$

- **Down-and-Out** if

$$P_{\mathrm{DO}}(T) = (K - S(T))^+ \mathbf{1}_{\{\min_{t \in [0,T]} S(t) \geq L\}},$$

- **Up-and-In** if

$$P_{\mathrm{UI}}(T) = (K - S(T))^+ \mathbf{1}_{\{\max_{t \in [0,T]} S(t) \geq L\}},$$

- **Down-and-In** if

$$P_{\mathrm{DI}}(T) = (K - S(T))^+ \mathbf{1}_{\{\min_{t \in [0,T]} S(t) \leq L\}}.$$

In all cases the payoff of a put applies only under an additional condition expressed by the event supporting the indicator function.

The 'Out' term means that the payoff becomes zero if the stock leaves a certain region. For 'Up' this region is the interval $(-\infty, L]$, so leaving it means going up, and 'Down' corresponds to $[L, +\infty)$ and departure is related to a decline of the stock prices.

The 'In' term means that the payoff is enabled by the stock entering some set: with 'Up' this set is $[L, +\infty)$ and for a positive payoff it is sufficient that the stock goes up to hit L at least once, while for 'Down' we take $(-\infty, L]$ and going down to hit L triggers the payoff.

The definitions show that, letting $A = \{\omega : \max_{t \in [0,T]} S(t, \omega) = L\}$, we have

$$P_{\mathrm{UO}}(T) + P_{\mathrm{UI}}(T) = (K - S(T))^+ (1 + \mathbf{1}_A).$$

The fact that $(K - S(T))^+ \mathbf{1}_A$ is counted twice on the left could be a serious inconvenience for general distributions. In the Black–Scholes model we will show that A is P-null (and also Q-null since the risk-neutral probability is equivalent to P) so that we can write

$$P_{\mathrm{UO}}(T) + P_{\mathrm{UI}}(T) = (K - S(T))^+,$$

since random variables are regarded the same if they are equal almost surely. Indeed, this holds in our setting as the price process S is driven by the Wiener process W, and this enables us to show – as we shall do shortly – that the distribution of the random variable $M_T = \max_{t\in[0,T]} S(t)$ is given by a density, so $P(A) = 0$.

Example 5.2
Suppose we own bonds issued by a company and fear that it may go bankrupt, as then the bonds may default. As a protection we can buy a put option of company's stock and to make this cheaper we choose the Down-and-In version with a low entrance level, close to zero, so that the put is active if the stock gets close to zero, which we assume to be a signal of likely default.

To obtain pricing formulae we apply the general theory, valid for any derivative security, where the no-arbitrage price is the discounted expected payoff, with expectation computed with respect to risk neutral probability:

$$P_{\text{UO}}(0) = e^{-rT}\mathbb{E}_Q\left((K - S(T))^+\mathbf{1}_{\{\max_{t\in[0,T]} S(t)\leq L\}}\right),$$
$$P_{\text{UI}}(0) = e^{-rT}\mathbb{E}_Q\left((K - S(T))^+\mathbf{1}_{\{\max_{t\in[0,T]} S(t)\geq L\}}\right).$$

Now either by adding these expressions or considering the sum $P_{\text{UO}} + P_{\text{UI}}$ as a derivative with payoff $(K - S(T))^+$, we obtain

$$P_{\text{UO}}(0) + P_{\text{UI}}(0) = e^{-rT}\mathbb{E}_Q((K - S(T))^+).$$

Therefore we need only compute one of the two option prices on the left and deduce the second from the Black–Scholes formula for the vanilla put option. Similarly,

$$P_{\text{DO}}(T) + P_{\text{DI}}(T) = (K - S(T))^+(1 + \mathbf{1}_B)$$

with $B = \{\omega : \min_{t\in[0,T]} S(t,\omega) = L\}$, and since the minimum also has continuous distribution, we have $P(B) = 0$, so we have to find a pricing formula for just one option from this pair.

5.2 Distribution of the maximum

In calculating pricing formulae for barrier options we will need to find the joint distribution of $S(T)$ and $\max_{t\in[0,T]} S(t)$. First consider the probability that $\max_{t \in [0,T]} S(t) \leq L$. Since the stock price is given by

$$S(t) = S(0)e^{\mu t - \frac{1}{2}\sigma^2 t + \sigma W(t)}$$

it is clear that for almost all paths the continuous functions $t \to S(t)$ and $t \to W(t)$ attain their maximum values on $[0, T]$ together.

So let us investigate the behaviour of $M(T) = \max_{t \in [0,T]} W(t)$. We first derive a property of the paths of W that may seem intuitively obvious, but nonetheless requires proof. Suppose that $c > 0$ is given and that τ_c is the first hitting time of c, so

$$\tau_c(\omega) = \min\{t > 0 : W(t) = c\} = \min\{t > 0 : W(t) \geq c\}.$$

Recall (Exercise 2.5) that τ_c is a stopping time for the natural filtration of W. The existence of the minima and their equality follows from the continuity of $t \to W(t)$.

We recall the following facts from [SCF]:
- for any finite stopping time $W(\tau)$ is measurable with respect to the σ-field $\mathcal{F}_\tau = \{A \in \mathcal{F} : A \cap P\{\tau \leq t) \in \mathcal{F}_t$ for all $t\}$,
- strong Markov property of W: for any finite stopping time τ, the process $W^*(t) = W(\tau + t) - W(\tau)$ is a Wiener process whose increments are independent of $\mathcal{F}_\tau$.

The reflection principle for the Wiener process uses these results to prove that reflecting each path at the level reached at an arbitrary stopping time will produce the paths of a new Wiener process. We can visualise this most clearly when the stopping time in question is a first hitting time such as τ_c: as the next theorem shows, combining the reflected path from time $\tau_c(\omega)$ onwards with the original path $\omega \to W(s, \omega)$ for $s \leq \tau_c(\omega)$ will yield a new Wiener process.

Theorem 5.3
Let W be a Wiener process and τ a finite stopping time for its natural filtration. Then the process $\bar{W}$ defined by

$$\bar{W}(t) = \begin{cases} W(t) & \text{for } 0 \leq t \leq \tau, \\ 2W(\tau) - W(t) & \text{for } \tau \leq t, \end{cases}$$

is also a Wiener process.

Proof The strong Markov property ensures that $W^*(t) = W(\tau + t) - W(\tau)$, $t \geq 0$ is a Wiener process, hence the same is true of $-W^*(t) = W(\tau) - W(t + \tau)$, and the increments of both these processes are independent of $\mathcal{F}_\tau$. For fixed ω, combining the continuous functions $f : t \to W(t)$, $t \leq \tau(\omega)$ and $g : t \to W^*(t)$, $t \geq \tau(\omega)$ will reproduce the process W, while combining f

with $-g$ will yield $\bar{W}$. We verify that the combined process $\bar{W}$ satisfies the definition of a Wiener process. For almost all paths ω, continuity at $\tau(\omega)$ is clear by construction, so the combined process is path-continuous. In particular, $(t, \omega) \rightarrow \bar{W}(t, \omega)$ is measurable for the product σ-field $\mathcal{B} \times \mathcal{F}$, since for each ω we can approximate it by step functions $(t, \omega) \rightarrow \bar{W}(t_k, \omega)$, constant on dyadic intervals. The increments of $\bar{W}$ are independent and normally distributed with the desired mean and variance within each part and if $s < t \le \tau < u < v$, the increments $\bar{W}(v) - \bar{W}(u)$ and $\bar{W}(t) - \bar{W}(s)$ are independent by construction of $\bar{W}$. Hence $\bar{W}$ is a Wiener process. $\qquad\square$

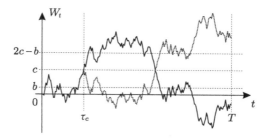

Figure 5.1

The trajectories of the new process are obtained by reflecting the trajectories of W about the horizontal line at c, as shown in Figure 5.1.

We return to our investigation of $M(T) = \max_{t \in [0,T]} W(t)$. Take $0 < c$ and $b \le c$.

We claim that

$$W(T) < b, M(T) \ge c \quad \text{if and only if} \quad \bar{W}(T) > 2c - b.$$

We consider both implications.

(i) Assume $W(T) < b$, $M(T) \ge c$. The inequality $M(T) \ge c$ implies $\tau_c \le T$ since τ_c is the first time t such that $W(t) = c$. So $\bar{W}(\tau_c) = c$ and since $W(T) < b$,

$$\bar{W}(T) = 2c - W(T) > 2c - b.$$

(ii) Assume $\bar{W}(T) > 2c - b$. Suppose $\tau_c \ge T$. Then $\bar{W}(T) = W(T) > 2c - b > c$ – a contradiction. So $\tau_c < T$, hence $M(T) \ge c$. Also, $\tau_c < T$ implies $\bar{W}(T) = 2c - W(T) > 2c - b$ (as assumed) so $W(T) < b$.

This equivalence implies

$$P(W(T) < b, M(T) \geq c) = P(\bar{W}(T) > 2c - b)$$

$$= 1 - N(\frac{2c - b}{\sqrt{T}}) \quad \text{(since } \bar{W} \text{ is a Wiener process)}$$

$$= N(\frac{b - 2c}{\sqrt{T}}),$$

where N is the cumulative distribution function of standard normal distribution.

Finding the joint density is now simply a matter of differentiation. We record the result for later use.

Proposition 5.4

The density of the joint distribution function of $W(T)$ and

$$M(T) = \max_{t \in [0,T]} W(t)$$

is given by

$$f(x, y) = \frac{2}{T} n' \left(\frac{x - 2y}{\sqrt{T}} \right), \quad \text{where } n(z) = \frac{1}{\sqrt{2\pi}} e^{-\frac{1}{2}z^2}.$$

Proof   So far we have shown that

$$P(W(T) < b, M(T) \geq c) = N \left(\frac{b - 2c}{\sqrt{T}} \right).$$

The joint cumulative distribution function of $W(T)$ and $M(T)$ is given by

$$F(b, c) = P(W(T) < b, M(T) < c) \quad \text{(by definition)}$$
$$= P(W(T) < b) - P(W(T) < b, M(t) \geq c)$$

since

$$\{W(T) < b\} = \{W(T) < b, M(T) < c\} \cup \{W(T) < b, M(T) \geq c\}$$

so

$$P(W(T) < b) = P(W(T) < b, M(T) < c) + P(W(T) < b, M(T) \geq c).$$

Next note that $W(T) < b$ if and only if $\frac{W(T)}{\sqrt{T}} < \frac{b}{\sqrt{T}}$ and $\frac{W(T)}{\sqrt{T}}$ is standard normal so

$$F(b, c) = N \left(\frac{b}{\sqrt{T}} \right) - N \left(\frac{b - 2c}{\sqrt{T}} \right).$$

The derivative of N is the density $n(x) = \frac{1}{\sqrt{2\pi}} e^{-\frac{1}{2}x^2}$ so the joint density is

$$f(b,c) = \frac{\partial^2 F(b,c)}{\partial c\, \partial b} = \frac{\partial}{\partial c}\left[\frac{1}{\sqrt{T}} n\left(\frac{b}{\sqrt{T}}\right) - \frac{1}{\sqrt{T}} n\left(\frac{b-2c}{\sqrt{T}}\right)\right]$$

$$= \frac{2}{T} n'\left(\frac{b-2c}{\sqrt{T}}\right),$$

which completes the proof. $\qquad\qquad\qquad\qquad\qquad\qquad\qquad$ □

Remark 5.5

Consider the case $b > c \geq 0$. Since $M(T) \geq W(T)$ by definition, and applying Proposition 5.4, we obtain

$$P(W(T) \leq b, M(T) \leq c) = P(W(T) \leq c, M(T) \leq c)$$
$$= F(c,c) = N(\frac{c}{\sqrt{T}}) - N(-\frac{c}{\sqrt{T}}).$$

When $c < 0$ we note, for any real b, that $P(W(T) \leq b, M(T) \leq c) = 0$, since $M(T) \geq W(0) = 0$.

Remark 5.6

We can now read off the joint distribution of W and its miminum $m_T = \min_{t \leq T} W(t) = \inf_{t \in [0,T]} W(t)$ from the relation

$$m_T = -\max_{t \leq T}(-W(t)),$$

since $-W$ is again a Wiener process. We have, again using the fact that W and $-W$ have the same distribution:

$$P(W(T) \geq b, m_T \geq c) = N\left(-\frac{b}{\sqrt{T}}\right) - N\left(\frac{2c-b}{\sqrt{T}}\right) \text{ for } c \leq \min(0,b)$$

$$P(W(T) \geq b, m_T \geq c) = N\left(-\frac{c}{\sqrt{T}}\right) - N\left(\frac{c}{\sqrt{T}}\right) \text{ for } c \leq 0, b \leq c$$

$$P(W(T) \geq b, m_T \geq c) = 0 \text{ for } c > 0 \text{ since } m_0 = W(0) = 0.$$

Note also that the right-hand side of the second equation is independent of $b \leq 0$, which, together with the third, implies that

$$P(m_T \geq c) = N\left(-\frac{c}{\sqrt{T}}\right) - N\left(\frac{c}{\sqrt{T}}\right) \text{ for } c \leq 0.$$

5.3 Pricing barrier and lookback options

As an example we price the Up-and-Out put with payoff

$$P_{\mathrm{UO}}(T) = (K - S(T))^+ \mathbf{1}_{\{\max_{t\in[0,T]} S(t)\le L\}}.$$

According to the general theory, the option price is

$$
\begin{aligned}
P_{\mathrm{UO}}(0) &= e^{-rT}\mathbb{E}_Q(P_{\mathrm{UO}}(T)) \\
&= e^{-rT}\mathbb{E}_Q\left((K - S(T))^+ \mathbf{1}_{\{\max_{t\in[0,T]} S(t)\le L\}}\right) \quad \text{(payoff inserted)} \\
&= e^{-rT}\mathbb{E}_Q\left(\mathbf{1}_{\{S(T)\le K\}}(K - S(T))\mathbf{1}_{\{\max_{t\in[0,T]} S(t)\le L\}}\right),
\end{aligned}
$$

where, as in the derivation of the Black–Scholes formula, we eliminate the set on which the payoff is zero. As a bonus we can dispose of the '+' to use the linearity of expectation:

$$
\begin{aligned}
P_{\mathrm{UO}}(0) &= e^{-rT}K\mathbb{E}_Q\left(\mathbf{1}_{\{S(T)\le K\}}\mathbf{1}_{\{\max_{t\in[0,T]} S(t)\le L\}}\right) \\
&\quad -e^{-rT}\mathbb{E}_Q\left(S(T)\mathbf{1}_{\{S(T)\le K\}}\mathbf{1}_{\{\max_{t\in[0,T]} S(t)\le L\}}\right). \quad (5.1)
\end{aligned}
$$

The computations of the expectations are a bit lengthy so it is best to split the argument into several steps.

Step 1. Introducing an auxiliary process.

The difficulty of computing the expectations is that the two random variables involved, $S(T)$ and $\max_{t\in[0,T]} S(t)$, are not independent. In the previous section we found the joint distribution of $W(T)$ and $\max_{t\in[0,T]} W(t)$ for any Wiener process, and we wish to use it here. Therefore the task is clear: express the events $\{S(T)\le K\}$ and $\{\max_{t\in[0,T]} S(t)\le L\}$ by means of similar inequalities involving some Wiener process.

To solve the inequalities it is convenient to write

$$S(t) = S(0)e^{\sigma Y(t)}$$

and according to the form of the stock price under the risk-neutral probability,

$$S(t) = S(0)\exp\left\{\left(r - \frac{1}{2}\sigma^2\right)t + \sigma W_Q(t)\right\}. \quad (5.2)$$

We introduce

$$Y(t) = \frac{r - \frac{1}{2}\sigma^2}{\sigma}t + W_Q(t).$$

Now the above events will be described by means of the auxiliary process Y:

$$S(T) \leq K \iff S(0)e^{\sigma Y(T)} \leq K$$
$$\iff Y(T) \leq \frac{1}{\sigma} \ln \frac{K}{S(0)},$$

and

$$\max_{t \in [0,T]} S(t) \leq L \iff \max_{t \in [0,T]} S(0)e^{\sigma Y(t)} \leq L$$
$$\iff \max_{t \in [0,T]} Y(t) \leq \frac{1}{\sigma} \ln \frac{L}{S(0)}.$$

As a result

$$\mathbf{1}_{\{S(T) \leq K\}} = \mathbf{1}_{\{Y(T) \leq b\}},$$
$$\mathbf{1}_{\{\max_{t \in [0,T]} S(t) \leq L\}} = \mathbf{1}_{\{\max_{t \in [0,T]} Y(t) \leq c\}},$$

with

$$b = \frac{1}{\sigma} \ln \frac{K}{S(0)},$$
$$c = \frac{1}{\sigma} \ln \frac{L}{S(0)}.$$

Step 2. Change of probability.

As we noticed, if Y were a Wiener process, we could draw on some earlier results. However, with our past experience, this is a task we successfuly dealt with previously: we can make Y a Wiener process after changing the probability.

The way we handled the volatility coefficient prepared the ground for a direct application of the Girsanov theorem. The process

$$Y(t) = vt + W_Q(t),$$

where

$$v = \frac{r - \frac{1}{2}\sigma^2}{\sigma},$$

is a Wiener process under a probability R given by

$$R(A) = \int_A e^{-\frac{1}{2}v^2 T - v W_Q(T)} dQ. \tag{5.3}$$

The expectations in (5.1) are with respect to Q but to benefit from the above maneuvre we need to work in the space with probability R.

In general (see [PF]), if $P_2(A) = \int_A f dP_1$, $f > 0$, then $P_1(A) = \int_A \frac{1}{f} dP_2$ as the density of P_1 with respect to P_2 is $\frac{1}{f}$. (The notation from the Radon–Nikodym theorem aids intuition here: $f = \frac{dP_2}{dP_1}$, and $\frac{dP_1}{dP_2} = \frac{1}{f}$.) As a consequence,

$$\mathbb{E}_{P_1}(X) = \mathbb{E}_{P_2}(\frac{1}{f}X).$$

So the density of Q with respect to R is

$$\frac{1}{e^{-vW_Q(T) - \frac{1}{2}v^2 T}} = e^{vW_Q(T) + \frac{1}{2}v^2 T} = e^{v(Y(T) - vT) + \frac{1}{2}v^2 T} = e^{vY(T) - \frac{1}{2}v^2 T}$$

and for any random variable X

$$\mathbb{E}_Q(X) = \mathbb{E}_R\left(e^{vY(T) - \frac{1}{2}v^2 T} X\right).$$

Step 3. The first term in (5.1).
By Step 1

$$\mathbb{E}_Q\left(\mathbf{1}_{\{S(T) \leq K\}} \mathbf{1}_{\{\max_{t \in [0,T]} S(t) \leq L\}}\right) = \mathbb{E}_Q\left(\mathbf{1}_{\{Y(T) \leq b\}} \mathbf{1}_{\{\max_{t \in [0,T]} Y(t) \leq c\}}\right)$$

and by Step 2 this is

$$\cdots = \mathbb{E}_R\left(e^{vY(T) - \frac{1}{2}v^2 T} \mathbf{1}_{\{Y(T) \leq b\}} \mathbf{1}_{\{\max_{t \in [0,T]} Y(t) \leq c\}}\right).$$

The density of the vector $(Y(T), \max_{t \in [0,T]} Y(t))$ is the same as found in the previous section, the argument being valid for any Wiener process. The form of the density is known, but at this stage it is irrelevant so we just use $f(x, y)$:

$$\mathbb{E}_R\left(e^{vY(T) - \frac{1}{2}v^2 T} \mathbf{1}_{\{Y(T) \leq b\}} \mathbf{1}_{\{\max_{t \in [0,T]} Y(t) \leq c\}}\right) = \int_{-\infty}^b \int_0^c e^{vx - \frac{1}{2}v^2 T} f(x, y) dx dy$$

$$= \int_{-\infty}^b e^{vx - \frac{1}{2}v^2 T} \int_0^c f(x, y) dy dx.$$

Note that we restricted the range of integration to $\{\max_{t \in [0,T]} Y(t) \leq c\}$ since a Wiener process is 0 at time $t = 0$ so the maximum has to be non-negative.
Step 3a. Computing $\int_0^c f(x, y) dy$.
Recall:

$$f(x, y) = \frac{2}{T} n'\left(\frac{x - 2y}{\sqrt{T}}\right) = \psi(y), \quad \text{say}$$

$$\psi(y) = \phi'(y),$$

where

$$\phi(y) = -\frac{\sqrt{T}}{2}\frac{2}{T}n\left(\frac{x-2y}{\sqrt{T}}\right).$$

Using elementary calculus we get

$$\int_0^c f(x,y)dy = \phi(c) - \phi(0) = \frac{1}{\sqrt{T}}n\left(\frac{x}{\sqrt{T}}\right) - \frac{1}{\sqrt{T}}n\left(\frac{x-2c}{\sqrt{T}}\right).$$

Here

$$n(z) = \frac{1}{\sqrt{2\pi}}e^{-\frac{1}{2}z^2}$$

and so

$$\int_0^c f(x,y)dy = \frac{1}{\sqrt{2\pi T}}e^{-\frac{x^2}{2T}} - \frac{1}{\sqrt{2\pi T}}e^{-\frac{(x-2c)^2}{2T}}.$$

Step 3b. Concluding calculations.
Recall that we have

$$\mathbb{E}_Q\left(1_{\{S(T)\le K\}}1_{\{\max_{t\in[0,T]}S(t)\le L\}}\right) = \int_{-\infty}^b e^{vx-\frac{1}{2}v^2T}\int_0^c f(x,y)dydx$$

and we can insert the result of the computations of Step 3a:

$$\mathbb{E}_Q\left(1_{\{S(T)\le K\}}1_{\{\max_{t\in[0,T]}S(t)\le L\}}\right)$$
$$= \frac{1}{\sqrt{2\pi T}}\int_{-\infty}^b e^{vx-\frac{1}{2}v^2T}e^{-\frac{x^2}{2T}}dx - \frac{1}{\sqrt{2\pi T}}\int_{-\infty}^b e^{vx-\frac{1}{2}v^2T}e^{-\frac{(x-2c)^2}{2T}}dx$$
$$= \frac{1}{\sqrt{2\pi T}}\int_{-\infty}^b e^{-\frac{(x-vT)^2}{2T}}dx - \frac{e^{2vc}}{\sqrt{2\pi T}}\int_{-\infty}^b e^{-\frac{(x-2c-vT)^2}{2T}}dx.$$

After the change of the variables: $u = (x - vT)/\sqrt{T}$, $v = (x - 2c - vT)/\sqrt{T}$
we obtain

$$\cdots = \frac{1}{\sqrt{2\pi}}\int_{-\infty}^{\frac{b-vT}{\sqrt{T}}}e^{-\frac{u^2}{2}}du - \frac{e^{2vc}}{\sqrt{2\pi}}\int_{-\infty}^{\frac{b-2c-vT}{\sqrt{T}}}e^{-\frac{v^2}{2}}dv$$
$$= N\left(\frac{b-vT}{\sqrt{T}}\right) - e^{2vc}N\left(\frac{b-2c-vT}{\sqrt{T}}\right).$$

Now insert

$$b = \frac{1}{\sigma}\ln\frac{K}{S(0)},$$
$$v = \frac{r-\frac{1}{2}\sigma^2}{\sigma},$$

for the final form

$$\cdots = N\left(\frac{\frac{1}{\sigma}\ln\frac{K}{S(0)} - \frac{r-\frac{1}{2}\sigma^2}{\sigma}T}{\sqrt{T}}\right)$$

$$- e^{2\frac{r-\frac{1}{2}\sigma^2}{\sigma}\frac{1}{\sigma}\ln\frac{L}{S(0)}}N\left(\frac{\frac{1}{\sigma}\ln\frac{K}{S(0)} - 2\frac{1}{\sigma}\ln\frac{L}{S(0)} - \frac{r-\frac{1}{2}\sigma^2}{\sigma}T}{\sqrt{T}}\right)$$

$$= N(d_1) - \left(\frac{L}{S(0)}\right)^{2\frac{r}{\sigma^2}-1}N(d_2),$$

where

$$d_1 = \frac{\ln\frac{K}{S(0)} - \left(r - \frac{1}{2}\sigma^2\right)T}{\sigma\sqrt{T}}, \qquad d_2 = \frac{\ln\frac{S(0)K}{L^2} - \left(r - \frac{1}{2}\sigma^2\right)T}{\sigma\sqrt{T}}. \tag{5.4}$$

Step 4. The second term of (5.1).

Just as for compound options, the presence of $S(T)$ poses some technical difficulties. Recall that, by introducing the process $Y(t)$, we have

$$\mathbb{E}_Q\left(S(T)\mathbf{1}_{\{S(T)\leq K\}}\mathbf{1}_{\{\max_{t\in[0,T]}S(t)\leq L\}}\right) = \mathbb{E}_Q\left(e^{\sigma Y(T)}\mathbf{1}_{\{Y(T)\leq b\}}\mathbf{1}_{\{\max_{t\in[0,T]}Y(t)\leq c\}}\right).$$

As above, we introduce the probability R

$$\cdots = S(0)\mathbb{E}_R\left(e^{vY(T)-\frac{1}{2}v^2T}e^{\sigma Y(T)}\mathbf{1}_{\{Y(T)\leq b\}}\mathbf{1}_{\{\max_{t\in[0,T]}Y(t)\leq c\}}\right)$$

and next the density $f(x,y)$ of the vector $(Y(T), \max_{t\in[0,T]}Y(t))$

$$\cdots = S(0)\int_{-\infty}^b\int_0^c e^{vx-\frac{1}{2}v^2T}e^{\sigma x}f(x,y)dxdy$$

$$= S(0)\int_{-\infty}^b e^{vx-\frac{1}{2}v^2T}e^{\sigma x}\int_0^c f(x,y)dydx.$$

We insert the form of $\int_0^c f(x,y)dy$ obtained in Step 3a and we have

$$\cdots = S(0)\frac{e^{\frac{1}{2}\sigma^2T+v\sigma T}}{\sqrt{2\pi T}}\int_{-\infty}^b e^{-\frac{(y-vT-\sigma T)^2}{2T}}dy$$

$$- S(0)\frac{e^{\frac{1}{2}\sigma^2T+v\sigma T+2cv+2c\sigma}}{\sqrt{2\pi T}}\int_{-\infty}^b e^{-\frac{(y-2c-vT-\sigma T)^2}{2T}}dy.$$

Changing variables:

$$u = \frac{x - vT - \sigma T}{\sqrt{T}},$$

$$v = \frac{x - 2c - T - \sigma T}{\sqrt{T}}$$

we obtain

$$\cdots = S(0)\frac{e^{\frac{1}{2}\sigma^2 T + v\sigma T}}{\sqrt{2\pi}} \int_{-\infty}^{\frac{b - vT - \sigma T}{\sqrt{T}}} e^{-\frac{u^2}{2}} du$$

$$- S(0)\frac{e^{\frac{1}{2}\sigma^2 T + v\sigma T + 2cv + 2c\sigma}}{\sqrt{2\pi}} \int_{-\infty}^{\frac{b - 2c - vT - \sigma T}{\sqrt{T}}} e^{-\frac{v^2}{2}} dv.$$

Despite its complicated appearance, this form is quite convenient, since we can make use of the standard cumulative distribution function: In the first integral on the right we have

$$\frac{1}{\sqrt{2\pi}} \int_{-\infty}^{\frac{b - vT - \sigma T}{\sqrt{T}}} e^{-\frac{u^2}{2}} du = N\left(\frac{b - vT - \sigma T}{\sqrt{T}}\right) \quad \text{(insert the form of } b, v\text{)}$$

$$= N\left(\frac{\frac{1}{\sigma}\ln\frac{K}{S(0)} - \frac{r - \frac{1}{2}\sigma^2}{\sigma}T - \sigma T}{\sqrt{T}}\right)$$

$$= N\left(\frac{\ln\frac{K}{S(0)} - \left(r + \frac{1}{2}\sigma^2\right)T}{\sigma\sqrt{T}}\right),$$

while in the second

$$\frac{1}{\sqrt{2\pi}} \int_{-\infty}^{\frac{b - 2c - vT - \sigma T}{\sqrt{T}}} e^{-\frac{v^2}{2}} dv = N\left(\frac{b - 2c - vT - \sigma T}{\sqrt{T}}\right) \quad \text{(insert the form of } b, v\text{)}$$

$$= N\left(\frac{\frac{1}{\sigma}\ln\frac{K}{S(0)} - 2\frac{1}{\sigma}\ln\frac{L}{S(0)} - \frac{r - \frac{1}{2}\sigma^2}{\sigma}T - \sigma T}{\sqrt{T}}\right)$$

$$= N\left(\frac{\ln\frac{S(0)K}{L^2} - \left(r + \frac{1}{2}\sigma^2\right)T}{\sigma\sqrt{T}}\right).$$

Therefore, going back to our derivation,

$$\mathbb{E}_Q\left(S(T)\mathbf{1}_{\{S(T)\leq K\}}\mathbf{1}_{\{\max_{t\in[0,T]} S(t)\leq L\}}\right) = S(0)e^{\frac{1}{2}\sigma^2 T + v\sigma T}N(d_3)$$

$$-S(0)e^{\frac{1}{2}\sigma^2 T + v\sigma T + 2cv + 2c\sigma}N(d_4)$$

where

$$d_3 = \frac{\ln\frac{K}{S(0)} - \left(r + \frac{1}{2}\sigma^2\right)T}{\sigma\sqrt{T}}, \quad d_4 = \frac{\ln\frac{S(0)K}{L^2} - \left(r + \frac{1}{2}\sigma^2\right)T}{\sigma\sqrt{T}} \qquad (5.5)$$

Finally inserting $v = \frac{r-\frac{1}{2}\sigma^2}{\sigma}$, $c = \frac{1}{\sigma} \ln \frac{L}{S(0)}$ we obtain

$$\mathbb{E}_Q \left(S(T) \mathbf{1}_{\{S(T) \leq K\}} \mathbf{1}_{\{\max_{t \in [0,T]} S(t) \leq L\}} \right)$$

$$= e^{\frac{1}{2}\sigma^2 T + \frac{r-\frac{1}{2}\sigma^2}{\sigma}\sigma T} S(0) N(d_3) - e^{\frac{1}{2}\sigma^2 T + \frac{r-\frac{1}{2}\sigma^2}{\sigma}\sigma T + 2\frac{1}{\sigma} \ln \frac{L}{S(0)} \frac{r-\frac{1}{2}\sigma^2}{\sigma} + 2\frac{1}{\sigma} \ln \frac{L}{S(0)} \sigma} N(d_4)$$

$$= e^{rT} S(0) N(d_3) - e^{rT} \left(\frac{L}{S(0)} \right)^{2\frac{r}{\sigma^2}+1} S(0) N(d_4),$$

which completes the computations.

Finally, and this is just a summary of the results obtained above, we have the following.

Theorem 5.7
The Up-and-Out put price is

$$P_{\mathrm{UO}}(0) = e^{-rT} K \left[N(d_1) - \left(\frac{L}{S(0)} \right)^{2\frac{r}{\sigma^2}-1} N(d_2) \right]$$

$$- S(0) \left[N(d_3) - \left(\frac{L}{S(0)} \right)^{2\frac{r}{\sigma^2}+1} N(d_4) \right],$$

where d_1, d_2, are given by (5.4) and d_3, d_4 by (5.5).

Exercise 5.1 Examine the case where $P_{\mathrm{UO}}(0) = P(0)$ (ordinary put).

Exercise 5.2 Consider $S(0) = 100$, $K = 100$, $T = 0.25$, $r = 5\%$, $\sigma = 25\%$. Is it possible to find L so that $P_{\mathrm{UO}}(0) = \frac{1}{2} P(0)$?

Exercise 5.3 Sketch the graphs of $P_{\mathrm{UO}}(0)$ and $P_{\mathrm{UI}}(0)$ as functions of L.

Next we compute the price of the Down-and-In put option in similar fashion, omitting steps in the calculation that are essentially the same as above. We can assume that $S(0) > L$, since otherwise the option becomes a vanilla put option. By general pricing theory we need to find

$$P_{\mathrm{DI}}(0) = e^{-rT} \mathbb{E}_Q \left[(K - S(T))^+ \mathbf{1}_{\{\min S(t) \leq L\}} \right],$$

which reduces, as in the calculation of $P_{\mathrm{UO}}(0)$, to

$$P_{\mathrm{DI}}(0) = e^{-rT} \mathbb{E}_Q \left[\left(K - S(0) e^{vY(T)} \right) \mathbf{1}_{\{Y(T) \leq b\}} \mathbf{1}_{\{\min_{t \leq T} Y(t) \leq c\}} \right],$$

where, as before, $b = \frac{1}{\sigma}\ln(\frac{K}{S(0)})$ and $c = \frac{1}{\sigma}\ln(\frac{L}{S(0)})$. Note that since $S(0) > L$ we have $c < 0$.

Note that $K \leq L$ is equivalent to $b \leq c$. The cases of a regular ($K \leq L$) and a reverse ($K > L$) option need to be treated separately, since, as we saw in Remark 5.6, the joint density of Y and $\min_{t\leq T} Y(t)$ takes different forms in these two situations. We will only consider the reverse case: assume that $K > L$, which means that

$$b = \frac{1}{\sigma}\ln\left(\frac{K}{S(0)}\right) > \frac{1}{\sigma}\ln\left(\frac{L}{S(0)}\right) = c.$$

Since we have assumed $S(0) > L$ we see that here $c < 0$, so $c \leq \min(0, b)$.

As previously we separate the two terms in the expectation. Write $m_T = \min_{t\leq T} Y(t)$ and compute

$$\mathbb{E}_Q\left[1_{\{Y(T)\leq b\}}1_{\{\min_{t\leq T} Y(t)\leq c\}}\right] = \mathbb{E}_{R_1}\left[e^{\nu Y(T)-\frac{1}{2}\nu^2 T}1_{\{Y(T)\leq b\}}1_{\{m_T\leq c\}}\right]$$

$$= e^{-\frac{1}{2}\nu^2 T}\mathbb{E}_{R_1}\left[e^{\nu Y(T)}1_{\{\{Y(T)\leq b\}}1_{\{m_T\leq c\}}\right]$$

$$= e^{\frac{1}{2}\nu^2 T}\int_{-\infty}^{b} e^{\nu x}\left(\int_{-\infty}^{c} g(x, y)dy\right)dx,$$

where $g(x, y)$ is the joint density of $Y(T)$ and m_T. Thus for $c \leq \min(0, b)$ we want to find the joint distribution

$$G(b, c) = P(Y(T) \leq c, m_T \leq b).$$

We can either repeat the discussion in Proposition 5.4 or we can use the first and final equations in Remark 5.6. Using the latter approach, let

$$A = \{Y(T) \leq b\}, B = \{m_T \leq c\}$$

and use the identities

$$P(A \cap B) = P(A) + P(B) - P(A \cup B)$$

$$N(x) = 1 - N(-x)$$

to find

$$P(Y(T) \leq b, m_T \leq c)$$

$$= P(Y(T) \leq b) + (1 - P(m_T \geq c)) - [1 - P(Y(T) \leq b, m_T \leq c)]$$

$$= N\left(\frac{b}{\sqrt{T}}\right) - \left(1 - 2N\left(\frac{c}{\sqrt{T}}\right)\right) - \left[N\left(-\frac{b}{\sqrt{T}}\right) - N\left(\frac{2c - b}{\sqrt{T}}\right)\right]$$

so that

$$g(b, c) = \frac{\partial^2}{\partial c \partial b}G(b, c) = \frac{d}{dc}\left[\frac{1}{\sqrt{T}}n\left(\frac{2c - b}{\sqrt{T}}\right)\right] = \frac{2}{T}n'\left(\frac{2c - b}{\sqrt{T}}\right).$$

Again, $g(x, y) = \frac{2}{T} n' \left(\frac{2y-x}{\sqrt{T}} \right)$ is the y-derivative of $\theta(y) = \frac{1}{\sqrt{T}} n \left(\frac{2y-x}{\sqrt{t}} \right)$, so

$$\int_{-\infty}^{c} g(x, y) dy = \theta(c) - \theta(-\infty) = \theta(c) = \frac{1}{\sqrt{T}} n \left(\frac{2c-x}{\sqrt{T}} \right),$$

and we can complete the computations of the expectations: $\mathbb{E}_Q[\mathbf{1}_{\{Y(T) \leq b\}} \mathbf{1}_{\{\min_{t \leq T} Y(t) \leq c\}}]$ and $\mathbb{E}_Q[S(T) \mathbf{1}_{\{Y(T) \leq b\}} \mathbf{1}_{\{\min_{t \leq T} Y(t) \leq c\}}]$. For the first we have

$$\mathbb{E}_Q[\mathbf{1}_{\{Y(T) \leq b\}} \mathbf{1}_{\{\min_{t \leq T} Y(t) \leq c\}}] = e^{\frac{1}{2}v^2 T} \int_{-\infty}^{b} e^{vx} \left(\int_{-\infty}^{c} g(x, y) dy \right) dx$$

$$= \frac{1}{\sqrt{2\pi T}} \int_{-\infty}^{b} e^{vx - \frac{1}{2}v^2 T} e^{-\frac{(2c-x)^2}{2T}} dx$$

$$= \frac{e^{2vc}}{\sqrt{2\pi T}} \int_{-\infty}^{b} e^{-\frac{(x-2c-vT)^2}{2T}} dx$$

and, using the change of variable $u = (x - 2c - vT)/\sqrt{T}$

$$\cdots = \frac{1}{\sqrt{2\pi}} \frac{e^{2vc}}{\sqrt{2\pi}} \int_{-\infty}^{\frac{b-2c-vT}{\sqrt{T}}} e^{-\frac{u^2}{2}} du$$

$$= e^{2vc} N \left(\frac{b - 2c - vT}{\sqrt{T}} \right)$$

but $b = \frac{1}{\sigma} \ln \frac{K}{S(0)}$ and $v = \frac{r - \frac{1}{2}\sigma^2}{\sigma}$, so this is

$$\cdots = e^{2 \frac{(r-\frac{1}{2}\sigma^2)}{\sigma} \frac{1}{\sigma} \ln \frac{L}{S(0)}} N \left(\frac{\frac{1}{\sigma} \ln \frac{K}{S(0)} - 2\frac{1}{\sigma} \ln \frac{L}{S(0)} - \frac{r-\frac{1}{2}\sigma^2}{\sigma} T}{\sqrt{T}} \right)$$

$$= \left(\frac{L}{S(0)} \right)^{\frac{2r}{\sigma^2}-1} N \left(\frac{\ln(\frac{KS(0)}{L^2}) - (r - \frac{1}{2}\sigma^2)T}{\sigma \sqrt{T}} \right)$$

$$= \left(\frac{L}{S(0)} \right)^{\frac{2r}{\sigma^2}-1} N(d_2).$$

The calculations for the second term are similar:

$$\mathbb{E}_Q \left(S(T) \mathbf{1}_{S(T) \leq K} \mathbf{1}_{\min_{t \in [0,T]} S(t) \leq L} \right)$$

$$= S(0) \mathbb{E}_Q \left(e^{\sigma Y(T)} \mathbf{1}_{Y(T) \leq b} \mathbf{1}_{\min_{t \in [0,T]} Y(t) \leq c} \right)$$

$$= S(0) \mathbb{E}_{R_1} \left(e^{vY(T) - \frac{1}{2}v^2 T} e^{\sigma Y(T)} \mathbf{1}_{Y(T) \leq b} \mathbf{1}_{\min_{t \in [0,T]} Y(t) \leq c} \right)$$

and the expectation equals

$$\cdots = \frac{1}{\sqrt{2\pi T}} \int_{-\infty}^{b} e^{(v+\sigma)x - \frac{1}{2}v^2 T} e^{-\frac{(2c-x)^2}{2T}} dx$$

$$= \frac{e^{\frac{1}{2}\sigma^2 T + v\sigma T + 2cv + 2c\sigma}}{\sqrt{2\pi T}} \int_{-\infty}^{b} e^{-\frac{(x-2c-vT-\sigma T)^2}{2T}} dx$$

changing the variable to $u = \frac{1}{\sqrt{T}}(x - 2c - (\sigma + v)T)$

$$\cdots = \frac{e^{\frac{1}{2}\sigma^2 T + v\sigma T + 2cv + 2c\sigma}}{\sqrt{2\pi}} \int_{-\infty}^{\frac{b-2c-vT-\sigma T}{\sqrt{T}}} e^{-\frac{v^2}{2}} dv$$

$$= e^{\frac{1}{2}\sigma^2 T + v\sigma T + 2cv + 2c\sigma} N\left(\frac{b - 2c - vT - \sigma T}{\sqrt{T}}\right).$$

Using the definitions of b, c and v as above, this becomes

$$e^{rT} \left(\frac{L}{S(0)}\right)^{\frac{2r}{\sigma^2}+1} N(d_4)$$

with d_4 as defined in (5.5). We have proved the following theorem.

Theorem 5.8

The price of the reverse Down-and-In put, where $K \geq L$, is given by

$$P_{\mathrm{DI}}(0) = e^{-rT} K \left(\frac{L}{S(0)}\right)^{\frac{2r}{\sigma^2}-1} N\left(\frac{\ln(\frac{KS(0)}{L^2}) - (r - \frac{1}{2}\sigma^2)T}{\sigma\sqrt{T}}\right)$$

$$-S(0) \left(\frac{L}{S(0)}\right)^{\frac{2r}{\sigma^2}+1} N\left(\frac{\ln \frac{S(0)K}{L^2} - (r + \frac{1}{2}\sigma^2)T}{\sigma\sqrt{T}}\right)$$

$$= \left(\frac{L}{S(0)}\right)^{\frac{2r}{\sigma^2}+1} \left[e^{-rT}\left(\frac{KS(0)^2}{L^2}\right) N(d_2) - S(0)N(d_4)\right]$$

where d_2, d_4 are defined in (5.4) and (5.5), respectively.

Note that, keeping r, T, σ fixed, with strike K the vanilla put has price

$$P(S(0), K) = e^{-rT} KN(-d_+) - S(0)N(-d_-).$$

Replacing K by $K_1 = K\left(\frac{S(0)}{L}\right)^2$, so that $-\ln\left(\frac{S(0)'}{K_1'}\right) = \ln\left(\frac{KS(0)}{L^2}\right)$ it follows that

$$d_2(S(0), K) = -d_-(S(0), K_1)$$

and similarly

$$d_4(S(0), K) = -d_+(S(0), K_1).$$

This leads to the following.

Corollary 5.9

Assuming that $S(0) > L$, the price of a reverse Down-and-In put option with strike K can be expressed as a fraction of the price of a vanilla put with strike $K_1 = K\left(\frac{S(0)}{L}\right)^2$, that is, with $P(S(0), K_1)$ as the vanilla put price we have

$$P_{\mathrm{DI}}(0) = \left(\frac{L}{S(0)}\right)^{\frac{2r}{\sigma^2}+1} P(S(0), K\left(\frac{S(0)}{L}\right)^2).$$

This barrier option can therefore be hedged using vanilla puts.

Exercise 5.4   Compute the initial price of an Up-and-In put option with price K and barrier L on a stock S.

Hedging

We conclude our discussion of barrier options by outlining how to hedge such an option.

We employ the PDE approach to pricing: if $u(t, z)$ satisfies

$$u_t + rxu_z + \frac{1}{2}\sigma^2 z^2 u_{zz} = ru$$

and the conditions

$$u(T, z) = (K - z)^+ \quad \text{for all } 0 < x \leq L, \quad \text{terminal condition,}$$
$$u(t, L) = 0 \quad \text{for all } 0 \leq t < T, \quad \text{boundary condition,}$$

then

$$P_{\mathrm{UO}}(0) = u(0, S(0))$$

– we claim that with the experience gathered so far it is pretty clear how to construct a formal proof of this result, which is left to the reader.

Exercise 5.5   Prove this formula.

The replicating strategy can be now constructed: let

$$\tau = \min\{t : S(t) = L\}.$$

Then

$$x(t) = u_z(t, S(t)),$$
$$y(t) = \frac{u(t, S(t)) - x(t)S(t)}{A(t)} \quad \text{for } t \leq \min\{\tau, T\},$$

and

$$x(t) = 0,$$
$$y(t) = 0 \quad \text{for } t > \min\{\tau, T\}.$$

Exercise 5.6 Prove that this strategy is admissible and replicates the payoff of Up-and-Out put.

Lookback option

Another popular derivative is the **lookback** option: here the payoff is not known in advance, but depends on the behaviour of the underlying over all or part of the trading period $[0, T]$. We consider the lookback put, where the payoff is $(\max_{t \leq T} S(t) - S(T))$. We will write $M^S(T) = \max_{t \leq T} S(t)$, so, with the risk-neutral probability Q the option premium is given by

$$P_L(0) = e^{-rT} \mathbb{E}_Q(M^S(T) - S(T)).$$

But the discounted price is a martingale under Q, so that $\mathbb{E}_Q(e^{-rT} S(T)) = S(0)$ and the second term above becomes $S(0)$. Also,

$$M^S(T) = S(0) \max_{t \leq T}(e^{\sigma Y(t)}) = S(0) M^Z(T),$$

where $Z(t) = \sigma Y(t) = (r - \frac{1}{2}\sigma^2)t + \sigma W_Q(t)$ for t in $[0, T]$. The option premium can now be written as

$$P_L(0) = e^{-rT} S(0) \mathbb{E}_Q(e^{M^Z(t)} - e^{rT}).$$

The calculation of $P_L(0)$ is similar to (but much shorter than) the above calculations for barrier options, so we shall leave the details as an exercise. First, note that we showed in (5.3) that Y is a Wiener process under the equivalent probability R defined by $\mathbb{E}_Q(\mathbf{1}_A) = \mathbb{E}_R(e^{vY(T) - \frac{1}{2}v^2 T} \mathbf{1}_A)$ for any $A \in \mathcal{F}$. Using $A = \{Y(T) < b, M^Y(T) < c\}$ for $0 \leq b < c$, the calculation of the distribution $F^Y(b, c) = \mathbb{E}_Q(\mathbf{1}_A)$ and hence the joint density $f^Y(b, c)$ is now routine.

Exercise 5.7 Show that the joint density of $(Y(T), M^Y(T))$ is given by

$$f^{Y,M^Y}(b, c) = \frac{2(2c - b)}{T\sqrt{T}} n\left(\frac{2c - b}{\sqrt{T}}\right) \exp\left(vb - \frac{1}{2}v^2 T\right).$$

Hence find the joint density of $(Z(T), M^Z(T))$, where $Z(t) = \sigma Y(t)$ on $[0, T]$ and use it to show that the premium of the lookback put is

$$P_L(0) = S(0)(N(-d) + e^{-rT} N\left(-d + \sqrt{T}\right)$$

$$+ \frac{\sigma^2}{2r} e^{-rT} \left[-N\left(d - \frac{2r}{\sigma}\sqrt{T}\right) + e^{-rT} N(d)\right],$$

where

$$d = \frac{2r + \sigma^2}{2\sigma\sqrt{T}}.$$

5.4 Asian options

A typical example of the application of options to hedge business activities is to guarantee the possibility of buying, at desired prices, assets like foreign currency or fuel. Typically, these purchases will be spread over time, so if we wanted to keep to path-independent derivatives, buying a series of call options with different exercise times would be needed. Such a strategy would be impractical and expensive, and financial markets have designed a product suitable for such cases. The underlying security is not the stock (say) prices at particular days $S(t_n)$ but their arithmetic averages

$$A_{\text{arithm}}(t_n) = \frac{1}{n} \sum_{k=1}^{n} S(t_k),$$

and the call payoff would be of the classical form $(A_{\text{arithm}}(T) - K)^+$. So such a single option, called an **Asian arithmetic** average option, would cover the business activities over the whole period $[0, T]$. Apart from convenience, such an option written on the total volume of transactions will be cheaper than a combination of simple call options aimed at a particular transaction. Intuition suggests that the average price will be smoother than the price itself. Figures 5.2 and 5.3 show that this is indeed true and so the average has much smaller volatility than the price, and as we know, volatility is the crucial factor responsible for the option premium. (Here we have daily prices of stock, $t_n = \frac{n}{365}$, in the Black–Scholes model with $\mu = 10\%$, $\sigma = 30\%$.)

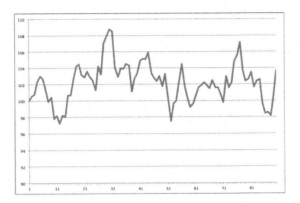

Figure 5.2 Daily prices $S(t_n)$.

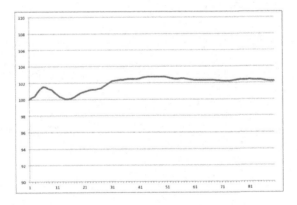

Figure 5.3 Averages $A_{\text{arithm}}(t_n)$.

For pricing it is convenient to use the geometric average as the underlying

$$A_{\text{geom}}(t_n) = \sqrt[n]{\prod_{k=1}^{n} S(t_k)}$$

and this gives a quite decent approximation of the arithmetic average (or at least we can use it as a proxy for the underlying on the basis of its good correlation with the arithmetic average).

Exercise 5.8 Investigate numerically the distance between geometric and arithmetic averages of daily stock prices.

If the distance between consecutive dates is small we can employ a further approximation:

$$A_{\text{geom}}(t_n) = \left(\prod_{k=1}^{n} \exp\{\ln S(t_k)\}\right)^{\frac{1}{n}} = \exp\left\{\frac{1}{n}\sum_{k=1}^{n}\ln S(t_k)\right\}$$

$$\approx \exp\left\{\frac{1}{t_n}\int_0^{t_n}\ln S(t)dt\right\}.$$

We shall use this continuous geometric average in the calculations below.

Continuous geometric average

First consider a put option with payoff

$$H(T) = \max\left\{0, K - \exp\left\{\frac{1}{T}\int_0^T \ln S(t)dt\right\}\right\}.$$

Applying the general scheme of no-arbitrage option pricing

$$H(0) = e^{-rT}\mathbb{E}_Q(H(T)).$$

Some transformations will allow us to use the classical Black–Scholes formula to find $H(0)$. Under the risk-neutral probability

$$S(t) = S(0)\exp\{(r - \frac{1}{2}\sigma^2)t + \sigma W_Q(t)\}$$

so

$$\int_0^T \ln S(t)dt = \int_0^T\left[\ln S(0) + \left(r - \frac{1}{2}\sigma^2\right)t + \sigma W_Q(t)\right]dt$$

$$= T\ln S(0) + \frac{T^2}{2}\left(r - \frac{1}{2}\sigma^2\right) + \sigma\int_0^T W_Q(t)dt.$$

Recall the product rule: $d\left[(T - t)W\right] = (T - t)dW - Wdt$ for any Wiener process, which gives

$$0 = \int_0^T (T - t)dW(t) - \int_0^T W(t)dt,$$

so, in particular,

$$\int_0^T W_Q(t)dt = \int_0^T (T-t)dW_Q(t).$$

We know that this is a normally distributed random variable (see [SCF]) with zero expectation and variance

$$\int_0^T (T-t)^2 dt = -\frac{1}{3}(T-t)^3 \big|_0^T = \frac{1}{3}T^3$$

and hence it can be written in the form

$$\int_0^T (T-u)dW_Q(u) = \frac{1}{\sqrt{3}}T^{\frac{3}{2}}Y,$$

where $Y \sim N(0,1)$. So we have

$$H(T) = \max\left\{0, K - S(0)\exp\left\{\frac{1}{2}\left(r - \frac{1}{2}\sigma^2\right)T + \sigma\frac{1}{\sqrt{3}}T^{\frac{1}{2}}Y\right\}\right\}$$

and consequently

$$H(0) = e^{-rT}\mathbb{E}_Q\left(\max\left\{0, K - S(0)\exp\left\{\frac{1}{2}\left(r - \frac{1}{2}\sigma^2\right)T + \sigma\frac{1}{\sqrt{3}}T^{\frac{1}{2}}Y\right\}\right\}\right)$$

$$= e^{-rT}\mathbb{E}_Q\left(\max\left\{0, K - \overline{S(0)}\exp\left\{\left(r - \frac{1}{2}\overline{\sigma}^2\right)T + \overline{\sigma}T^{\frac{1}{2}}Y\right\}\right\}\right)$$

with

$$\overline{S(0)} = S(0)\exp\left\{-\frac{1}{2}rT - \frac{1}{12}\sigma^2 T\right\},$$

$$\overline{\sigma} = \sigma\frac{1}{\sqrt{3}}.$$

If we compare this with the derivation of the Black–Scholes formula, where we computed exactly the same expectation, we can conclude as follows.

Theorem 5.10

The prices of the Asian integral geometric average call and put are given by

$$C\left(r, T, K, \overline{S(0)}, \overline{\sigma}\right) = \overline{S(0)}N\left(d_+(\overline{S(0)})\right) - Ke^{-rT}N\left(d_-(\overline{S(0)})\right),$$

$$P\left(r, T, K, \overline{S(0)}, \overline{\sigma}\right) = -\overline{S(0)}N\left(-d_+(\overline{S(0)})\right) + Ke^{-rT}N\left(-d_-(\overline{S(0)})\right),$$

where

$$d_+(z) = \frac{\ln\frac{z}{K} + \left(r + \frac{1}{2}\overline{\sigma}^2\right)T}{\overline{\sigma}\sqrt{T}},$$

$$d_-(z) = \frac{\ln\frac{z}{K} + \left(r - \frac{1}{2}\overline{\sigma}^2\right)T}{\overline{\sigma}\sqrt{T}}.$$

Exercise 5.9 Compare the cost of a series of 10 calls for a single share to be exercised over next 10 weeks, with the cost of 10 Asian calls.

Discrete geometric average

Now take t_k evenly spaced, $t_k = \frac{k}{n}T$, and consider the payoff

$$H(T) = \max\left\{0, K - \exp\left\{\frac{1}{n}\sum_{k=1}^{n}\ln S(t_k)\right\}\right\}.$$

As before, we want to make use of the Black–Scholes formula so we begin with inserting the risk-neutral values of stock prices

$$S(t_k) = S(0)\exp\left\{\left(r - \frac{1}{2}\sigma^2\right)t_k + \sigma W_Q(t_k)\right\}$$

to the payoff. We first analyse the exponential

$$\frac{1}{n}\sum_{k=1}^{n}\ln S(t_k) = \frac{1}{n}\sum_{k=1}^{n}\left(\ln S(0) + \left\{\left(r - \frac{1}{2}\sigma^2\right)t_k + \sigma W_Q(t_k)\right\}\right)$$

$$= \ln S(0) + \frac{1}{n}\left(r - \frac{1}{2}\sigma^2\right)\sum_{k=1}^{n}\frac{k}{n}T + \sigma\frac{1}{n}\sum_{k=1}^{n}W_Q(t_k).$$

Now

$$\sum_{k=1}^{n}k = \frac{1}{2}n(n+1),$$

and guessing that the increments of Wiener process will be easier to handle, we introduce the telescoping sums

$$W(t_k) = \sum_{i=1}^{k}\left[W_Q(t_i) - W_Q(t_{i-1})\right]$$

and then, counting the repeated terms,

$$\sum_{k=1}^{n} W_Q(t_k) = \sum_{k=1}^{n} \sum_{i=1}^{k} [W_Q(t_i) - W_Q(t_{i-1})]$$

$$= \sum_{k=1}^{n} (n + 1 - k) [W_Q(t_k) - W_Q(t_{k-1})].$$

These, inserted, give

$$\frac{1}{n} \sum_{k=1}^{n} \ln S(t_k) = \ln S(0) + \frac{1}{2} \left(r - \frac{1}{2}\sigma^2 \right) \frac{n(n+1)}{n^2} T$$

$$+ \sigma \frac{1}{n} \sum_{k=1}^{n} (n + 1 - k) [W_Q(t_k) - W_Q(t_{k-1})].$$

We know that the sum of the (independent) increments $W_Q(t_k) - W_Q(t_{k-1})$ is a normally distributed random variable (see [SCF]) with zero expectation and variance

$$\sum_{k=1}^{n} (n + 1 - k)^2 \mathrm{Var} [W_Q(t_k) - W_Q(t_{k-1})] = \sum_{k=1}^{n} (n + 1 - k)^2 \frac{T}{n}$$

$$= \frac{T}{n} \sum_{j=1}^{n} j^2$$

$$= \frac{T}{n} \frac{n(n+1)(2n+1)}{6}$$

employing the well-known formula for the sum of the squares of consecutive integers. Therefore we can write

$$\frac{1}{n} \sum_{k=1}^{n} (n + 1 - k) [W_Q(t_k) - W_Q(t_{k-1})] = \frac{1}{n} \sqrt{T \frac{(n+1)(2n+1)}{6}} Y$$

with $Y \sim N(0, 1)$. We can now insert these pieces into the payoff $H(T)$ which takes the form

$$\max \left\{ 0, K - S(0) \exp \left\{ \frac{1}{2} \left(r - \frac{1}{2}\sigma^2 \right) \frac{n(n+1)}{n^2} T + \sigma T^{\frac{1}{2}} \sqrt{\frac{(n+1)(2n+1)}{6n^2}} Y \right\} \right\}.$$

It is time for the final touch: to have the payoff of the form suited for the Black–Scholes formula, i.e.

$$H(T) = \max \left\{ 0, K - \widehat{S(0)} \exp \left\{ \left(r - \frac{1}{2}\widehat{\sigma}^2 \right) T + \widehat{\sigma} T^{\frac{1}{2}} Y \right\} \right\}$$

we first let

$$\widehat{\sigma} = \sigma \sqrt{\frac{(n+1)(2n+1)}{6n^2}}$$

and then find $\widehat{S(0)} = S(0)\exp\{x\}$ for some x, so that the first term is of the required form:

$$\frac{1}{2}\left(r - \frac{1}{2}\sigma^2\right)\frac{n(n+1)}{n^2}T = \left(r - \frac{1}{2}\widehat{\sigma}^2\right)T + x,$$

which easily gives (first insert $\widehat{\sigma}$ and then do some elementary, tedious algebra)

$$\widehat{S(0)} = S(0)\exp\left\{rT\left(\frac{1}{2}\frac{n(n+1)}{n^2} - 1\right) + \frac{1}{12}\sigma^2 T\left(\frac{1}{n^2} - 1\right)\right\}.$$

We finally get

$$H(0) = e^{-rT}\mathbb{E}_Q\left(\max\left\{0, K - \widehat{S(0)}\exp\left\{\left(r - \frac{1}{2}\widehat{\sigma}^2\right)T + \widehat{\sigma}T^{\frac{1}{2}}Y\right\}\right\}\right)$$

and we can conclude the following, as above.

Theorem 5.11
The prices of the Asian discrete geometric average call and put are given by the Black–Scholes expressions $C(r, T, K, \widehat{S(0)}, \widehat{\sigma})$, $P(r, T, K, \widehat{S(0)}, \widehat{\sigma})$.

Exercise 5.10   Solve the version of Exercise 5.9 for the discrete geometric average.

6

General models

We generalise the Black–Scholes model in two directions: several assets and general coefficients in the equations describing the stock price dynamics. First we stick to the simple case where the equations for stock prices are linear. It seems pretty clear that all new features will be captured by the case of two assets. The extension from two to more assets is not likely to surprise us so we begin with a detailed discussion of some effects arising from one added dimension. Then we prepare the grounds for more general models and our objective here is to prove the Girsanov Theorem which enables us to find a risk-neutral probability. The celebrated Lévy Theorem, which characterises Wiener processes among continuous martingales, is used, together with a multi-dimensional version of the Itô formula, to prove this important result. Finally, we briefly consider some applications of these theorems to a multi-stock market.

6.1   Two assets

First we need a probability space $(\Omega, \mathcal{F}, P)$ on which two independent Wiener processes W_1, W_2 are defined. For its construction it is natural to consider two probability spaces, $(\Omega_i, \mathcal{F}_i, P_i)$, $i = 1, 2$, each accommodating a Wiener process, and take the product $\Omega = \Omega_1 \times \Omega_2$ as the sample space, the product σ-field $\mathcal{F} = \mathcal{F}_1 \times \mathcal{F}_2$ (the smallest σ-field containing all rectangles $A_1 \times A_2$, $A_i \in \mathcal{F}_i$) and the product probability $P = P_1 \times P_2$ (the extension of $P(A_1 \times A_1) = P_1(A_1)P_2(A_2)$ from rectangles to the whole $\mathcal{F}$). Now for $i = 1, 2$ the processes $W_i : \Omega_i \times [0, T] \to \mathbb{R}$ can be extended to Ω by setting $W_i(t, (\omega_1, \omega_2)) = W_i(t, \omega_i)$, using the same letter for the extension, a minor and justified abuse of notation.

The filtration $\mathcal{F}_t^{(W_1, W_2)}$ is taken as the natural filtration of W_1, W_2, i.e. $\mathcal{F}_t^{(W_1, W_2)} = \sigma(W_1(s), W_2(s) : s \le t)$ for each $t \in [0, T]$. Note that $\mathcal{F}_t^{(W_1, W_2)}$ is generated by sets of the form $A \times B$, where $A \in \mathcal{F}_t^{W_1} = \sigma(W_1(s) : s \le t)$, and $B \in \mathcal{F}_t^{W_2} = \sigma(W_2(s) : s \le t)$. Following the abuse of notation used for $W_i(t, (\omega_1, \omega_2))$, $i = 1, 2$, on the product $\Omega_1 \times \Omega_2$ we again write $\mathcal{F}_t^{W_1}$ to denote $\{A \times \Omega : A \in \sigma(W_1(s) : s \le t)\}$, and similarly for $\mathcal{F}_t^{W_2}$. It is then clear that $\mathcal{F}_t^{W_1}$ and $\mathcal{F}_t^{W_2}$ are sub-σ-fields of $\mathcal{F}_t^{(W_1, W_2)}$. Clearly, W_i is a martingale with respect to $\mathcal{F}_t^{W_i}$, but we need to verify this property with respect to $\mathcal{F}_t^{(W_1, W_2)}$.

Proposition 6.1
For $i = 1, 2$, for each $s \le t$, we have

$$\mathbb{E}\left(W_i(t)|\mathcal{F}_s^{(W_1, W_2)}\right) = W_i(s).$$

Proof   First we observe that

$$\mathbb{E}\left(W_i(t)|\mathcal{F}_s^{(W_1, W_2)}\right) = \mathbb{E}\left(W_i(t)|\mathcal{F}_s^{(W_1, W_2)} \cap \mathcal{F}_t^{W_i}\right)$$

by working from right to left: $\mathbb{E}\left(W_i(t)|\mathcal{F}_s^{(W_1, W_2)} \cap \mathcal{F}_t^{W_i}\right) = Y$ if for $A \in \mathcal{F}_s^{(W_1, W_2)} \cap \mathcal{F}_t^{W_i}$

$$\int_A Y dP = \int_A W_i(t) dP,$$

but for such A (which are in $\mathcal{F}_s^{(W_1, W_2)}$)

$$\int_A W_i(t) dP = \int_A \mathbb{E}\left(W_i(t)|\mathcal{F}_s^{(W_1, W_2)}\right) dP$$

so $Y = \mathbb{E}\left(W_i(t)|\mathcal{F}_s^{(W_1, W_2)}\right)$ since it is $\mathcal{F}_t^{W_i}$-measurable.

It is now sufficient to show that $\mathcal{F}_s^{(W_1, W_2)} \cap \mathcal{F}_t^{W_i} = \mathcal{F}_s^{W_i}$ since then we use the fact that $W_i(t)$ is an $\mathcal{F}_t^{W_i}$-martingale and so

$$\mathbb{E}\left(W_i(t)|\mathcal{F}_s^{(W_1, W_2)} \cap \mathcal{F}_t^{W_i}\right) = \mathbb{E}\left(W_i(t)|\mathcal{F}_s^{W_i}\right) = W_i(s).$$

To show that $\mathcal{F}_s^{(W_1, W_2)} \cap \mathcal{F}_t^{W_i} = \mathcal{F}_s^{W_i}$ note that the inclusion $\supset$ is obvious. For $\subset$ we use the fact that $\mathcal{F}_t^{W_i}$ is generated by rectangles with Ω_j as one of the factors ($j \ne i$), so the same is true about the elements of the intersection.

Now $\mathcal{F}_s^{(W_1,W_2)}$ is the smallest σ-field so that both families $W_i(u)$, $u \le s$ are measurable. For $j \ne i$ the set in the j-coordinate for any set in the intersection with sets in $\mathcal{F}_t^{W_i}$ is Ω_j, so the intersection is generated by sets of the form $\{W_i(u), u \le s\}$, which completes the argument. □

The market

We assume that the market model contains three underlying securities.

- The **risk-free** asset (money-market account), described as before by a deterministic function

$$dA(t) = rA(t)dt,$$

with $A(0) = 1$ (for convenience), where $r > 0$, and so $A(t) = e^{rt}$.

- The **risky** assets S_1, S_2, given by Itô processes of the form

$$dS_1(t) = \mu_1 S_1(t)dt + c_{11}S_1(t)dW_1(t) + c_{12}S_1(t)dW_2(t),$$
$$dS_2(t) = \mu_2 S_2(t)dt + c_{21}S_1(t)dW_1(t) + c_{22}S_2(t)dW_2(t),$$

with $S_1(0), S_2(0)$ given, where $\mu_i \in \mathbb{R}$, $c_{ij} > 0$ (without loss of generality we can assume this since the sign of the volatility coefficient is actually irrelevant: if it is negative then we change W to $-W$ and we have an equation with positive coefficient but with respect to $(-W)$, which is again a Wiener process). The matrix $C = [c_{ij}]$ is assumed to be invertible.

Though we use the letter S, these assets do not have to be stocks, for instance, one can be a stock and the other the rate of exchange of foreign currency.

The process of prices generates a natural filtration $\mathcal{F}_t^{(S_1,S_2)}$, which plays an important role in identifying derivative securities and trading strategies.

These equations describe the processes S_i separately; they are linked by the reference to the Wiener processes. We can solve them with the tools available, namely by considering equations involving a single Wiener process.

Exercise 6.1 Show that $aW_1 + bW_2$ is a Wiener process if and only if $a^2 + b^2 = 1$.

Now we can introduce auxiliary Wiener processes in the equations for
$S_i, i = 1, 2,$

$$W_i'(t) = \frac{c_{i1}}{\sqrt{c_{i1}^2 + c_{i2}^2}} W_1(t) + \frac{c_{i2}}{\sqrt{c_{i1}^2 + c_{i2}^2}} W_2(t)$$

and the equations take the form

$$dS_i(t) = \mu_i S_i(t) + \sigma_i S_i(t) dW_i'(t)$$

where

$$\sigma_i = \sqrt{c_{i1}^2 + c_{i2}^2}, \quad \text{for } i = 1, 2.$$

This explains why we used the notation c_{ij} rather than σ_{ij} in the basic equations. We can apply the existence and uniqueness theorem for stochastic
differential equations (given in [SCF]) separately for each i, and the Itô
formula, also applied to each i, allows us to identify the unique solutions

$$S_i(t) = S_i(0) \exp\left\{\mu_i t - \frac{1}{2}\sigma_i^2 t + \sigma_i W_i'(t)\right\}$$

so for $i = 1, 2$

$$S_i(t) = S_i(0) \exp\left\{\mu_i t - \frac{c_{i1}^2 + c_{i2}^2}{2} t + c_{i1} W_1(t) + c_{i2} W_2(t)\right\}. \qquad (6.1)$$

With the form of stock prices to hand we find that the filtrations generated by the Wiener processes and by the stock prices coincide. This is
a consequence of the fact that the pairs $(W_1(t), W_2(t)$ and $(S_1(t), S_2(t))$ are
linked by means of an invertible deterministic mapping of $\mathbb{R}^2$ to $\mathbb{R}^2$. The
assumption of the invertibility of the matrix C plays a crucial role here.

Exercise 6.2 Prove carefully that $\mathcal{F}_t^{(W_1, W_2)} = \mathcal{F}_t^{(S_1, S_2)}$ if C is invertible.

Exercise 6.3 Find the correlation coefficient for $W_1'(t)$ and $W_2'(t)$.

Exercise 6.4 Suppose that W_1, W_2 are independent Wiener processes. Show that $\rho \in [-1, 1]$ is the correlation coefficient between
the random variables $W_1(t)$ and $\rho W_1(t) + \sqrt{1 - \rho^2} W_2(t)$ for any t.

Remark 6.2

In the case discussed in the previous exercise, we can formulate the equations for stock pricess by using just three parameters: ρ, σ_1, σ_2 with clear meanings, namely for independent W_1, W_2 we take $W_1' = W_1, W_2' = \rho W_1 + \sqrt{1 - \rho^2} W_2$, and consider the following equations

$$dS_i = \mu_i S_i dt + \sigma_i S_i dW_i', \quad i = 1, 2.$$

Going back to the original formulation, we can see that above equation corresponds to

$$C = \begin{bmatrix} \sigma_1 & 0 \\ \sigma_2 \rho & \sigma_2 \sqrt{1 - \rho^2} \end{bmatrix}$$

and this matrix is invertible in non-trivial cases, that is, when $\rho \in (-1, 1)$, $\sigma_i > 0$.

Strategies and risk-neutral probabilities

A strategy (in the basic market) will be a triple $x_1(t), x_2(t), y(t)$ of $\mathcal{F}_t^{(S_1, S_2)}$-adapted processes, with value

$$V_{(x_1, x_2, y)}(t) = x_1(t) S_1(t) + x_2(t) S_2(t) + y(t) A(t),$$

We write $V_{(x_1, x_2, y)}(t) = V(t)$ to simplify the notation, and the self-financing condition takes the form

$$dV(t) = x_1(t) dS_1(t) + x_2(t) dS_2(t) + y(t) dA(t).$$

The two-dimensional versions of most of the results we proved for the one-dimensional case are straightforward. For example:

> **Exercise 6.5** Given $V(0)$ and $x_i(t), i = 1, 2$, find $y(t)$ so that the strategy is self-financing.

The next exercise provides a link to portfolio theory. Consider a portfolio built of S_1 and S_2 with time-independent weights $w_1, w_2, w_1 + w_2 = 1$ and define a strategy

$$x_1(t) = \frac{w_1 V(t)}{S_1(t)}, \quad x_2(t) = \frac{w_2 V(t)}{S_2(t)}.$$

Exercise 6.6 Prove that if $x_1(t)$, $x_2(t)$ is self-financing then

$$dV(t) = [w_1\mu_1 + w_2\mu_2] V(t)dt$$
$$+ [w_1\sigma_{11} + w_2\sigma_{21}] V(t)dW_1(t) + [w_1\sigma_{12} + w_2\sigma_{22}] V(t)dW_2(t),$$

Conversely, prove that if V satisfies the above equation, then the strategy $x_1(t)$, $x_2(t)$ is self-financing.

Definition 6.3

A derivative security of European type is an $\mathcal{F}_T^{(S_1,S_2)}$-measurable random variable.

With invertible C we can use $\mathcal{F}_T^{(W_1,W_2)}$ instead of $\mathcal{F}_T^{(S_1,S_2)}$, as noted above.

Our first task is to obtain martingale properties for (discounted) stock prices. Following the ideas of Chapter 2 we write

$$dS(t) = rS(t)dt + S(t)((\mu - r)dt + CdW(t)),$$

where

$$C = \begin{bmatrix} c_{11} & c_{12} \\ c_{21} & c_{22} \end{bmatrix}, \quad S(t) = \begin{bmatrix} S_1(t) \\ S_2(t) \end{bmatrix}, \quad \mu = \begin{bmatrix} \mu_1 \\ \mu_2 \end{bmatrix}, \quad W(t) = \begin{bmatrix} W_1(t) \\ W_2(t) \end{bmatrix},$$

and for invertible C

$$dS(t) = rS(t)dt + S(t)C\left(C^{-1}(\mu - r)dt + dW(t)\right).$$

If $W^Q(t) = C^{-1}(\mu - r)t + W(t)$ is a two-dimensional Wiener process under some new probability Q (a fact we will confirm below, as an extension of the Girsanov Theorem 2.1), then

$$dS_1(t) = rS_1(t)dt + c_{11}S_1(t)dW_1^Q(t) + c_{12}S_1(t)dW_2^Q(t),$$
$$dS_2(t) = rS_2(t)dt + c_{21}S_1(t)dW_1^Q(t) + c_{22}S_2(t)dW_2^Q(t),$$

and by modifying the derivation of (6.1) we find that

$$S_i(t) = S_i(0)\exp\left\{rt - \frac{c_{i1}^2 + c_{i2}^2}{2}t + c_{i1}W_1^Q(t) + c_{i2}W_2^Q(t)\right\}, \quad i = 1, 2,$$

so each discounted stock price process S_i ($i = 1, 2$) is a martingale.

Exercise 6.7 Prove the last claim. (Hint: use independence and Proposition 6.1.)

> **Exercise 6.8** Show that under Q the process of discounted values of a strategy is a martingale.

Two stocks, one Wiener process

We will now justify the decision of taking the same number of Wiener processes as the number of assets, and in particular the assumption about invertibility of C, by considering two degenerate cases. Suppose we take one Wiener process to drive two stock prices

$$dS_1(t) = \mu_1 S_1(t)dt + \sigma_1 S_1(t)dW(t),$$
$$dS_2(t) = \mu_2 S_2(t)dt + \sigma_2 S_2(t)dW(t).$$

This corresponds to the basic equations with the degenerate matrix C having the form

$$C = \begin{bmatrix} c_{11} & 0 \\ c_{21} & 0 \end{bmatrix},$$

which is not invertible, of course, and we write $\sigma_i = c_{i1}$ since these numbers represent volatilities now.

As far as the probability setup is concerned, we can work on a single space $(\Omega, \mathcal{F}, P)$ and with our experience of the one-dimensional setting we know that $\mathcal{F}_t^{S_1} = \mathcal{F}_t^{S_2} = \mathcal{F}_t^W$, so $\mathcal{F}_t^{(S_1,S_2)} = \mathcal{F}_t^W$, and each equation can be solved uniquely.

The stock prices are perfectly correlated, and motivated by the considerations of [DMFM], where we discussed two stocks in a binomial model, we formulate

Proposition 6.4
No-arbitrage implies that market prices of risk for two stocks are the same

$$\frac{\mu_1 - r}{\sigma_1} = \frac{\mu_2 - r}{\sigma_2}. \tag{6.2}$$

Proof First we show that we can replicate one stock by means of the other combined with the risk-free asset. The goal is to find $x(t), y(t)$ such that

$$S_2(t) = V_{(x,y)}(t) = x(t)S_1(t) + y(t)A(t).$$

The self-financing condition implies

$$dS_2(t) = x(t)dS_1(t) + y(t)dA(t),$$

which gives

$$\mu_2 S_2(t)dt + \sigma_2 S_2(t)dW(t) = \mu_1 S_1(t)x(t)dt + \sigma_1 S_1(t)x(t)dW(t) + ry(t)A(t)dt.$$

The uniqueness of Itô characteristics implies that the dt and dW coefficients on both sides are the same:

$$\mu_2 S_2(t) = \mu_1 S_1(t)x(t) + ry(t)A(t),$$
$$\sigma_2 S_2(t) = \sigma_1 S_1(t)x(t),$$

so that

$$x(t) = \frac{\sigma_2 S_2(t)}{\sigma_1 S_1(t)},$$
$$y(t) = \frac{1}{rA(t)}\left(\mu_2 S_2(t) - \mu_1 S_1(t)\frac{\sigma_2 S_2(t)}{\sigma_1 S_1(t)}\right).$$

The initial values must be the same (otherwise there is an obvious arbitrage opportunity) so

$$S_2(0) = \frac{\sigma_2 S_2(0)}{\sigma_1 S_1(0)}S_1(0) + \frac{1}{rA(0)}\left(\mu_2 S_2(0) - \mu_1 \frac{\sigma_2 S_2(0)}{\sigma_1}\right)A(0)$$
$$= S_2(0)\left(\frac{\sigma_2}{\sigma_1} + \frac{\mu_2}{r} - \frac{\mu_1\sigma_2}{r\sigma_1}\right),$$

and simple algebra gives the result. □

This implies that the risk neutral probability is the same for each stock since as we know it is determined by the market price of risk. We can also prove the converse.

Proposition 6.5
If condition (6.2) is violated, we can find arbitrage opportunities.

Proof We construct an arbitrage strategy by designing a self-financing strategy with zero noise term and return beating the risk free rate. Suppose

$$\frac{\mu_1 - r}{\sigma_1} > \frac{\mu_2 - r}{\sigma_2},$$

and we seek a self-financing portfolio $x_1(t)$, $x_2(t)$, $y(t)$, that is, a portfolio satisfying

$$dV = x_1 dS_1 + x_2 dS_2 + ydA$$

with $V(0) = 0$ and with deterministic growth higher than r. The self-financing condition implies (by an easy modification of Proposition 2.9)

$$d\tilde{V} = x_1(t)d\tilde{S}_1 + x_2(t)d\tilde{S}_2$$
$$= x_1(\mu_1 - r)\tilde{S}_1 dt + x_1\sigma_1\tilde{S}_1 dW(t) + x_2(\mu_2 - r)\tilde{S}_2 dt + x_2\sigma_2\tilde{S}_2 dW(t)$$

and to obtain deterministic growth we choose x_1, x_2 so that the noise term vanishes:

$$x_1\sigma_1\tilde{S}_1 = -x_2\sigma_2\tilde{S}_2,$$

or, after multiplying by e^{rt}

$$x_1\sigma_1 S_1 = -x_2\sigma_2 S_2.$$

This is guaranteed if

$$x_1(t) = \frac{1}{\sigma_1 S_1(t)},$$
$$x_2(t) = -\frac{1}{\sigma_2 S_2(t)}.$$

The risk free position is (modifying Corollary 2.10)

$$y(t) = \int_0^t x_1(u)d\tilde{S}_1(u) + \int_0^t x_2(u)d\tilde{S}_2(u) - e^{-rt}\left(\frac{1}{\sigma_1} - \frac{1}{\sigma_2}\right)$$
$$= \int_0^t x_1(u)(\mu_1 - r)S_1(u)e^{-ru}du + \int_0^t x_1(u)\sigma_1 S_1(u)e^{-ru}dW(u)$$
$$+ \int_0^t x_2(u)(\mu_2 - r)S_2(u)e^{-ru}du + \int_0^t x_2(u)\sigma_2 S_2(u)e^{-ru}dW(u)$$
$$- e^{-rt}\left(\frac{1}{\sigma_1} - \frac{1}{\sigma_2}\right)$$
$$= \left(\frac{\mu_1 - r}{\sigma_1} - \frac{\mu_2 - r}{\sigma_2}\right)\int_0^t e^{-ru}du - e^{-rt}\left(\frac{1}{\sigma_1} - \frac{1}{\sigma_2}\right).$$

Finally

$$V(t) = \left(\frac{1}{\sigma_1} - \frac{1}{\sigma_2}\right) + y(t)A(t)$$
$$= A(t)\left(\frac{\mu_1 - r}{\sigma_1} - \frac{\mu_2 - r}{\sigma_2}\right)\int_0^t e^{-ru}du$$

hence

$$dV(t) = rV(t)dt + \left(\frac{\mu_1 - r}{\sigma_1} - \frac{\mu_2 - r}{\sigma_2}\right)dt > rV(t)dt,$$

which creates arbitrage: we borrow risk-free and invest in V with sure positive profit. $\qquad\square$

Remark 6.6

The market built of S_1, S_2, A is complete since $\mathcal{F}_T^{(S_1,S_2)} = \mathcal{F}_T^W$ and any payoff H can be replicated by means of S_1 (and also by S_2).

One stock, two Wiener processes

Now suppose that a single stock is driven by two Wiener processes. As we may suspect (motivated by the trinomial example, see [DMFM]), the model will not be complete. However, some complications will emerge and this example will highlight the relevance of some aspects of the basic definitions of derivative security and strategy. Assume that W_1, W_2 are independent Wiener processes, and

$$dS(t) = \mu S(t)dt + c_1 S(t)dW_1(t) + c_2 S(t)dW_2(t)$$

so we have a special case of the general 2-stock Black–Scholes model with a degenerate, non-invertible matrix

$$C = \begin{bmatrix} c_1 & c_2 \\ c_1 & c_2 \end{bmatrix}.$$

As we know, with

$$W'(t) = \frac{c_1}{\sqrt{c_1^2 + c_2^2}} W_1(t) + \frac{c_2}{\sqrt{c_1^2 + c_2^2}} W_2(t),$$

$$dS(t) = \mu S(t) + \sigma S(t)dW'(t),$$

where $\sigma = \sqrt{c_1^2 + c_2^2}$. This equation can be solved,

$$S(t) = S(0)\exp\left\{\mu t - \frac{c_1^2 + c_2^2}{2}t + c_1 W_1(t) + c_2 W_2(t)\right\},$$

all $\mathcal{F}_T^{W'} = \mathcal{F}_T^S$-measurable payoffs can be replicated by means of $\mathcal{F}_t^S$-adapted strategies, so we have completeness in this market.

The filtration $\mathcal{F}_t^{(W_1,W_2)}$ is richer that $\mathcal{F}_t^S$ and this will create some room for incompleteness. However, we begin with a related feature: we show that the risk neutral probability is not unique in this model.

Proposition 6.7

In this model there are many risk-neutral probabilities with respect to the filtration $\mathcal{F}_t^{(W_1,W_2)}$.

Proof We begin with an informal construction of risk-neutral probabilities along the same lines as before: we wish to write $S(t)$ in the form $S(0) \exp\{rt - \frac{1}{2}\sigma^2 t + \sigma W_Q(t)\}$. After discounting we have a martingale provided that W_Q is a Wiener process. Fix $\alpha \in [0,1]$, and write

$$
\begin{aligned}
S(t) &= S(0) \exp \left\{ rt - \frac{c_1^2}{2}t + c_1 \left[\alpha \frac{\mu - r}{c_1}t + W_1(t) \right] \right. \\
&\qquad \left. - \frac{c_2^2}{2}t + c_2 \left[(1-\alpha)\frac{\mu - r}{c_2}t + W_2(t) \right] \right\} \\
&= S(0) \exp \left\{ rt - \frac{c_1^2}{2}t + c_1 W_1^\alpha(t) - \frac{c_2^2}{2}t + c_2 W_2^\alpha(t) \right\},
\end{aligned}
$$

where (with α denoting an index, not a power)

$$
W_1^\alpha(t) = \alpha \frac{\mu - r}{c_1}t + W_1(t),
$$

$$
W_2^\alpha(t) = (1-\alpha)\frac{\mu - r}{c_2}t + W_2(t).
$$

The processes W_1, W_2 are independent and we may regard them as living on a product probability space $\Omega = \Omega_1 \times \Omega_2$, W_i living on Ω_i. Then by applying the Girsanov Theorem to each i we find Q_i^α where the densities $\frac{dQ_i^\alpha}{dP_i}(i = 1, 2)$ are of the form

$$
M_1^\alpha(T) = \exp \left\{ -\frac{1}{2}\left(\alpha\frac{\mu - r}{c_1}\right)^2 T - \alpha\frac{\mu - r}{c_1}W_1(T) \right\},
$$

$$
M_2^\alpha(T) = \exp \left\{ -\frac{1}{2}\left((1-\alpha)\frac{\mu - r}{c_2}\right)^2 T - (1-\alpha)\frac{\mu - r}{c_2}W_2(T) \right\},
$$

so that the W_i^α are Wiener processes under Q_i^α. As a consequence

$$
W^\alpha(t) = \frac{c_1}{\sqrt{c_1^2 + c_2^2}}W_1^\alpha(t) + \frac{c_2}{\sqrt{c_1^2 + c_2^2}}W_2^\alpha(t)
$$

is also a Wiener process, taken with respect to $Q^\alpha = Q_1^\alpha \times Q_2^\alpha$, with density relative to $P = P_1 \times P_2$ given by $M^\alpha(T) = M_1^\alpha(T)M_2^\alpha(T)$. Now

$$
S(t) = S(0) \exp \left\{ rt - \frac{c_1^2 + c_2^2}{2}t + \sqrt{c_1^2 + c_2^2}W^\alpha(t) \right\}
$$

so $\tilde{S}(t)$ is a martingale. More explicitly, by Fubini's Theorem, for $A = A_1 \times A_2$ in $\mathcal{F}_T^{(W_1, W_2)}$ and a non-negative integrable function f on $\Omega = \Omega_1 \times \Omega_2$

we have

$$\int_A f(\omega_1, \omega_2) dQ^\alpha(\omega_1, \omega_2) = \int_{A_2} \left(\int_{A_1} f(\omega_1, \omega_2) dQ_1^\alpha(\omega_1) \right) dQ_2^\alpha(\omega_2).$$

When $f(\omega_1, \omega_2) = f_1(\omega_1) f_2(\omega_2)$ we can split the two integrals. This is the case with $f = \tilde{S}(t) = S(0) \exp\left\{-\frac{c_1^2}{2} t + c_1 W_1^\alpha(t)\right\} \exp\left\{-\frac{c_2^2}{2} t + c_2 W_2^\alpha(t)\right\}$, and in the proof of Proposition 6.1 we saw that, for $t > s$, $i = 1, 2$, conditioning $W_i(t)$ (and therefore also $W_i^\alpha(t)$) on $\mathcal{F}_s^{(W_1, W_2)}$ amounts to the same as conditioning it on $\mathcal{F}_s^{(W_1, W_2)} \cap \mathcal{F}_t^{W_i}$. So, if we take $A_1 \in \mathcal{F}_t^{W_1}$ in the Fubini identity it is clear that the conditional expectation involving W_1 also does not depend on ω_2, so the integrals can be split, and then the martingale property proved in Proposition 6.1 can be applied in each factor. In other words,

$$\mathbb{E}_{Q^\alpha}(\tilde{S}(t) | \mathcal{F}_s^{(W_1, W_2)})$$

$$= S(0) \mathbb{E}_{Q_1} \left(\exp\left\{ -\frac{c_1^2}{2} t + c_1 W_1^\alpha(t) \right\} \Big| \mathcal{F}_s^{(W_1, W_2)} \cap \mathcal{F}_t^{W_1} \right)$$

$$\times \mathbb{E}_{Q_2} \left(\exp\left\{ -\frac{c_2^2}{2} t + c W_2^\alpha(t) \right\} \Big| \mathcal{F}_s^{(W_1, W_2)} \cap \mathcal{F}_t^{W_2} \right)$$

$$= S(0) \mathbb{E}_{Q_1} \left(\exp\left\{ -\frac{c_1^2}{2} s + c_1 W_1^\alpha(s) \right\} \right) \mathbb{E}_{Q_2} \left(\exp\left\{ -\frac{c_2^2}{2} s + c W_2^\alpha(s) \right\} \right)$$

$$= \tilde{S}(s). \qquad \square$$

One could try to conclude that the fact that the risk-neutral probability is not unique will imply incompleteness of the model. However, the situation is slightly more complicated. Let us see how the argument would go. In our earlier derivation non-uniqueness of the risk-neutral probabilities implied incompleteness: if $\mathbf{1}_A$ can be replicated for each event A, the discounted value process of the replicating strategy is a martingale, hence has constant expectation and so $Q(A) = V(0)e^{rT}$ gives uniqueness of the risk-neutral probability. This classical argument does not work here due to the incompatibility of the various filtrations involved. We outline the reasons, leaving some of the details as exercises.

First, we observed that this model is complete in the sense that $\mathcal{F}_T^S$-measurable payoffs can be replicated by means of $\mathcal{F}_t^S$-adapted strategies and here there exists a unique risk-neutral probability Q with respect to $\mathcal{F}_t^S$ with density determined by

$$\sigma = \sqrt{c_1^2 + c_2^2}, \quad b = \frac{\mu - r}{\sigma},$$

and taking the form

$$M^Q(T) = \exp\left\{-\frac{1}{2}b^2T - bW'(T)\right\}$$

$$= \exp\left\{-\frac{1}{2}\frac{(\mu-r)^2}{c_1^2 + c_2^2}T - (\mu - r)\frac{c_1}{c_1^2 + c_2^2}W_1(t) + (\mu - r)\frac{c_2}{c_1^2 + c_2^2}W_2(t)\right\}.$$

We do not have any contradiction, since $M^Q(t)$ is not a martingale with respect to the larger filtration $\mathcal{F}_t^{(W_1,W_2)}$ and Q is not risk-neutral with respect to $\mathcal{F}_t^{(W_1,W_2)}$.

Exercise 6.9   Prove this statement.

To find claims that cannot be replicated we have to consider $\mathcal{F}_T^{(W_1,W_2)}$-measurable payoffs and restrict to $\mathcal{F}_t^S$-measurable strategies. Now $H = W_1(T)$ is not replicable since $x(T)S(T) + y(T)A(T)$ is not $\mathcal{F}_T^{W_1}$-measurable (we may take $|W_1(T)|$ instead if we wish to require payoffs to be non-negative).

Exercise 6.10   Prove this statement.

Allowing $\mathcal{F}_t^{(W_1,W_2)}$-adapted strategies, we can replicate such a claim easily: take $x(t) = \frac{W_1(t)}{S(t)}$, $y(t) = 0$.

6.2   Many assets

Guided by the above example we restrict our attention to the case where the number d of risky assets matches the number of driving Wiener processes. These are now assumed to live on a product space $\Omega = \Omega_1 \times \cdots \times \Omega_d$, with W_j defined on Ω_j but considered on Ω. The vector of independent Wiener processes will be denoted by $\mathbf{W} = (W_1, \ldots, W_d)$ and the filtration generated by $\mathbf{W}$ will be simply written as $\mathcal{F}_t$. It is straightforward to prove the counterpart of Proposition 6.1 giving the martingale property of each W_j with respect to $\mathcal{F}_{t:}$ for $j = 1, \ldots, d$, for each $s \leq t$ we have $\mathbb{E}(W_j(t)|\mathcal{F}_s) = W_j(s)$.

The d-dimensional version of the Black–Scholes market will by composed of the risk-free asset

$$dS_0(t) = rS_0(t)dt$$

and d risky assets

$$dS_i(t) = \mu_i S_i(t)dt + \sum_{j=1}^{d} c_{ij} S_i(t)dW_j(t), \quad i = 1, \ldots, d$$

with invertible matrix $C = [c_{ij}]$. The solution can be guessed to be of the form

$$S_i(t) = S_i(0) \exp \left\{ \mu_i t - \frac{\sum_{j=1}^{d} c_{ij}^2}{2} t + \sum_{j=1}^{d} c_{ij} W_j(t) \right\}$$

and this could be justified by repeating the trick of introducing auxiliary Wiener processes, one by one, reducing the system to a set of decoupled equations. We prefer to adopt an alternative approach, and will develop multi-dimensional Itô processes below, which will provide a method of immediate verification of the above formula.

A gentle further generalisation would allow the coefficients to be time-dependent deterministic functions and set

$$dS_0(t) = r(t)S_0(t)dt,$$

$$dS_i(t) = \mu_i(t)S_i(t)dt + \sum_{j=1}^{d} c_{ij}(t)S_i(t)dW_j(t), \quad i = 1, \ldots, d. \tag{6.3}$$

To make sure that the stochastic integrals make sense we can assume that c_{ij} are bounded, in which case an explicit formula is easily provided (see [SCF]).

For many purposes we need further generalisation allowing non-linearities and stochastic coefficients.

Example 6.8

The assumption of constant volatility is not realistic since it contradicts the data, and so we need a model where volatility is given by a process. The simplest possibility is to consider the system of equations

$$dS(t) = \mu S(t)dt + \sigma(t)S(t)dW_1(t),$$

$$d\sigma(t) = a(\sigma(t))dt + b(\sigma(t))dW_2(t),$$

where the form of the coefficients will need to guarantee realistic performance of the process σ: it should have positive values, not escaping to infinity. Of course, strictly speaking, such a process does not represent a traded asset but since option prices depend on volatility and vice versa (as with implied volatility, mentioned in Section 3.3), volatility may be treated like a market security for modelling purposes.

Hence it is natural to consider a general system of coupled equations

$$dS_i(t) = \mu_i(t, S_1(t), \ldots, S_d(t))dt + \sum_{j=1}^{d} c_{ij}(t, S_1(t), \ldots, S_d(t))dW_j(t),$$

which can be written concisely in vector notation (see the theorem below), with the convention

$$\int_0^t \mathbf{C}(t)d\mathbf{W}(t) = \left(\sum_{j=1}^{d} \int_0^t c_{1j}(s)dW_j(s), \ldots, \sum_{j=1}^{d} \int_0^t c_{dj}(s)dW_j(s) \right).$$

Since in general no closed form solutions will be available, we restrict our attention to existence and uniqueness.

Theorem 6.9

If

$$\mu : [0, \infty) \times \mathbb{R}^d \to \mathbb{R}^d,$$
$$C : [0, \infty) \times \mathbb{R}^d \to \mathbb{R}^{d \times d},$$

are Lipschitz continuous with linear growth:

$$|\mu(t, x) - \mu(t, y)|_{\mathbb{R}^d} + |C(t, x) - C(t, y)|_{\mathbb{R}^{d \times d}} \leq c \left(|x - y|_{\mathbb{R}^d} \right),$$
$$|\mu(t, x)|_{\mathbb{R}^d} + |C(t, x)|_{\mathbb{R}^{d \times d}} \leq c \left(1 + |x|_{\mathbb{R}^d} \right),$$

then the equation

$$dS(t) = \mu(t, S(t))dt + C(t, S(t))dW(t)$$

has a unique solution.

Proof The proof of the one-dimensional case given in [SCF] can be repeated word for word with proper interpretation of the notation, in particular, with $|\cdot|$ being the norm in $\mathbb{R}^n$ rather then the absolute value. □

6.3 Itô formula

We will give a proof of the multi-dimensional version of the Itô formula. Take integrable processes a_i and a matrix $[b_{ij}(t)]$, $j = 1, \ldots, n$, $i = 1, \ldots, k$, of $\mathcal{P}^2$-processes, all with continuous paths. Define a multi-dimensional Itô process $X(t) = (X_1(t), \ldots, X_k(t))$ by prescribing its coordinates

$$dX_i = a_i dt + \sum_{j=1}^{n} b_{ij} dW_j, \quad i = 1, \ldots, k.$$

Theorem 6.10 (Itô – general)
If $F : [0, \infty) \times \mathbb{R}^k \to \mathbb{R}$, of class C^1 in the first variable and of class C^2 in the others, and if $Y(t) = F(t, X(t))$, then Y is an Itô process with

$$dY(t) = F_t(t, X(t))dt + \sum_{i=1}^{k} F_{x_i}(t, X(t))a_i(t)dt$$

$$+ \sum_{i=1}^{k} F_{x_i}(t, X(t)) \sum_{j=1}^{n} b_{ij}(t)dW_j(t)$$

$$+ \frac{1}{2} \sum_{j=1}^{n} \sum_{i,l=1}^{k} F_{x_i x_l}(t, X(t))b_{ij}(t)b_{lj}(t)dt.$$

Exercise 6.11 Prove that the processes

$$S_i(t) = S_i(0) \exp \left\{ \int_0^t \mu_i(t)dt - \frac{1}{2} \sum_{j=1}^{d} \int_0^t \sigma_{ij}^2(t)dt + \sum_{j=1}^{d} \int_0^t \sigma_{ij}(t)dW_j(t) \right\}$$

solve (6.3), where $i = 1, \ldots, d$.

In the proof we will concentrate on new features as compared with the one-dimensional case, though we will repeat all the steps in abbreviated form (we are assuming that the reader is familiar with the argument given in [SCF]). The idea of the proof in the general case is similar to that in one dimension: decomposition of $Y(t) - Y(0)$ into a telescoping sum with some intermediate times $t_k = \frac{kt}{N}$, Taylor formula, limit passage. Clearly the cross-terms involving the product of increments of different processes: $[X_i(t_{k+1}) - X_i(t_k)][X_j(t_{k+1}) - X_j(t_k)]$ are new here, so we precede the proof with some tools needed to handle these.

For two processes X, Y we define their cross-variation to be

$$[X, Y](t) = \lim \sum_{i=0}^{n-1} [X(t_{i+1}) - X(t_i)][Y(t_{i+1}) - Y(t_i)] \tag{6.4}$$

where $0 = t_0 < t_1 < \cdots < t_n = t$ and the limit is in probability as max $|t_{i+1} - t_i| \to 0$. Using the elementary polarisation identity $ab = \frac{1}{4}(a+b)^2 - \frac{1}{4}(a-b)^2$, we can immediately deduce that

$$[X, Y](t) = \frac{1}{4}[X + Y, X + Y](t) - \frac{1}{4}[X - Y, X - Y](t)$$

where $[X, X]$ is the quadratic variation of X defined by (6.4) with $X = Y$, provided that the right-hand side exists.

If $X(t) = \int_0^t b_X(s)dW(s)$, then $[X, X](t) = \int_0^t b_X^2(s)ds$ (see [SCF]) and if $Y(t) = \int_0^t b_Y(s)dW(s)$ then

$$[X, Y](t) = \int_0^t b_X(s)b_Y(s)ds,$$

again by polarisation.

Exercise 6.12   Prove this property.

Using the cross-variation processes the Itô formula correction term can be written in the form

$$\frac{1}{2} \sum_{i,l=1}^{k} F_{x_i x_l}(t, X(t))d[X_i, X_l](t),$$

where the integral is understood in the Stieltjes sense.

Finally, since the compensator for $X^2(t)$ is the quadratic variation $[X, X](t)$, i.e. the process $X^2(t) - [X, X](t)$ is a martingale, the same role for the product $X(t)Y(t)$ is played by the cross-variation $[X, Y](t)$.

Exercise 6.13   Prove that $X(t)Y(t) - [X, Y](t)$ is a martingale.

We will prove the two-dimensional version, where all the new features are captured. We formulate it separately for convenience, in slightly abbreviated form.

Theorem 6.11 (Itô – two dimensions)
Consider two Itô processes with continuous characteristics

$$dX_k = a_k(t)dt + b_{1k}(t)dW_1(t) + b_{2k}(t)dW_2(t), \quad k = 1, 2$$

and sufficiently regular $F(t, x_1, x_2)$. Then $Y(t) = F(t, X_1(t), X_2(t))$ is an Itô process with

$$F(X_1(t), X_2(t)) - F(0, 0)$$
$$= \int_0^t [F_t(X_1(s), X_2(s)) + F_{x_1}(X_1(s), X_2(s))a_1(s) + F_{x_2}(X_1(s), X_2(s))a_2(s)] \, dt$$
$$+ \sum_{k=1}^2 \int_0^t [F_{x_1}(X_1(s), X_2(s))b_{1k}(s) + F_{x_2}(X_1(s), X_2(s))b_{2k}(s)] \, dW_k(s)$$
$$+ \frac{1}{2} \sum_{k=1}^2 \int_0^t \Big[F_{x_1 x_1}(X_1(s), X_2(s))b_{1k}^2(s) + 2F_{x_1 x_2}(X_1(s), X_2(s))b_{1k}(s)b_{2k}(s)$$
$$+ F_{x_2 x_2}(X_1(s), X_2(s))b_{2k}^2(s) \Big] \, dt.$$

Proof Application of the localisation technique allows us to assume that F is bounded. We restrict attention to F independent of t, as the extension to F depending also on time is routine and can be done in exactly the same way as for one dimension.

Step 1. Taylor expansion. Fix t, let $t_i = i\frac{t}{n}$, $i = 0, 1, \ldots, n$. We decompose the left-hand side of the claim and use the Taylor formula to get

$$F(X_1(t), X_2(t)) - F(0, 0)$$
$$= \sum_{i=0}^{n-1} [F(X_1(t_{i+1}), X_2(t_{i+1})) - F(X_1(t_i), X_2(t_i))]$$
$$= \sum_{i=0}^{n-1} (F_{x_1}(X_1(t_i), X_2(t_i))[X_1(t_{i+1}) - X_1(t_i)]$$
$$+ F_{x_2}(X_1(t_i), X_2(t_i))[X_2(t_{i+1}) - X_2(t_i)])$$
$$+ \frac{1}{2} \sum_{i=0}^{n-1} \Big(F_{x_1 x_1}(y_i, z_i)[X_1(t_{i+1}) - X_1(t_i)]^2$$
$$+ 2F_{x_1 x_2}(y_i, z_i)[X_1(t_{i+1}) - X_1(t_i)][X_2(t_{i+1}) - X_2(t_i)]$$
$$+ F_{x_1 x_1}(y_i, z_i)[X_2(t_{i+1}) - X_2(t_i)]^2 \Big)$$

for some y_i, z_i between $X_1(t_i)$ and $X_1(t_{i+1})$, $X_2(t_{i+1})$ and $X_2(t_i)$, respectively.

Step 2. Terms with F_{x_i}. These can be dealt with in the same way as in the one-dimensional case.

Step 3. Terms with $F_{x_j x_k}$. We have to show

$$\sum_{i=0}^{n-1} F_{x_j x_k}(y_i, z_i)[X_j(t_{i+1}) - X_j(t_i)][X_k(t_{i+1}) - X_k(t_i)]$$

$$\to \sum_{n=1}^{2} \int_0^t F_{x_j x_k}(X_1(s), X_2(s))b_{jn}(s)b_{kn}ds.$$

Step 3a. Disposing of y_i, z_i.
We prove that y_i, z_i can be replaced by $X_1(t_i), X_2(t_i)$, respectively, showing that

$$\sum_{i=0}^{n-1} [F_{x_j x_k}(y_i, z_i) - F_{x_j x_k}(X_1(t_i), X_2(t_i)))][X_j(t_{i+1}) - X_j(t_i)][X_k(t_{i+1}) - X_k(t_i)] \to 0.$$
(6.5)

This follows from the uniform continuity of F and of the paths of an Itô process. Working pathwise, for $\varepsilon > 0$ we can find $\delta > 0$ such that

$$|t_{i+1} - t_i| < \delta \text{ implies } |F_{x_j x_k}(y_i, z_i) - F_{x_j x_k}(X_1(t_i), X_2(t_i)))| < \varepsilon,$$

so for $n \geq N$ with N large enough,

$$\sum_{i=0}^{n-1} [F_{x_j x_k}(y_i, z_i) - F_{x_j x_k}(X_1(t_i), X_2(t_i)))][X_j(t_{i+1}) - X_j(t_i)][X_k(t_{i+1}) - X_k(t_i)]$$

$$\leq \varepsilon \sum_{i=0}^{n-1} [X_j(t_{i+1}) - X_j(t_i)][X_k(t_{i+1}) - X_k(t_i)].$$

Since the quadratic variation of X_i is finite, the right-hand side converges in probability so a subsequence converges almost surely, and it is bounded. Letting $\varepsilon \to 0$ shows that (6.5) holds with almost sure convergence.

In the same way as in the one-dimensional case we can show that in L^2-norm, for $k = 1, 2$

$$\sum_{i=0}^{n-1} F_{x_k x_k}(X_1(t_i), X_2(t_i))[X_k(t_{i+1}) - X_k(t_i)]^2 \to \int_0^t F_{x_k x_k}(X_1(s), X_2(s))b_{kk}^2(s)ds$$

so the task is reduced to proving

$$\sum_{i=0}^{n-1} F_{x_1 x_2}(X_1(t_i), X_2(t_i))[X_1(t_{i+1}) - X_1(t_i)][X_2(t_{i+1}) - X_2(t_i)]$$

$$\to \int_0^t F_{x_1 x_2}(X_1(s), X_2(s)) \sum_{k=1}^{2} b_{1k}(s)b_{2k}(s)ds.$$

Step 3b. Links. The convenient link between the sum and the integral is provided by the mixed-form sums

$$\sum_{i=0}^{n-1} F_{x_1 x_2}(X_1(t_i), X_2(t_i)) \sum_{k=1}^{2} \int_{t_i}^{t_{i+1}} b_{1k}(s) b_{2k}(s) ds$$

since by continuity of the paths of b_{1k}, b_{2k} they can be easily proved to be close to the approximating sums of the integral:

$$\sum_{i=0}^{n-1} F_{x_1 x_2}(X_1(t_i), X_2(t_i))$$

$$\times \left(\int_{t_i}^{t_{i+1}} \sum_{k=1}^{2} b_{1k}(s) b_{2k}(s) ds - \sum_{k=1}^{2} b_{1k}(t_i) b_{2k}(t_i)[t_{i+1} - t_i] \right) \to 0.$$

We have reduced the problem to showing that

$$\sum_{i=0}^{n-1} F_{x_1 x_2}(X_1(t_i), X_2(t_i))[X_1(t_{i+1}) - X_1(t_i)][X_2(t_{i+1}) - X_2(t_i)]$$

$$- \sum_{i=0}^{n-1} F_{x_1 x_2}(X_1(t_i), X_2(t_i)) \sum_{k=1}^{2} \int_{t_i}^{t_{i+1}} b_{1k}(s) b_{2k}(s) ds \to 0$$

Step 3c. Disposing of the drift. Each process X_k has two components: the drift and the stochastic integral, and we show that the first is irrelevant here. Inserting

$$X_k(t_{i+1}) - X_k(t_i) = \int_{t_i}^{t_{i+1}} a_k(s) ds + \int_{t_i}^{t_{i+1}} b_{1k}(s) dW_1(s) + \int_{t_i}^{t_{i+1}} b_{2k}(s) dW_2(s)$$

and multiplying (consider the sum of stochastic integrals as one term, resulting in four terms) one can easily prove that the terms involving a_k go to zero. Namely, boundedness of $F_{x_1 x_2}$ gives

$$\sum_{i=0}^{n-1} F_{x_1 x_2}(X_1(t_i), X_2(t_i)) \int_{t_i}^{t_{i+1}} a_1(s) ds \int_{t_i}^{t_{i+1}} a_2(s) ds \to 0$$

and uniform continuity of paths of stochastic integrals and integrability of a_k implies $(k \neq j)$

$$\sum_{i=0}^{n-1} F_{x_1 x_2}(X_1(t_i), X_2(t_i)) \int_{t_i}^{t_{i+1}} a_k(s)ds$$

$$\times \left(\int_{t_i}^{t_{i+1}} b_{1j}(s)dW_1(s) + \int_{t_i}^{t_{i+1}} b_{2j}(s)dW_2(s) \right)$$

$$\leq C \max_i \left| \int_{t_i}^{t_{i+1}} b_{1j}(s)dW_1(s) + \int_{t_i}^{t_{i+1}} b_{2j}(s)dW_2(s) \right| \sum_{i=0}^{n-1} \int_{t_i}^{t_{i+1}} |a_k(s)|ds \to 0.$$

Step 3d. The final step. It remains to show

$$\sum_{i=0}^{n-1} F_{x_1 x_2}(X_1(t_i), X_2(t_i))$$

$$\times \left([Y_1(t_{i+1}) - Y_1(t_i)][Y_2(t_{i+1}) - Y_2(t_i)] - \sum_{k=1}^{2} \int_{t_i}^{t_{i+1}} b_{1k}(s)b_{2k}(s)ds \right) \to 0,$$

where

$$Y_k(t) = \int_0^t b_{1k}(s)dW_1(s) + \int_0^t b_{2k}(s)dW_2(s).$$

This convergence is based on two facts: $F_{x_1 x_2}$ is bounded and, similarly as observed before, the cross-variation of $Y_1(t)Y_2(t)$ is

$$[Y_1, Y_2](t) = \int_0^t (b_{11}(s)b_{21}(s) + b_{12}(s)b_{22}(s)) \, ds. \qquad \square$$

Exercise 6.14   Prove the above formula.

Exercise 6.15   Verify the uniqueness of Itô process characteristics, i.e. prove that $X_1 = X_2$ implies $a_1 = a_2$, $b_{11} = b_{21}$, $b_{12} = b_{22}$ by applying the Itô formula to find the form of $(X_1(t) - X_2(t))^2$.

6.4   Lévy's Theorem

Recall that if $W(t)$ is a Wiener process, then $W(t)$ and $W^2(t) - t$ are martingales. As it turns out these properties are almost sufficient to characterise a

Wiener process. A version of the following theorem, more common in the literature, assumes the martingale property of $M(t)$ and $M^2(t) - t$, so the result we are going to prove is stronger, but this is what we shall need later.

Theorem 6.12
Suppose that for $i = 1, \ldots, d$, $M_i(0) = 0$, $M_i(t) \in L^2(\Omega)$, $M_i(t)$ and $M_i^2(t) - t$ are local martingales with respect to the Wiener filtration $\mathcal{F}_t$, $i = 1, \ldots, d$, with common localising sequence. If in addition $[M_i, M_j](t) = 0$, for $i \neq j$, then $(M_1(t), \ldots, M_d(t))$ is a Wiener process.

Proof **Step 1. Representation.**
First we will find a sequence of processes $f_i \in \mathcal{P}^2$ such that

$$M_i(t) = \int_0^t f_i(s) dW(s).$$

Write $L_i(t) = M_i^2(t) - t$. By the assumption, there exists a sequence of stopping times $\tau_n \nearrow \infty$ such that

$$M_{in}(t) = M_i(\min\{t, \tau_n\})$$
$$L_{in}(t) = L_i(\min\{t, \tau_n\})$$

are martingales. Note that $L_{in}(t) = M_{in}^2(t) - t$.

By the martingale representation theorem, which applies since $\mathbb{E}(M_{in}^2(t) - t)$ is finite so $M_{in} \in L^2(\Omega)$, for each $i \leq d$ and $n \geq 1$,

$$M_{in}(t) = \int_0^t f_{in}(s) dW_i(s)$$

for some $f_{in} \in \mathcal{M}^2$. Write

$$f_i(t) = \sum_{n=1}^{\infty} \mathbf{1}_{(\tau_n, \tau_{n+1}]}(t) f_{in}(t).$$

Since with probability one $\tau_n(\omega) = T$ for $n \geq N(\omega)$, for almost all ω the above sum is reduces to adding finitely many components. To show that $f_i \in \mathcal{P}^2$ we have to estimate the integral of its square for fixed ω

$$\int_0^T f_i^2(t) dt = \int_0^T \left(\sum_{n=1}^{N} \mathbf{1}_{(\tau_n, \tau_{n+1}]}(t) f_{in}(t) \right)^2 dt$$
$$= \sum_{n=1}^{N(\omega)} \int_{\tau_n}^{\tau_{n+1}} f_{in}^2(t) dt < \infty$$

since all f_{in}^2 are integrable for almost all ω. The representation of M_i follows directly from the representation of M_{in}.

Step 2. Quadratic variation of M_i.

By the Itô formula

$$dM_i^2(t) = 2M_i(t)f_i(t)dW_i(t) + f_i^2(t)dt.$$

In integral form this gives (subtracting t on both sides)

$$M_i^2(t) - t = 2\int_0^t M_i(s)f_i(s)dW_i(s) + \int_0^t f_i^2(s)ds - t$$

We know that $M_i^2(t) - t$ is a local martingale, $\int_0^t M_i(s)f_i(s)dW(s)$ is a local martingale (as a stochastic integral), so

$$\int_0^t f_i^2(s)ds - t = \int_0^t (f_i^2(s) - 1)ds$$

is a local martingale with bounded variation. It is a local martingale as a difference of local martingales and this is an ordinary integral and the function of the upper limit has finite variation. The quadratic variation of $\int_0^t f_i^2(s)ds$ is zero (since the variation is finite) so this process is constant: for all t

$$\int_0^t (f_i^2(s) - 1)ds = 0$$

hence

$$f_i^2(t) = 1 \quad \text{all } t.$$

This also shows that $f_i \in \mathcal{M}^2$. Unfortunately, we cannot conclude that f_i is equal to one, which would finish the proof. What we have achieved so far is this: we found the quadratic variation of $M_i(t) = \int_0^t f_i(s)dW(s)$, which is

$$[M_i, M_i](t) = \int_0^t f_i^2(s)ds = t.$$

Step 3. Normal distribution.

Next we will show that the characteristic function of the vector $M(t)$ has the proper form guaranteeing normal distribution:

$$\mathbb{E}\left(\exp\left\{i\sum_{i=1}^d y_i M_i(t)\right\} | \mathcal{F}_s\right) = \exp\left\{-\frac{1}{2}(t - s)\sum_{i=1}^d y_i^2(t - s)\right\}, \quad y \in \mathbb{R}^d.$$

We want to apply the Itô formula to a complex-valued function which follows from the multi-dimensional version since the set of complex numbers can be identified with the plane. Let $F(x) = \exp\{i\sum x_i y_i\}$, so that

$F_{x_i}(x) = iy_i F(x)$, $F_{x_i x_j}(x) = -y_i y_j F(x)$ and using the fact that the cross-variations of M_i and M_j vanish by assumption, we get

$$\exp\left\{i \sum_{i=1}^{d} y_i M_i(t)\right\}$$

$$= \exp\left\{i \sum_{i=1}^{d} y_i M_i(s)\right\} + i \sum_{i=1}^{d} y_i \int_s^t \exp\left\{i \sum_{i=1}^{d} y_i M_i(u)\right\} f_i(u) dW_i(u)$$

$$- \sum_{i,j=1}^{d} \frac{1}{2} y_i y_j \int_s^t \exp\left\{i \sum_{i=1}^{d} y_i M_i(u)\right\} f_i^2(u) du$$

$$= \exp\left\{i \sum_{i=1}^{d} y_i M_i(s)\right\} + i \sum_{i=1}^{d} y_i \int_s^t \exp\left\{i \sum_{i=1}^{d} y_i M_i(u)\right\} f_i(u) dW_i(u)$$

$$\sum_{i,j=1}^{d} \frac{1}{2} y_i y_j \int_s^t \exp\left\{i \sum_{i=1}^{d} y_i M_i(u)\right\} du$$

since $f_{in}^2 = 1$. Multiply by $\mathbf{1}_A$ for $A \in \mathcal{F}_s$ and then by $\exp\{-i \sum_{i=1}^{d} y_i M_i(s)\}$,

$$\exp\left\{i \sum_{i=1}^{d} y_i [M_i(t) - M_i(s)]\right\} \mathbf{1}_A$$

$$= \mathbf{1}_A + i \sum_{i=1}^{d} y_i \mathbf{1}_A \int_s^t \exp\left\{i \sum_{i=1}^{d} y_i [M_i(u) - M_i(s)]\right\} f_i(u) dW_i(u)$$

$$- \frac{1}{2} \sum_{i,j=1}^{d} y_i y_j \mathbf{1}_A \int_s^t \exp\left\{i \sum_{i=1}^{d} y_i [M_i(u) - M_i(s)]\right\} du.$$

The complex exponential is bounded by one, so $\exp\{i \sum_{i=1}^{d} y_i M_i(t)\} f(t)$ is in $\mathcal{M}^2$.

Now take the conditional expectation $\mathbb{E}(\cdot|\mathcal{F}_s)$ on both sides. The conditional expectation of stochastic integral is zero, so

$$\mathbb{E}\left(\exp\left\{i \sum_{i=1}^{d} y_i [M_i(t) - M_i(s)]\right\} \mathbf{1}_A|\mathcal{F}_s\right)$$

$$= P(A) - \frac{1}{2} \sum_{i,j=1}^{d} y_i y_j \int_s^t \mathbb{E}\left(\exp\left\{i \sum_{i=1}^{d} y_i [M_i(u) - M_i(s)]\right\} \mathbf{1}_A|\mathcal{F}_s\right) du.$$

Write

$$\psi(t, y_1, \ldots, y_d) = \mathbb{E}\left(\exp\left\{i \sum_{i=1}^{d} y_i \left[M_i(t) - M_i(s)\right]\right\} \mathbf{1}_A | \mathcal{F}_s\right).$$

It is a random function, but as will turn out, in fact it is deterministic. It satisfies

$$\psi(t, y) = P(A) - \frac{1}{2} \sum_{i,j=1}^{d} y_i y_j \int_s^t \psi(u, y) du,$$

or, in other words.

$$\frac{\partial}{\partial t}\psi(t, y) = \frac{1}{2} \sum_{i,j=1}^{d} y_i y_j \psi(t, y) \text{ with } \psi(s, y) = P(A).$$

This equation has a unique solution:

$$\psi(t, y) = P(A) \exp\left\{-\frac{1}{2}(t - s) \sum_{i,j=1}^{d} y_i y_j\right\}$$

so

$$\mathbb{E}\left(\exp\left\{i \sum_{i=1}^{d} y_i \left[M_i(t) - M_i(s)\right]\right\} | \mathcal{F}_s\right) = \exp\left\{-\frac{1}{2}(t - s) \sum_{i,j=1}^{d} y_i y_j\right\}. \quad (6.6)$$

Take the expectation to get

$$\mathbb{E}\left(\exp\left\{i \sum_{i=1}^{d} y_i \left[M_i(t) - M_i(s)\right]\right\}\right) = \exp\left\{-\frac{1}{2}(t - s) \sum_{i,j=1}^{d} y_i y_j\right\}. \quad (6.7)$$

The characteristic function determines the distribution. On the right we can see the characteristic function of the normal distribution, so $M_i(t) - M_i(s)$ is normally distributed with mean 0 and variance $t - s$. We can see that the independence of M_i and M_j follows from vanishing cross-variation since we have the proper diagonal form of the characteristic function of the vector $M(t)$.

Step 4. Increments.

What remains to show is the independence of the increments of M_i. Here we work in one dimension, with one coordinate M_i. Take $t_1 < t_2 \leq t_3 < t_4$, consider the vector $(M_i(t_4) - M_i(t_3), M_i(t_2) - M_i(t_1))$, and compute the characteristic function

$$\mathbb{E}\left(e^{iy_1(M_i(t_4)-M_i(t_3))+iy_2(M_i(t_2)-M_i(t_1))}\right)$$

$$= \mathbb{E}\left(\mathbb{E}\left(e^{iy_1(M_i(t_4)-M_i(t_3))+iy_2(M_i(t_2)-M_i(t_1))}|\mathcal{F}_{t_3}\right)\right) \quad \text{(tower property)}$$

$$= \mathbb{E}\left(e^{iy_2(M_i(t_2)-M_i(t_1))}\mathbb{E}\left(e^{iy_1(M_i(t_4)-M_i(t_3))}|\mathcal{F}_{t_3}\right)\right) \quad \text{(taking out the known)}$$

$$= \mathbb{E}\left(e^{iy_2(M_i(t_2)-M_i(t_1))}e^{-\frac{1}{2}y_1^2(t_4-t_3)}\right) \quad \text{(by (6.6))}$$

$$= e^{-\frac{1}{2}y_1^2(t_4-t_3)}\mathbb{E}\left(e^{iy_2(M_i(t_2)-M_i(t_1))}\right)$$

$$= e^{-\frac{1}{2}y_1^2(t_4-t_3)}e^{-\frac{1}{2}y_2^2(t_2-t_1)} \quad \text{(by (6.7))}$$

so the increments are independent, have zero means, variances t_4-t_3, t_2-t_1 respectively. This follows form the fact that the vector has normal distribution as the characteristic function shows. In addition, we can see that the increments have zero correlation, again from the form of the characteristic function. Uncorrelated normal random variables are independent. A similar argument works for n increments.

We conclude that $(M_1, \ldots, M_n)$ satisfies all condition of the definition of Wiener process. □

Remark 6.13
The assumption about the common localising sequence is not necessary. Suppose $L_n(t) = L(\min\{t, v_n\})$ are martingales with $v_n \nearrow \infty$. Let $\eta_n = \min\{\tau_n, v_n\}$, $\eta_n \nearrow \infty$.

If $\tau \le T$ is a stopping time, Y is a martingale then $Y_\tau(t) = Y(\min\{t, \tau\})$ is a martingale by the optional stopping theorem. Therefore

$$M_n'(t) = M_n(\min\{t, \eta_n\}),$$
$$L_n'(t) = L_n(\min\{t, \eta_n\})$$

are martingales. The reason we are imposing the assumption about the common sequence of stopping times is that we want to avoid proving this fact. The proof is easy for discrete time and covered in [DMFM]. However, the extension to continuous time requires a somewhat longer argument. In the applications we will be able to satisfy this additional condition.

6.5　Girsanov Theorem

This section will provide us with a powerful tool which enables a conversion of a general Itô process into a martingale by changing the reference probability. But first recall a result from [PF].

Lemma 6.14 (Bayes formula)

If $Q(A) = \mathbb{E}_P(\mathbf{1}_A f)$, $f \geq 0$, $\mathbb{E}_P(f|X|) < \infty$, $\mathbb{E}_Q(|X|) < \infty$ and $\mathcal{G} \subset \mathcal{F}$ then

$$\mathbb{E}_P(fX|\mathcal{G}) = \mathbb{E}_Q(X|\mathcal{G})\mathbb{E}_P(f|\mathcal{G}).$$

As before, we consider a d-dimensional Wiener process

$$W(t) = (W_1(t), \ldots, W_d(t))$$

living on $(\Omega, \mathcal{F}, P)$ and let a_i be $\mathcal{F}_t$-adapted processes (filtration generated by W), $i = 1, \ldots, d$.

Theorem 6.15 (Girsanov)
Write

$$Y_i(t) = \int_0^t a_i(s)ds + W_i(t)$$

and assume that

$$M(t) = \exp\left\{-\sum_{i=1}^d \int_0^t a_i(s)dW_i(s) - \frac{1}{2}\sum_{i=1}^d \int_0^t a_i^2(s)ds\right\}$$

is a martingale. Let

$$Q(A) = \int_A M(T)dP.$$

Then Y is a d-dimensional Wiener process on the probability space $(\Omega, \mathcal{F}, Q)$.

The process Y has non-zero expectation since we added a term to the Wiener process. As was the case for Theorem 2.1 this added term can be eliminated by changing the measure. The exponential martingale M has constant expectation

$$\mathbb{E}_P(M(T)) = \mathbb{E}_P(M(0)) = 1$$

so $M(T)$ is a density.

Before proving the Girsanov theorem we mention two conditions, each guaranteeing that M is a martingale.

(1) a_i are deterministic (this will be proved below).

(2) The Novikov condition:

$$\mathbb{E}\left(\exp\left\{\frac{1}{2}\sum_{i=1}^d \int_0^T a_i^2(s)ds\right\}\right) < \infty.$$

The proof that the Novikov condition suffices for the martingale property of M is difficult, but we will not need it, as in our applications a_i will be deterministic.

Proposition 6.16
If the a_i are deterministic, then $M(t)$ is a martingale.

Proof The multi-dimensional Itô formula applied to $M(t) = \exp\left\{\sum_{i=1}^{d} X_i(t)\right\}$ with $F(t, x_1, \ldots, x_d) = \exp\{x_1 + \cdots + x_d\}$ ($F_{x_i} = F$), $b_{ij} = \delta_{ij}a_i$, and

$$dX_i(t) = -\frac{1}{2}a_i^2(t)dt - a_i(t)dW_i(t)$$

gives

$$dM(t) = -\sum_{i=1}^{d} F(t, X(t))\frac{1}{2}a_i^2(t)dt + \sum_{i=1}^{d} F(t, X(t))a_i dW_i(t)$$

$$+\frac{1}{2}\sum_{i=1}^{d} F(t, X(t))a_i^2(t)dt.$$

$$= -\exp\left\{\sum_{i=1}^{d} X_i(t)\right\}\sum_{i=1}^{d} a_i(t)dW_i(t),$$

so M is a local martingale. It is non-negative so it is a supermartingale.

Lemma 2.20 tells us that for each $i \leq d$, $\int_0^t a_i(s)dW_i(s)$ has normal distribution with zero mean and variance $\int_0^t a_i^2(s)ds$ and, of course, the random variable $-\int_0^t a_i(s)dW_i(s)$ has the same properties. But if X has normal distribution with $\mathbb{E}(X) = 0$, then $\mathbb{E}(\exp\{X\}) = \exp\left\{\frac{1}{2}\mathrm{Var}(X)\right\}$.

To see that $M(t)$ is a martingale it is sufficient to show that it has constant expectation. Since the a_i are deterministic, the integrals $\int_0^t a_i(s)dW_i(s)$ are independent so

$$\mathbb{E}\left(\exp\left\{-\sum_{i=1}^{d}\int_0^t a_i(s)dW_i(s) - \frac{1}{2}\sum_{i=1}^{d}\int_0^t a^2(s)ds\right\}\right)$$

$$= \exp\left\{-\frac{1}{2}\sum_{i=1}^{d}\int_0^t a^2(s)ds\right\}\mathbb{E}\left(\prod_{i=1}^{d}\exp\left\{-\int_0^t a_i(s)dW_i(s)\right\}\right)$$

$$= \exp\left\{-\frac{1}{2}\sum_{i=1}^{d}\int_0^t a^2(s)ds\right\}\prod_{i=1}^{d}\mathbb{E}\exp\left\{-\int_0^t a_i(s)dW_i(s)\right\}$$

$$= 1,$$

which completes the proof. $\square$

We now prove the Girsanov Theorem.

Proof of Girsanov Theorem 6.15 We show that $Y_i(t) = \int_0^t a_i(s)ds + W_i(t)$ and $Y_i^2(t) - t$ are local martingales, with a common sequence of localising stopping times, with respect to Q and $\mathcal{F}_t$, and also that $[Y_i, Y_j](t) = 0$ for $i \neq j$, which is sufficient in view of the Lévy Theorem.

Step 1. Martingale property of Y_i (under Q).

Assume Y_i and M are bounded. We employ integration by parts to find $d(Y_i(t)M(t))$ where

$$dM(t) = -\sum_j M(t)a_j(t)dW_j(t)$$

$$dY_i(t) = a_i(t)dt + dW_i(t)$$

and we get

$$d(Y_i(t)M(t)) = M(t)dY_i(t) + Y_i(t)dM(t) - a_i(t)M(t)dt$$

$$= M(t)(a_i(t)dt + dW_i(t)) - \sum_{j=1}^d Y(t)M(t)a_j(t)dW_j(t) - a_i(t)M(t)dt$$

$$= \sum_{j=1}^d M(t)[\delta_{ij} - Y(t)a_j(t)]dW_j(t).$$

So $Y_i(t)M(t)$ is a local martingale hence a martingale (as we know, a stochastic integral is a local martingale and a bounded local martingale is a martingale).

Next, if $Q(A) = \mathbb{E}_P(\mathbf{1}_A f)$, then $\mathbb{E}_P(fX|\mathcal{G}) = \mathbb{E}_Q(X|\mathcal{G})\mathbb{E}_P(f|\mathcal{G})$. Take $M = f$, $Y_i = X$, $\mathcal{G} = \mathcal{F}_s$ to get

$$\mathbb{E}_Q(Y_i(t)|\mathcal{F}_s) = \frac{\mathbb{E}_P(M(t)Y_i(t)|\mathcal{F}_s)}{\mathbb{E}_P(M(t)|\mathcal{F}_s)}$$

$$= \frac{M(s)Y_i(s)}{M(s)} \quad \text{(both } M \text{ and } MY_i \text{ are martingales)}$$

$$= Y_i(s)$$

so Y_i is a martingale.

Step 2. Martingale property of $Y_i^2(t) - t$.

Again assume Y_i and M are bounded. By the Itô formula

$$d(Y_i^2(t) - t) = 2Y_i(t)dY_i(t) = 2a_i(t)Y_i(t)dt + 2Y_i(t)dW_i(t).$$

Integration by parts gives (recall $dM(t) = -M(t)\sum_{i=1}^{d} a_i(t)dW_i(t)$)

$$d(M(t)(Y_i^2(t) - t)) = M(t)d(Y_i^2(t) - t) + (Y_i^2(t) - t)dM(t) - 2a_i(t)Y_i(t)M(t)dt$$
$$= M(t)(2a_i(t)Y_i(t)dt + 2Y_i(t)dW_i(t))$$
$$- (Y_i^2(t) - t)M(t)\sum_{j=1}^{d} a_j(t)dW_j(t) - 2a_i(t)Y_i(t)M(t)dt$$
$$= 2M(t)Y_i(t)dW_i(t) - 2M(t)(Y_i^2(t) - t)\sum_{j=1}^{d} a_j(t)dW_j(t).$$

So $M(t)(Y_i^2(t) - t)$ is a local martingale hence a martingale (since bounded). We can now conclude in the similar way as in Step 1. We use the Bayes formula with $Q(A) = \mathbb{E}_P(1_A f)$ where $M = f$, $Y_i^2 - t = X$, $\mathcal{G} = \mathcal{F}_s$,

$$\mathbb{E}_Q(Y_i^2(t) - t|\mathcal{F}_s) = \frac{\mathbb{E}_P(M(t)(Y_i^2(t) - t)|\mathcal{F}_s)}{\mathbb{E}_P(M(t)|\mathcal{F}_s)}$$
$$= \frac{M(s)(Y_i^2(s) - s)}{M(s)} \quad \text{(martingale property)}$$
$$= Y_i^2(s) - s.$$

So $Y_i^2(t) - t$ is a martingale.
Step 3. General Y_i, M.
Let

$$\tau_n = \inf\{t : |Y_i(t)| \geq n \text{ for some } i \text{ or } M(t) \geq n\}.$$

Almost all paths of Y_i and M are continuous so for each such path we have an upper bound, since we are working on a bounded time interval. So $\tau_n \to \tau$ almost surely as $n \to \infty$. For fixed i let

$$Y_{in}(t) = Y_i(\min\{\tau_n, t\})$$
$$M_n(t) = M(\min\{\tau_n, t\}).$$

The processes M_n, Y_{in} are bounded:

$$|Y_{in}| \leq n$$
$$M_n \leq n$$

and by Steps 1, 2, Y_{in}, $Y_{in}^2 - t$ are martingales. Hence Y_i, $Y_i^2 - t$ are local martingales

Step 4. Cross-variations.

Finally

$$[Y_i, Y_j](t) = \left[\int_0^t a_i(s)ds + W_i(t), \int_0^t a_j(s)ds + W_j(t) \right] = 0$$

since the integral of a_i is a process with finite variation and $[W_i, W_j](t) = 0$ by independence.

These steps prove that Y is a Wiener process by Lévy's Theorem. Observe that a single sequence of stopping times is good for both processes, so the additional assumption imposed in the proof of the Lévy Theorem is satisfied. □

6.6 Applications

We conclude this volume by applying the above general results to the study of the multi-asset Black–Scholes model with variable coefficients:

$$dS_i(t) = \mu_i(t)S_i(t)dt + \sum_{j=1}^d c_{ij}(t)S_i(t)dW_j(t), \quad i = 1, \dots, d,$$

keeping the risk-free assets in a simple form $A(t) = e^{rt}$, i.e. assuming that the risk-free rate is constant. For the above equations to make sense we assume that the processes $\mu_i(t)$, $c_{ij}(t)$ are adapted with respect to the filtration generated by the d-dimensional Wiener process, have continuous paths, and are bounded by deterministic constants (we are not aiming for the most general set-up).

With the multi-dimensional Itô formula at hand we can easily verify that a solution is given by

$$S_i(t) = S_i(0) \exp \left\{ \int_0^t \mu_i(t)dt - \frac{1}{2} \sum_{j=1}^d \int_0^t c_{ij}^2(t)dt + \sum_{j=1}^d \int_0^t c_{ij}(t)dW_j(t) \right\}.$$

Exercise 6.16 Prove this fact.

This solution is unique as a result of Theorem 6.9.

Our next goal is to find sufficient conditions for the existence of risk-neutral probability.

Theorem 6.17

Suppose $\theta_i(t)$ is a d-dimensional process such that

(1) $\sum_{j=1}^{d} c_{ij}(t)\theta_j(t) = \mu_i(t) - r$,

(2) $M(t) = \exp\{-\frac{1}{2}\int_0^t \sum_{i=1}^d \theta_i^2(s)ds - \int_0^t \sum_{i=1}^d \theta_i(s)dW_i(s)\}$ is a martingale.

Then $Q(A) = \mathbb{E}(\mathbf{1}_A M(T))$ is a probability such that the discounted price process is a martingale.

Proof The product rule gives

$$d(M(t)\tilde{S}_i(t)) = -MS_i \frac{1}{2} \sum_j \theta_j^2 dt - MS_i \sum_j \theta_j dW_j$$
$$+ M(t)(\mu_i - r)S_i dt + MS_i \sum c_{ij} dW_j$$
$$+ \frac{1}{2} MS$$

so $M(t)\tilde{S}_i(t)$ is a martingale. Consequently

$$\mathbb{E}_P(M(t)\tilde{S}_i(t)|\mathcal{F}_s) = M(s)\tilde{S}_i(s). \tag{6.8}$$

By Lemma 6.14 with $f = M(t)$, $\mathcal{G} = \mathcal{F}_s$, $X = \tilde{S}_i(t)$ we have $Q(A) = \mathbb{E}_P(\mathbf{1}_A M(T)) = \mathbb{E}_P(\mathbf{1}_A M(t))$ (as M is a martingale) so

$$\mathbb{E}_P(M(t)\tilde{S}_i(t)|\mathcal{F}_s) = \mathbb{E}_Q(\tilde{S}_i(t)|\mathcal{F}_s)\mathbb{E}_P(M(t)|\mathcal{F}_s)$$

By (6.8) the left-hand is equal to $M(s)\tilde{S}_i(s)$ and by the martingale property of M the right-hand side is $\mathbb{E}_Q(\tilde{S}_i(t)|\mathcal{F}_s)M(s)$ and since $M(s) > 0$ this gives the martingale property of discounted stock prices. □

Next note that as a direct consequence of the Girsanov Theorem we know that the processes

$$W_i^Q(t) = \int_0^t \theta_i(s)ds + W_i(t)$$

are the coordinates of a d-dimensional Wiener process in the probability space $(\Omega, \mathcal{F}, Q)$. The dynamics of stock prices with respect to W^Q amounts to a direct generalisation of the one-dimensional equation derived earlier.

Exercise 6.17 Prove that

$$dS_i(t) = rS_i(t)dt + \sum_{j=1}^{d} c_{ij}(t)S_i(t)dW_j^Q(t), \quad i = 1, \ldots, d.$$

We expect that the pricing formula for options written on many stocks (so-called basket options) should be given by means of expected discounted payoff computed with respect to Q. For a European path-independent derivative we have $H(T) = h(S_1(T), \ldots, S_d(T))$ with some $h : \mathbb{R}^d \to \mathbb{R}$, and

$$H(0) = e^{-rT} \mathbb{E}_Q(H(T)).$$

Practical consequences of the general pricing formula are limited since the joint distribution of the future stock prices has to be used and an explicit expression, like the Black–Scholes formula, is rarely available so that Monte-Carlo methods are used to approximate the expectation.

To justify this formula we need multi-dimensional counterparts of some basic definitions and facts.

Strategies are adapted processes $(x_1(t), \ldots, x_d(t), y(t))$ satisfying the self-financing condition: $dV(t) = \sum_{i=1}^d x_i(t)dS_i(t) + y(t)dA(t)$, where the value process $V(t) = \sum_{i=1}^d x_i(t)S_i(t) + y(t)A(t)$ is above some level $-L$ and is a martingale with respect to Q, to eliminate the pathologies known from the one-dimensional case. Then we need a version of the martingale representation theorem to find replicating strategies. Finally, introducing the extended market with extended strategies, we define the process $H(t)$ to be the price of the derivative if this process, assumed Itô, does not lead to arbitrage. Finally, we have to prove that $H(t)$ is the same as the process of values of a unique replicating strategy. All these facts can be proved along the same lines as the one-dimensional counterparts.

Example 6.18
Consider a two-dimensional Black–Scholes market with constant coefficients and the payoff function $h(x_1, x_2) = \max\{x_1 - x_2, 0\}$, the so-called exchange option. Assume that the matrix $C = [c_{ij}]$ is invertible with $C^{-1} = [d_{ij}]$, and this gives a risk neutral probability Q by Theorem 6.17 with constant $\theta_i = \sum d_{ij}(\mu_j - r)$, and the Wiener process $W_i^Q(t) = t\theta_i + W_i(t)$. Clearly $S_1(T) - S_2(T) > 0$ if and only if $Y(t) = \frac{S_2(T)}{S_1(T)} < 1$.

$$e^{-rT} \mathbb{E}_Q(\max\{S_1(T) - S_2(T), 0\}) = e^{-rT} \mathbb{E}_Q(\mathbf{1}_{\{Y(T)<1\}}S_1(T)(1 - Y(T))) \quad (6.9)$$

In the Bayes formula (Lemma 6.14) take $f = e^{-rT}\frac{S_1(T)}{S_1(0)}$ then with $Q_f(A) = \mathbb{E}_Q(\mathbf{1}_A f)$, $(P = Q)$, $X = \mathbf{1}_{\{Y(T)<1\}}(1 - Y(T))$ and $\mathcal{G} = \mathcal{F}_0$ we have the right-hand side of (6.9) equal to

$$e^{-rT}\mathbb{E}_Q\left(\mathbf{1}_{\{Y(T)<1\}}S_1(T)(1-Y(t))\right)$$
$$= S_1(0)\mathbb{E}_Q(fX)$$
$$= S_1(0)\mathbb{E}_{Q_f}(X)\mathbb{E}_Q(f)$$
$$= S_1(0)\mathbb{E}_{Q_f}\left(\mathbf{1}_{\{Y(T)<1\}}(1-Y(T))\right)\mathbb{E}_Q\left(\frac{S_1(T)}{S_1(0)}e^{-rT}\right).$$

But $\tilde{S}_1$ is a Q-martingale so $\mathbb{E}_Q\left(\frac{S_1(T)}{S_1(0)}e^{-rT}\right) = 1$ and $\mathbf{1}_{\{Y(T)<1\}}(1-Y(T)) = \max\{1 - Y(T), 0\}$ so $H(0)$ can be found using the Black–Scholes formula for the put option with Y as the underlying asset, 1 being the strike price:

$$H(0) = S_1(0)\mathbb{E}_{Q_f}(\max\{1 - Y(T), 0\}).$$

The evaluation of this basket option thus reduces to the one-dimensional analysis of some auxiliary asset.

Exercise 6.18 Derive the equation for the process Y and find the explicit formula for the exchange option.

Finally, we outline the PDE approach to the pricing problem. Assuming existence of a regular function $u : \mathbb{R}^d \to \mathbb{R}$ such that $H(t) = u(S_1(t), \ldots, S_d(t))$, by routine application of the Itô formula we can derive a partial equation satisfied by u :

$$u_t(t, z_1, \ldots, z_d) + r\sum_{i=1}^{d} z_i u_{z_i}(t, z_1, \ldots, z_d)$$

$$+\frac{1}{2}\sum_{i,j,k=1}^{d} z_i z_j u_{z_i z_j}(t, z_1, \ldots, z_d)c_{ik}c_{jk}$$
$$= ru(t, z_1, \ldots, z_d), \quad t < T,$$

with terminal condition

$$u(T, z_1, \ldots, z_d) = h(z_1, \ldots, z_d).$$

In the simple Black–Scholes model, existence of such a u was obtained by the Black–Scholes formula. In many dimensions, such an explicit formula is not available except from some special payoffs. The advantage of this approach is that we can derive a similar equation for the case of non-linear coefficients in the model. If the underlying securities prices follow

$$dS_i(t) = \mu_i(t, S_1(t), \ldots, S_d(t))dt + \sum_{j=1}^{d} c_{ij}(t, S_1(t), \ldots, S_d(t))dW_j(t),$$

then the candidate for the pricing function u would be a solution to a linear PDE

$$u_t(t, z_1, \ldots, z_d) + r \sum_{i=1}^{d} \mu_i(t, z_1, \ldots, z_d)u_{z_i}(t, z_1, \ldots, z_d)$$

$$+\frac{1}{2} \sum_{i,j,k=1}^{d} u_{z_i z_j}(t, z_1, \ldots, z_d)c_{ik}(z_1, \ldots, z_d)c_{jk}(z_1, \ldots, z_d)$$

$$= ru(t, z_1, \ldots, z_d), \quad t < T,$$

with the same terminal condition.

Index

Printed in the United States
by Baker & Taylor Publisher Services